I0105222

WOMEN MUSICIANS OF ZIMBABWE:

A Celebration of Women's Struggle for Voice and Artistic Expression

©Joyce Jenje Makwenda 2013

©Joyce Jenje Makwenda

Published by Joyce Jenje (Storytime)
Tel: +263 (04) 306336 / 306236
Cel: +263 773 468 378 / 775 220 026
Email: joycejenje@gmail.com
Harare, Zimbabwe 2013

ISBN -079743476-3

A record for this book is also available at the National Archives, Zimbabwe.

Research/Author: Joyce Jenje Makwenda
Editor: Sarudzayi Chifamba-Barnes
Layout/Index: Yolanda Birivadi
Cover design: Josh Sithole
Graphic Design: Jeffrey Milanzi
Printing: SP Design & Print

Joyce Jenje-Makwenda

WOMEN MUSICIANS OF ZIMBABWE:

A Celebration of Women's Struggle for Voice and Artistic Expression

GRATITUDE

THIS book was made possible with a fund from the FORD FOUNDATION; thank you for the generous fund which went a long way towards writing, editing, research, final publishing, and also my Masters program at the University of Witwatersrand.

In addition I would like to thank the following people at the Ford Foundation – Nume (Farai) Mashinini and John Butler Adams, for believing in this project, Betty Amunga for assisting wherever possible. I would like to thank Alice Brown the Ford Foundation Country Representative (during the time I was funded), for seeing the importance of the project and funding it. The project took more time than I had anticipated. Thank you so much FORD FOUNDATION for giving me time and space to dream in order to bring out – THE VOICE AND ARTISTIC EXPRESSION OF WOMEN IN THIS BOOK.

Initially the project included the book and thesis but because of the time and space I had, a diary notebook and a children's book on Women Musicians of Zimbabwe were added. A film documentary is on the way.

In 1994/1995 I received a grant from NOVIB for research and writing the first draft, but unfortunately NOVIB could not fund the project beyond the first draft. At NOVIB I would like to thank in particular Judith Uyerterland who made it possible for me to get funding for the early research and writing. I had to shelve the project until 2006 when I got funding from the Ford Foundation. However, from 1995 to 2006, a lot had changed on the music scene and I had to carry out new research to incorporate the new changes in a fast changing industry. The book took a new angle which was no longer narrative, but is written thematically.

The National Archives of Zimbabwe played an all-embracing role as an invaluable store house of historical material.

DEDICATION

TO my late parents, David (Murehwa) Jenje and Canaan (MaDube) Jenje, for the support, encouragement and guiding me in my career path since I was young.

While writing this book I realized how important family encouragement is for the development of women artists and I am grateful that I am one of the lucky ones.

To various artists who contributed to the unfolding of women musicians in Zimbabwe.

Joyce Jenje-Makwenda

Women Musicians

Flame celebrations

Prelude

I FELT the need to explore the role played by women in the development of music genres in Zimbabwe and to explore why there are very few women musicians in Zimbabwe compared to men.

I was born in 1958 and grew up in Mbare, Harare, one of the oldest townships for black people from Zimbabwe and neighbouring countries. I belong to an urban culture and a social hybrid of different cultural mix. What struck me most during my youth days, and a trend which has continued today, is that in Zimbabwe very few women take music as a career, unlike men. If they do, they are either employed as backing vocalists for male musicians, or dancers.

The few who lead their own bands do not last on the music scene. As a young person, I grew up listening to the music from both local and international women musicians, including Dorothy Masuka, Miriam Makeba, Susan Chenjerayi, Susan Mapfumo, Diana Ross, Tina Turner and Gladys Night. Of the three Zimbabwean women that I have mentioned, only Dorothy Masuka continued with her musical role till today. After asking myself numerous questions and finding no answers, I sought on a journey of research to find answers. I visited the National Archives of Zimbabwe, interviewed some women and male musicians. All the evidence I uncovered highlighted the negative influence of patriarchal Zimbabwe cultures on women and music.

I interviewed more than 100 women (young and old; new and seasoned) musicians, and corroborated the interviews with oral history and archival material, which included newspapers and books.

The research is not about developing on the writings of other people (secondary research), but is a primary research based on observations and the interviews I conducted with female musicians and other stakeholders in the music industry. These have been corroborated by newspaper articles, newsreels, and other oral history interviews. I formulated a hypothesis based on my own personal observations. I therefore want to share my observations with you, and where I felt the need to back my observations and interviews, I incorporated secondary literature written by other authors. Secondary literature is incorporated sparingly as this is not meant to be an academic research.

I believe that experience is the best teacher; with my observations, journalistic skills and interviews I decided to come up with a comprehensive piece of the role played by women in the music industry of Zimbabwe.

My work is ongoing as I continue to interview women in the music industry. I have collected a personal archive with interviews on audio-tapes, video tapes, press cuttings and photos.

I started the research on Women Musicians concurrently with Zimbabwe Township Music in 1984. While I was doing the research some scholars interviewed me on the topic as they were carrying out research related topics. Caleb Dube, Emmanuel Chiwome and Thomas Turino were some of the scholars who were interested in the research that I was doing particularly Zimbabwe Township Music. While I was working on the research on Women

Musicians scholars and researchers also interviewed me and to seek my opinion on a number of issues as I had been working on the research for some time. Some of the scholars are Mwenda Ntarangwi and Angela Impey.

It is important to mention that when I started my work in 1984, the idea was mainly to document my culture, and to make it accessible in a more dynamic way and to pass it on to the next generations so that they appreciate their culture, and the contributions of women musicians to the development of music in Zimbabwe. This book also informs my Masters Degree thesis which I am currently studying with the University of the Witwatersrand.

Last but not least, the book is written in a simple way. It fuses journalism with an artistic approach and academic writing.

From left to right: Tabeth Kapuya, Joyce Jenje Makwenda (author) and Victoria Chingate of the Gay Gaieties (16/10/91)

Contents

Chapter 1

Brief History of Women and Music in Zimbabwe

MUSIC, has been part of African women's lives since time immemorial. Zimbabwean women sang songs to communicate, express their feelings or celebrate life changes. During pasichigare (pre-colonial times) women used the song to cope with the day to day challenges of life, to manage their daily chores, to deal with their emotions, to air their grievances, to challenge oppression, and to celebrate womanhood. Through music, women were able to put themselves at the centre-stage of their communities. They were an integral part of the structures of the society and they found it easier to use music as a communication tool.

Women in Zimbabwe in more general terms assume the role of mothers, carers, planting crops, preparing food and feeding the family. In the pre-colonial times some tasks such as pounding millet (grain) were very tedious and carried out using mortars and pestles, and the millie-meal was then separated from the chaff using chaff-separators. On the other hand men assumed the roles of providers (shelter, food through hunting, clearing the bushes for farming and protecting the families from external enemies).

The Task of Motherhood: Managing Daily Chores: Pre-colonial Era

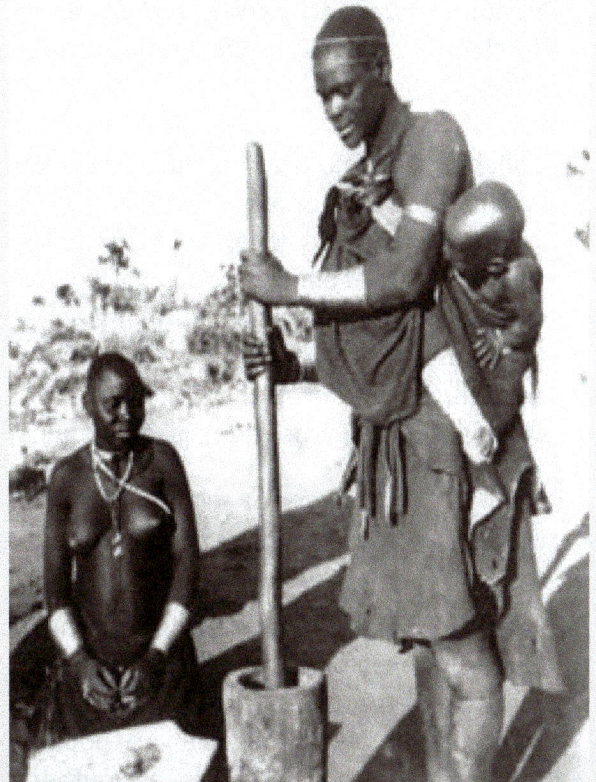

Shona women pounding corn (1900c)

Singing helped women to cope with their day-to-day work, such as when they were working in the fields, grinding, pounding and thrashing (maize, millet or sorghum). The song was used to alleviate stress and make tasks simpler and easier to accomplish as women sang songs in a rhythm way depending on the particular task they were doing.

Pounding grain was usually done by two or three women pounding in the same mortar, while taking turns to do so. Their pestles produced nice, rhythmic sounds.

Song as a parenting tool

African women used, and still use song as a tool for parenting through singing lullabies. Zimbabwe, like most African countries, is a patriarchal society with distinct roles for men and women. The woman's main role is seen as giving birth and looking after the children while men provide for the families. Women in many African traditions use lullabies to enjoy motherhood and to communicate with children. Lullabies were used to comfort young children, to persuade them to go to sleep, as well as to communicate with them.

Lullabies were passed from one generation to the other as mothers passed this art to children and future generations. However, while the art of singing lullabies has been passed from generation to generation, unfortunately, and in general, women musicians have not been able to transform this legacy into the domain of popular music.

The first person to translate women's musical heritage into popular music effectively was the South African singer, Miriam Makeba. She recorded the widely known Nguni lullaby 'Thula Sana Lwami' in the 1950's, which became very popular and is now recognised as a Southern African jazz standard. She reclaimed this song on behalf of women in general.

Thula Sana Lwami in Nguni

Thula Thula sana lwami
Thul'u papa uzofika ekuseni
Angilali ebusuku nawe sana lwami
Angilali ebusuku nawe sana lwami
Thula Thula mama thula sana lwami
Thul' upapa uzofika ekuseni
Thula sana lwami

English Version

Don't cry my baby
Please don't cry
Your father will be here
Very soon
Please don't cry my baby
Don't cry
I don't sleep at night
Because of you my baby
Please don't cry
Your father will be here
Very soon

Miriam Makeba inspired other women to also record lullabies and other children's songs. In 1994, Tendai Makura recorded Shona lullabies and other children's songs. She recruited nine children to sing with her and they took part in the recording. By so doing, Makura passed the music to today's generations. Some of the songs on this recording are Usachema Mwana (Do not cry child), Mwana Wangu Chivata (Sleep my child), E-ru-ru-re. E-ru-ru-re (Hush-hush, my baby, don't you cry). E-ru-ru-re, is a popular Shona lullaby. When we were growing up in the township we used to sing this song while babysitting.

E-ru-ru-re

E-ru-ru-re nyarara mhana mwana
Unochemeyiko
Unochemera amai vako
Vakaenda mhiri kwaruKweza
KwaruKweza kunabanga jena
Banga jena rokucheke nyama
Cheke nyama yeparuware

E-ru-ru-re nyarara mhana (mwana)

English Translation

Hush Hush my baby dont you cry
Why are you crying
You are crying for your mother
She has gone to work

Tendayi Makura also recorded songs for children's games, *Chumushunye shunye, Mushana Mushana, Tsuro Kanga Tsuro.*

Song and Story-telling

African societies have a rich culture of story-telling, which was usually dominated by women. It was women's role to pass on family history, which they often did through the medium of song/ music. The song is widely used in the art of story-telling, which in turn played an integral role in the education of children. Folktales were used to teach children moral values. According to author Chifamba-Barnes (2008), music was used to energise children before a story-telling session, so that they would not lose concentration. In a way, the use of songs as prelude and during the story-telling session energised both the storyteller and the audience.

In many stories, children were asked to punctuate the stories with *Dzepfunde*, 'Yes we are listening', or 'we have heard you'. *Dzepfunde* was used as a way of reassuring the story-teller that the children were listening. In a way, this was also a way of involving both the audience and the storyteller in the story-telling session.

The *rungano* (storytelling) was educational because it taught children the skills of hunting, singing, courtship and counting as well.

Song –Motsiro

Motsiro-o, (one)
Dendere--e (two)
wagara- (three)
Mashangwe (four)
Mbirimbidzwa (five)
pamuromo (six)
Pegange (seven)
Ngangaidzwa (eight)
Chindori (nine)
Gumirawa (Gumi rakwana) (ten)

(Source: Chifamba-Barnes, 2008).

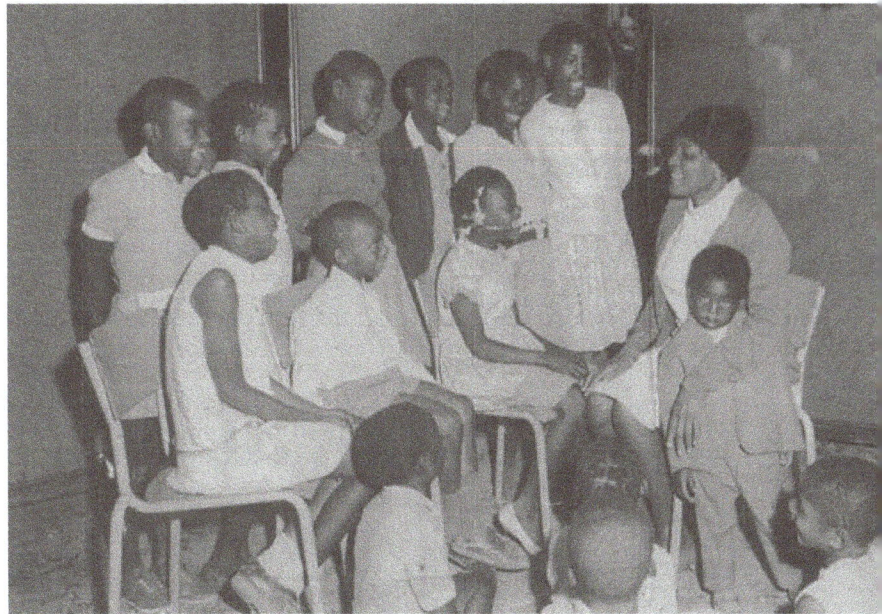

In a morden day set up - Ambuya Mlambo narrates a story in the broadcast studio in the c1950's

Music (through the song), therefore, can be argued to have enabled children to learn basic arithmetic/mathematics in a non-formal and relaxed way. Today's education has become too formal and for some children it is boring and they do not concentrate as much than when it is done through music.

Lifecycle Stories and Music: Warning and Advising

STORIES were told to all age groups, from small children to adults, depending on the moral values the story-tellers wanted to impart to their audiences. More often, songs accompanied these stories to suit with the mood of the story. These stories passed from one generation to another. Stories were told to warn children about the pot-holes of life, while others imparted general knowledge of nature to children; the myth of creation and an insight into understanding the supernatural world.

One particular story was about girls who had gone to look for firewood and met a man whom they had never seen in their area. The man proposed to one of the girls, who readily fell in love with him. The man turned into a lion and ate the girl. The other girls escaped unhurt and told their parents what had happened. This story was told to me by Malandu (Mangena) Mateza (my maternal grandmother). She was a great storyteller who lived in the area of Gwatemba, Filabusi in Bulawayo (Zimbabwe).

This kind of story was told to adolescent girls in an attempt to warn them about the dangers of falling in love with strangers. It was part of the tradition to encourage young people to court people they knew. Boys were also told similar stories, for example, of beautiful girls (strangers) who turned into snakes or animals at night and devoured their suitors. Story-telling thus played an important role in reinforcing moral values.

The Tonga , people who occupy the Zambezi valley in the north of Zimbabwe have a rich tradition of storytelling. Below is an example of one of their tales. It is about a second wife who was not shown love by her husband. The story/song does not only warn girls to be careful when choosing their partners, but also demonstrates how women can use performance to protest against ill-treatment and oppression from their husbands in particular. The song also empowers women and encourages them not to give in to oppression and ill treatment. Stories and songs long functioned as mediums of defense for women.

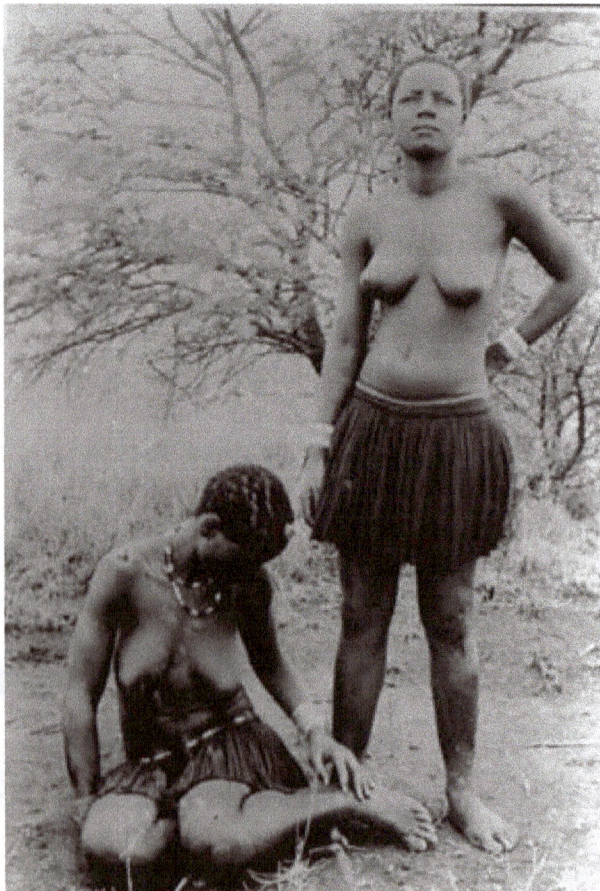

Ndebele Girls (1900c)

Nhamiwa's Magic Stick

As Told by Maria Munsaka (WICSA Diary 1992 –August)

Once there was a polygamist who had two wives. He loved the first wife very much, but treated the second wife cruelly. Her name was Nhamiwa and she had spiritual powers. With her magic stick she could separate the waters of the Zambezi. Every day she accompanied the polygamist to the riverbank. She beat the water with her stick and immediately the river parted, leaving a dry pathway in the centre. Her husband could walk across without even getting wet. As soon as he reached the other side of the river, the waters closed. He made this daily journey to steal cattle. At sunset he would call across to Nhamiwa (singing):

"Nhamiwa, Nhamiwa,
Beat and part water!
I have three fat cattle
And the middle one is yours!"

Nhamiwa would beat the water so he would cross. But when the succulent meat had been cooked and was ready to eat, she was always given bones.

One day the polygamist went down to the river as usual. Nhamiwa went with him and beat the water with her stick, just as he requested. He made the crossing and, at sunset, Nhamiwa heard him calling from the opposite shore:

"Nhamiwa, Nhamiwa,
Whose strength can part the water
Use your stick to let me cross
And you'll eat meat tonight!"

But Nhamiwa's ears were deaf. The polygamist called again, and again.

Eventually Nhamiwa sang to him across the river:

"I will not beat the water
I will not let you cross
Today you will be fixed!"

Suddenly there was a great commotion. The owners of the beasts had discovered who was stealing their cattle. Brandishing spears, they surrounded the polygamist. He called to Nhamiwa yet again, very desperate:

"Nhamiwa, Nhamiwa
They've come with sharp spears!
Beat the water with your stick
So I may safely cross!"

 Nhamiwa did nothing. The owners of the cattle set upon the polygamist and killed him. His body was thrown into the river. *(WICSA Diary 1992-August).*

Today some young women musicians are advocating a similar approach. For

example, Patience Musa's song *Zvirinani Ndigare Ndega* (It is better that I stay alone {than to have an abusive husband like you}) is a typical example of how women use music to air their grievances and empower others.

Women challenging injustices in society: Protest Music

PROTEST music was used as a means of complaining about certain injustices in the society. It could be complaining about other women or sending a message in riddles to another woman who would have aggrieved them. They conveyed these messages to each other at various gathering places, for instance, in the fields where they took turns to help each other carry out their duties. The process would be started with a provocative song in order to create an atmosphere for the other woman to express her grievances. There would be two or more factions hurling insults at each other, and there were those who added wood to the fire, secretly fuelling the tension. Another typical venue for such song dueling was the river, where women met to wash clothes or bath.

Such pre-colonial/rural traditions of conveying grievances through women's groups or gatherings were carried over into the townships where black people lived communally, and used communal toilets and bathing facilities.

This way of conveying grievances through song and ridicule somehow helped create a generally peaceful atmosphere among women. Conflicts or misunderstandings could easily be communicated through music, which was also used as a way of alerting other friends to come to their rescue and play the role of peacemaker. This ensured that the antagonists remained friends, although on the surface they wanted to play tough.

In the 1960s, the Rhodesian government used women's clubs as a way of 'educating' African women about good cooking, hygiene and better ways of raising families. Different women's clubs sang songs as they competed with rival clubs (National Archives of Zimbabwe).

During pasichigare women also used music to air their grievances to their husbands. For instance while grinding or pounding, a woman might sing a song to her husband's family informing them that her husband was not treating her well, or was not performing well in bed. This resulted in the husband's relatives talking to him or even just administering some herbs to the man in order to help him to function properly.

In an interview with ethnomusicologist Mwesa Mapoma, he confirmed that a woman might sing to alert her husband's relatives to her discontent and this would diffuse tension and help avoid conflict between the two as the relatives became the peace makers. Francisca Muchena, a Zimbabwean female traditional musician agrees with Mapoma, and explained

that if a woman confronted her husband directly the couple was likely to end up fighting. For this reason she used music to communicate her grievances, including intimate sexual issues to the relatives, in order that they might rescue the situation. This shows that in the past pleasurable sexual intercourse was taken as one of the most important aspects of a successful marriage, as opposed to today where singing such a song would probably result in the woman (singer) being seen as someone of loose morals.

In another aspect, women sang praise songs (totems) for their husbands after a pleasurable sexual encounter, (Fortune, 1982) (Muchena int 1994) . This genre is popularly known as 'madanha omugudza'.

Music was also used as a form of romance or alerting a wife especially when a husband was coming from beer drinking or had been away from home for a long time. According to Amai Muchena the husband would sing to soften his wife as the wife would be unhappy with the husband's absence. The husband would start to sing as he approached his home and by the time he gets into the house the wife would be happy and this would have prepared her for pleasurable sex.

A man would also sing a song to warn his wife that he was on his way home and in case there was someone in the house; friends, relatives or children. This was supposed to make sure that the visitors left so that the two would be left together to enjoy a conjugal engagement.

Daughters-in-law and mothers-in-law also communicated their grievances through song. The relationship between the two is usually contentious. A daughter-in-law could challenge her mother-in-law in a song, and also using language that was metaphorical. She would do this where there was a gathering of people that included the mother-in-law and other important members of the family. As a result, relatives would come together and solve the problem between the two. In some instances music makes it possible for the less powerful to communicate with the more powerful, (Herbert Simemeza–Epworth Theatrical Strutters Film Documentary 1994).

A mother-in-law and a daughter-in-law sometimes swap roles, with the mother-in-law being the daughter-in-law. This enabled them to tease each other and the same time airing their grievances against each other in a relaxed, non-confrontational manner. Grievances were also communicated through the names given to children, such as Sarudzayi (discrimination), Tambudzayi (you make me suffer), Muchaneta (you will get tired), Nyarai (be ashamed).

In recent times some of the names are in English-Godknows, Norest, Nodivorce, Last etc.

Extraordinarily Gifted Women - Community Leaders

MUSIC was/has also been used to enhance status in the community for women who were extraordinarily musically gifted. It is these kinds of women musicians who were asked to lead traditional events by the community. They sang at weddings and also led proceedings at traditional ceremonies.

When a girl reached puberty the women leaders organised a ceremony to celebrate her womanhood. Before a girl was accepted as a full, mature woman she had to go through initiation. Female initiation rites are concerned with the regeneration and continuity of life.

All over Africa, these rites enact a symbolic rebirth into adulthood, a process through which the community passes on knowledge and symbolic metaphors
In contemporary, particularly urban life, kitchen parties serve as surrogate

Shona Girls (1880s)

initiation ceremonies to prepare a woman for marriage. Like baby-showers and baby welcomes, at kitchen tea (party) the woman's friends, relatives and connoisseurs are invited to give advice to the young woman on how to look after her home and husband. Music is played at these parties, and the participants dance to the music imitating a sexual activity, which helps in explaining any issues regarding motherhood and womanhood. These parties are restricted to women.

According to Amadiuni (1995: 72), the women sang "lewd songs reproducing the sound and rhythm of copulation", which is the same as women in Zimbabwe would sing and dance at baby-showers, that is, imitating sexual activities.

After an initiation process (during pasichigare), gatherings were organized for girls and boys to meet and choose their life partners. In the Shona culture Jenaguru was organized where girls and boys would sing and dance the whole night. Jenaguru was organized when the moon was set/full moon as it was believed that certain positions of the moon determine the ideal time to look for one's life partner. Hence Jena meaning light, and guru, meaning a big event, (Jenaguru is still being practiced particularly in certain rural areas although it is no longer purely traditional and some of the songs played are jiti).

Marriage Songs and Gender Roles

After courtship the girl would be ready to get married, and the wedding day was an important event as women celebrate wifehood.

In a Nguni wedding, women were in charge of welcoming the bride into her parents-in-law's home. Amadiuni (1995, page 72), argues that among the Nnobi of Nigeria, "wives as initiates and custodians of the fertility cult reigned supreme" at wedding ceremonies. They sang and danced at both the ritual dance performed for the new wife and also at the birth of a new baby.

In Ndebele (Nguni) culture the welcoming ceremony was called *ukuhaya. Ukuhaya* was delegated to women of high standing in their communities who were professionals in this regard. According to Canaan (Mateza) Jenje (my mother), her mother (my grandmother) Malandu Mangena Mateza, who was also a story teller, would be invited to welcome the bridegroom in *ukuhaya.* She was of big built but when she was involved in *ukuhaya* she would jump and do all that was necessary to perform *ukuhaya* well. Therefore she was always invited in her home area to welcome the bride into her new family. Malandu Mateza was also reputed to have been one of the best *dombo* (bride price negotiators between the bridegroom and the bride's family) in the community, even though negotiating for bride price was a role mostly assigned to men.

Women, and not men, performed Ukuhaya in order to make another woman feel at ease in her new home and family. *Halala halala halala, 'Hoza laye, hoza laye !' (Halala halala halala, 'bring her, bring her !').* They would sing, mentioning the name of the bridegroom (her husband) who would be holding her as they walk into his family home. The leader of the welcoming group of women would then jump jubilantly towards the bride reciting

poetry, backed by song by the other women who she would be leading and making gestures symbolising 'welcome home' amid ululations and the waving of a (traditional) cow's tail.

DORIC SITHOLE, who comes from a family of women who practice *ukuhaya,*

Malandu Mateza Dube (Mangena)

explained, *"Ukuhaya is a celebration which is done so as to welcome the new bride into the family. Very often other women who are her in-laws in song and in dance welcome the bride. An interesting point to note about this celebration is the fact that the lyrics of the songs are a reflection of the roles of the bride/woman in the family. An example of some of the* lyrics that are sung include that of the Ndebele song "Umakoti ngowethu" which means the "Bride Is Ours" and in this song the bride is described as someone who will cook for the family and wash their clothing through Ndebele words such as "Uzasiwatshela" (You will wash clothes for us) and "Asiphekele" (Cook for us).

The bride is met at the gate on her arrival and some of the in-laws who are women, gather together and start singing carrying the kitchen utensils used for cooking. For instance traditional cooking utensils may include "Uphini" which is a Ndebele word used to describe a utensil made out of wood used to make traditional meals such as "isitshwala" in Ndebele or "sadza" in Shona, a thick porridge which is prepared using mealie meal. Some of the women carry pots and spoons, which signifies the role of the woman as someone who is supposed to be in the kitchen and is able to cook traditional meals.

The main reason why women take part in this celebration and not men is because women who welcome the bride have more experience about what is expected from a woman hence it is always best to be welcomed by people who will give you advice about how to do things when one is married. It would be a strange sight to see men singing and dancing welcoming the bride carrying the kitchen utensils during this celebration because 'culturally' their place is not in the kitchen. Hence it can be said that women welcome the bride because the celebration is about making the bride realize what her role is in the family by being introduced to the family by people of her own gender who have more experience."

Like the Ndebele, in Shona culture the husband's relatives sang songs welcoming the new daughter-in-law. The husband's sisters usually performed the welcoming ceremonies. The Shona call it "kushonongora mwenga" (to show acceptance of the bride by giving her money, and also to honour her) (Glandina

Nhamo [Ethnomusicologist] int.2006). The songs they sang included *Tauya naye muroora* (We have brought the daughter in-law home). The female relatives of the husband to welcome the new bride, to her new home and family usually sang the songs.

Tauya naye muroora
Muroora tauya naye
Tauya naye nemagumbezi
Muroora tauya naye
Tauya naye nemagumbezi

Tauya Naye muroora (English meaning)
We have brought the
daughter in law
We have brought her
With all her blankets

David Chifunyise rearranged the song *Tauya naye muroora* in 2000 and gave it

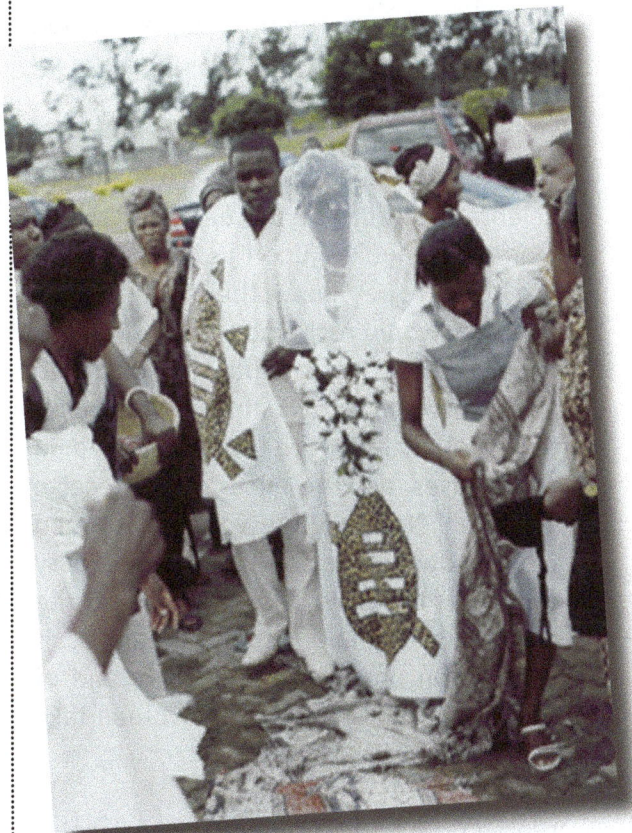

Women welcoming the bride to the family of her husband. The bride is being accompanied to her husband and the family of her husband by her brother. *(A wedding that I attended in 2006)*

a new urban grooves feel. The other song often sung was Muroora ndewedu (The bride is ours).

Women would sing songs praising their marriages. However, if they did not approve of the marriage they would sing songs of protest. They gave advice through song, warning the bride and bridegroom of the dangers of infidelity and other related issues. This tradition is still going on today.

At a wedding that I attended in 2006 the singer, **Dudu Manhenga,** sang songs of warning and advice. She played the song *Zvakapresa*, prefacing it by communicating with the audience and the newlyweds in a humorous way. This was to enable her to convey the subject of the song, which is about the deadly Virus HIV. She warned the newlyweds about HIV and AIDS. She said, "Shadhi, I don't want to meet my young sister tomorrow and she will tell me about the words that I am going to sing in this song. If I ever hear her saying these words, let me warn you ... People laughed and then she went on to sing the song *Zvakapresa* (Things are not well).

Women also lead songs at funerals to celebrate the life of the deceased. Since women are looked upon as custodians of the society they knew the family history and they would recite how the individuals had lived their lives and how they had died and this would be accompanied by music. They would also recite their totem and, in some cases, ask the ancestors to receive the dead. Naturally the voices of women were known to be sharp and it was easy for others to follow once they had set the tone in a call-and-response manner. It is common practice in Zimbabwe and of some parts in Africa to have women take the lead in songs.

Women who led traditional ceremonies of any kind were respected members of society. Young girls would be lured to marry into families of such powerful women, in order to communicate their intention (of marrying into the family) the aspiring daughter-in-law would fetch them water or firewood. The mother-in-law to be then alerted her son about a nice girl in the community. This in turn created a healthy relationship between the mother-in-law and the daughter-in-law as the mother-in-law would have acknowledged her daughter–in-law from the beginning. Leonard Dembo's song *Chitekete* (The Loved One) confirms this as it says: *Kudzai muroora waamai* (respect the daughter-in-law of my mother), meaning the woman she marries (the wife my mother approves of). This showed that the man's mother was regarded as having or playing an integral part in her relationship with her son's wife. A mother-in-law had, and still has, vested interest in her son's wife in the African traditional way of life and this has continued into the present day.

> *Women would sing songs praising their marriages. However, if they did not approve of the marriage they would sing songs of protest. They gave advice through song, warning the bride and bridegroom of the dangers of infidelity and other related issues. This tradition is still going on today.*

Francisca Muchena maintains that a friendly relationship between the daughter-in-law and her mother-in-law worked to the advantage of the younger woman who would get told secrets of the family. This helps her deal with the particular family in a more informed manner. But in some cases some mothers in-law can be difficult to handle and in such cases the daughter-in-law has to find other family members who can help her understand the politics of the particular family she is marrying into.

Leaders in Traditional Music

SOME of the women musicians who led traditional ceremonies were also good at playing instruments. The use of different instruments in women's music was very important as it made the music richer. Some of the instruments that women played were mbira, marimba and drums. However, due to colonisation and the so-called civilisation and Christianity, women no longer play some traditional instruments, particularly the *ngoma* (drum) and the mbira, as this was regarded as un-womanly and barbaric.

The churches also discouraged both men and women from playing drums. Women were particularly discouraged from playing the small drums that are usually placed between the thighs. They were seen as unlady-like.

Putting the drum between the legs was also viewed as thus. **Irene Chigamba**, a female drummer, repudiated this assertion and argues that she has the right to play all types of drums, whether or not they were placed between the thighs or legs.

Elizabeth Ncube, a Ndebele praise poet, also maintains that she has a right to play any drum. She is/was the first female Imbongi (praise poet) in Zimbabwe. However, Ncube was nearly attacked by a male imbongi because he was upset by the way she performed on stage. The male imbongi is said to have accused her of - *"wake wabona ngaphi umfazi otanyula inyawo pambili kwabantu?"* Where on earth did you see a woman who opens her legs in front of people? This comment shows how women's sexuality is controlled by society.

Putting the drum between the legs was also viewed as thus. Irene Chigamba, a female drummer, repudiated this assertion and argues that she has the right to play all types of drums, whether or not they were placed between the thighs or legs.

Women's freedom to communicate freely was destroyed by foreign religions. Challenging male's impotence through song was seen as un-Christian and un-womanly. One can argue, therefore, that western civilisation contributed to the erosion of women's power (Amadiuni, 1995)

Venda girls playing drums

Chapter 2

The Economic and Political history of Women and Power in Zimbabwe

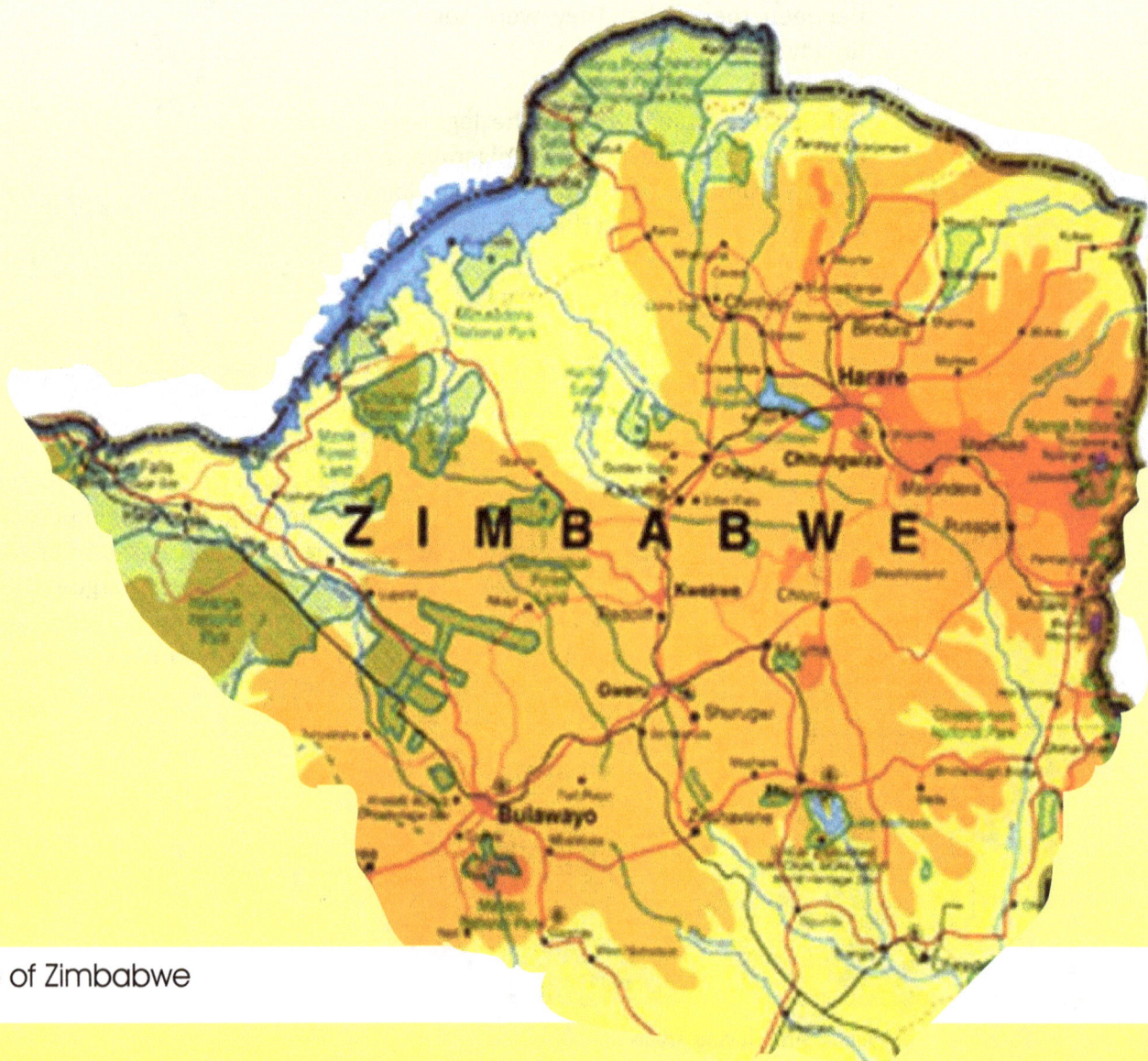

Map of Zimbabwe

HISTORICALLY, Zimbabwean women have played a significant role both in the political and economic sphere either by being 'allowed' that space or through societal structures provided for women; or by simply forcing their way through. The pre-colonial period produced some of the most powerful women in the history of Zimbabwean politics, such as Modjadji, Nehanda and Lozikeyi.

The participation in, and the understanding of politics by women has also affected their 'voice' in general, and how it is represented in music. The history and politics of Zimbabwe as a country has contributed to the shaping of women's political voice and their artistic expression. Women's musical journey has been influenced by politics.

Zimbabwe went through different political stages; from pre-colonial when the land was ruled by chiefs and Kings, through to Southern Rhodesia under the Federation of Rhodesia and Nyasaland, Rhodesia under UDI, Zimbabwe-Rhodesia and lastly Zimbabwe, with each political era leaving a mark on women and politics thus shaping their voice politically, economically and musically.

Pre-colonial Era

Zimbabwe as a state rose to prominence in the 15th century, when the country throve under the Mutapa Empire which ruled over the loose confederations of what make the Shona people today (Oliver, 2004).

The Munhumutapa (ruler) traded gold and ivory with the Portuguese, the Swahili traders and other rulers in the region making the kingdom the richest (ibid).

Magnificent structures now called Great Zimbabwe still stands as testimony to the Kingdom's civilization (Mudenge 1988).

Powerful women during the Mutapa Empire

The reign of Munhumutapa produced one of the most respected woman leaders in Southern Africa Modjadji –The Rain Queen (Krige et al, 1943). In 1800 she left the Great Zimbabwe under controversial and mysterious circumstances and headed South to what is South Africa today. She founded a people known as the Balobedi, who have been ruled by a matrineal line of queens. The fifth Queen Modjadji died in 2005 and she has not yet been replaced (by the time the book went to print).

From the first Modjadji in the eighteenth century the Modjadji Queen Dom is well known for supernatural powers that bring about rain. The Queen Dom still practices the rain making ceremony, which is also part of Zimbabwean (Shona) culture from which Mojaji people originated. The Balobedu Queen Dom is situated north of South Africa, within the Limpopo Province, between Venda and Northern Sotho speaking people. The Mutapa Empire was eventually weakened by infighting, foreign infiltration and Portuguese influence.

Colonialism and foreign invasions led to the marginalisation of women. Between 1830 and 1896 Zimbabwe experienced invasions first from the Nguni speaking people fleeing from Shaka Zulu and later from the Europeans Cecil John Rhodes' Pioneer Column occupied the country in 1890, leading to the colonisation of Zimbabwe. This was followed by a series of resistance (uprisings), first in 1893 and later in 1896 to 1897 marking the First Chimurenga. It is important to note that since the occupation of Zimbabwe by whites, the composition of women now included Ndebele, Shona and white women, the latter who were also marginalised, partially because they were very few in number compared to white males, as shown by the Southern Rhodesian census figures.

In 1904 there were approximately 406

white females to every 1000 males, and the figures rose to 796 white females to every 1000 white males in 1926 (Southern Rhodesia Report of the Director of Census, May 1926). Blake (1977:159) argues that "Rhodesia was a white male-dominated society", with divisions also common not only among blacks and whites, but between immigrants of English heritage with other European or white immigrants (Venables, 2003).

When white women became more visible in later years they were still regarded as second class citizens compared to their male counterparts. When Zimbabwe attained its independence white women, just like their black counterparts, got better jobs that were more challenging and they were paid the same as men.

Nehanda (c. 1863-1898)

Ambuya Nehanda, who inspired a revolt against the British in 1896, is one of the very few prominent women documented in pre-colonial Zimbabwean history.

Nehanda Charwe Nyakasikana, or Ambuya Nehanda, of the Hwata Zezuru clan, was the female incarnation of the oracle spirit Nyamhika Nehanda. Nehanda Charwe Nyakasikana coordinated the first Chimurenga and was captured in December 1897 and charged with the murder of a Native Commissioner Pollard. She was hanged together with Kagubi in April 1898.

Before Ambuya Nehanda was taken to the gallows, a Roman Catholic priest asked to baptise her in order to convert her to Christianity but she refused and said, 'My bones will surely rise again!'. Kaguvi agreed to be baptized. Nehanda was thus a gallant, defiant fighter and fierce heroine of the First Chimurenga. She was one of the first brave women to emerge in the history of Zimbabwean politics.

It is argued that her spirit guided the First Chimurenga in 1896 and the second Chimurenga from the 1960's to 1979. In the Second Chimurenga, ZANLA Forces asked for guidance from Mbuya Nehanda.

Mbuya Nehanda

NEHANDA NYAKASIKANA

She not only inspired the struggle, but according to David Lan, she also inspired literary and musical works and other artefacts. After independence her face was on a specially printed banner that was hung wherever the new nation state was welcomed, Nehanda's head and shoulders hovered above those of Robert Mugabe. Her influence in Zimbabwe history and politics is symbolised by the many institutions named after her, which include the Mbuya Nehanda Maternity Hospital, and some schools and roads.

Songs were also composed in her honour. The Mbuya Nehanda song became so popular during the liberation struggle and after independence that it became almost like a national anthem. This song was sung by the freedom fighters and when Zimbabwe got its independence in 1980 it was rearranged and fused with popular music and sung by Virginia Sillah and backed by the Harare Mambos Band.

Mbuya Nehanda
Grandmother Nehanda
Mbuya Nehanda kufa vachitaura shuwa
Grandmother Nehanda died telling us
Mbuya Nehanda kufa vachishereketa
Grandmother Nehanda died performing tricks
Kuti tinotora sei nyika ino
So that we could take our country
Shoko rimwe ravakatiudza tora gidi uzvitonge
The only word she told us is take the gun and liberate yourself
Vauya kuhondo shuwa here
They have come back from the war, is it true really
Vakamhanya mhanya nemasabhu
They ran around with machine guns
Vakatora anti air kuti ruzhinji ruzvitonge
They took anti air so that Zimbabweans can rule themselves

THE Ndebele people who occupied north western Zimbabwe were ruled by King Lobengula after his father Mzilikazi. In 1893 the Ndebele people rose up in arms against the whites. Lobengula resisted

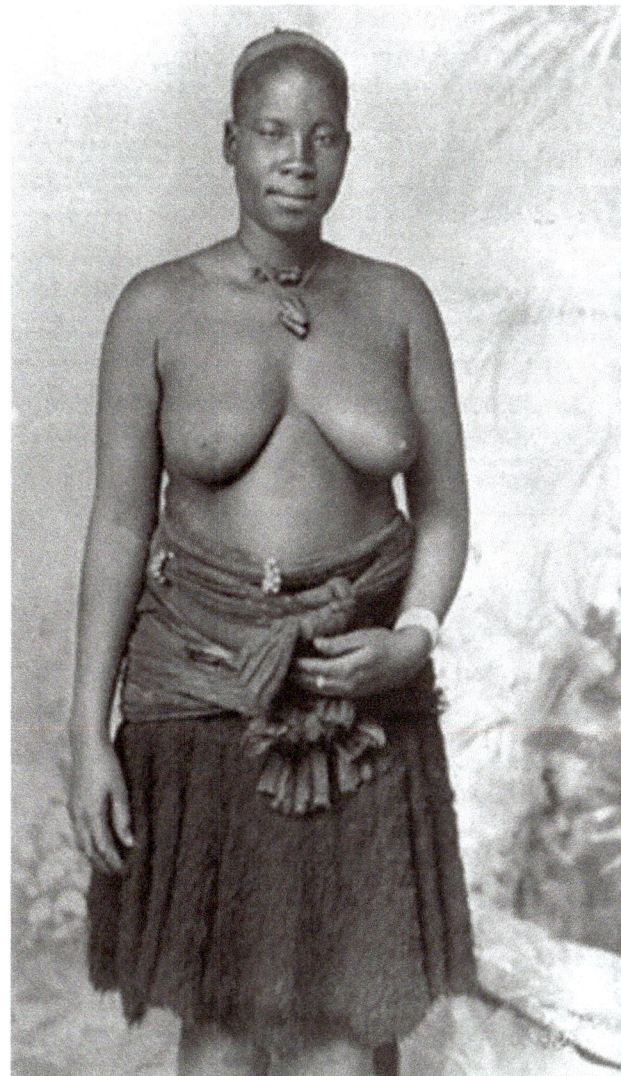

Lozikeyi Dlodlo c.1860 (First wife of King Lobengula)

capture by the whites by burning down his village and fled northwards where he died. The causes of his death are not known and the whereabouts of his grave are also unknown.

His disappearance created tremendous commotion amongst the Ndebele nation as his soldiers wept and demanded from the ancestors to know where their king was so that they could follow him. When Lobengula disappeared his first wife took over the leadership and led the Ndebele nation. She is said to have been one of the best political strategists in the history of Zimbabwean politics.

According to Marieke Clarke a researcher on Lozikeyi,: "During the 1896 Revolt she (Lozikeyi) made sure that the military was well equipped. While she was organizing the attack on the white soldiers with her military, everything was kept a secret. There was no leak whatsoever. This meant that when they attacked the whites they were taken completely by surprise.

It is argued that the 1896 uprising was more organised than the 1893 War, and the white settlers would have been defeated had the British imperial troops not intervened. Like with the Zanla forces (mainly Shona) were inspired by Nehanda, the Zipra forces were also inspired by Lozikeyi's spirit, she inspired her people to lay down the pen and pick up the guns again." (Clarke 2006).

Queen Lozikeyi remains an icon for the Ndebele people in Zimbabwe. Like

Nehanda, she is also a foremother/ pioneer of Zimbabwe's liberation struggle. According to Jeremy Brickhill (ZIPRA Force), (Zimbabwe People's Revolutionary Army), the ZIPRA fighters buried two bullets at the queen's grave; one FN rifle (Fabrique Nationale rifle) and one AK (Avtomat Kalashnikova 1947) rifle. The FN bullet represented the Rhodesian forces, while the AK bullet represented the Guerrillas (freedom fighters): The ZIPRA soldiers did this to inform Queen Lozikeyi's spirit that the country was at war and to ask her for strength.

There were songs composed in her honour and in praise of her leadership qualities. Today's composers and musicians have composed songs in her honour and some of them are: *Gogo Lozikeyi Uliqawe* (Grandmother Lozikeyi you are a hero), and *Siyakubonga Gogo MaDlodlo* (We thank you Grandmother MaDlodlo).

Nehanda and Lozikeyi are the formothers of the Zimbabwe liberation struggle.

Early Administrative History and its impact on the African Family

IN order to control Africans a law was passed in 1902 requiring all Blacks/ Africans to register and carry passes which facilitated the collection of hut taxes and labour recruitment. This destabilised the African family further, affecting women and children. The rule of the BSAC was terminated in 1923, and Southern Rhodesia was annexed as a British colony with internal self-government, and they held their first elections in 1924. The country was divided into African and European areas under the Land Apportionment Act in 1930. This included laws on how African land was to be used. (e.g. Forced de-stocking of livestock and changing traditional land tenure practices.)

It meant that the country was divided into subsistence farming, commercial farming

QUEEN LOZIKEYI (Later years)

and urban areas. The urban areas were further divided into townships for blacks and suburbia for whites. Black people were forced to leave their traditional homes to pave way for commercial farming. Most of those dispossessed were settled in the rural areas designated for black subsistence farmers but some migrated to the city (urban) in protest because they had been relocated to arid or uncultivatable areas (Marko Jenje Mhembere).

In 1931 when my paternal grandparents, Agnes and Marko Jenje Mhembere were forced to leave their home in Chishawasha and were required to settle in an arid place, they decided to move to the city as they felt there were more opportunities to establish a better life for their family. They were among the early urban black settlers who were settled in Mbare (Harare) township the first black township in the then Salisbury now Harare.

In the rural areas black people lived communally (extended families who shared the same values and beliefs), and carried on practicing their traditional beliefs, though Christianity (other foreign religions) and the so-called civilisation diluted these beliefs. With the introduction of colonialism, industrialisation, Christianity and urbanisation, women no longer had the authority they previously enjoyed as a result of their positions as teachers in their families. It was women's role to pass on family history, which they often did through the medium of song/music.

The new dispensation brought many challenges to women. For instance they were no longer considered as important in the family structures. Although they continued to being 'entrusted' with the responsibility of being custodians of the society's culture, they had little power to make decisions. It was not easy for women to be involved in

the new structures, which worked against them.

Women could no longer use music like in the past as a means of communication in all spheres, especially about their husbands' shortcomings as fathers, and husbands. It became un-Christian and indecent. Anyway, most husbands were not at home most of the time working in the city where they ended up indulging in extramarital relationships, sometimes leaving their wives with a sense of uncertainty and insecurity.

Lawrence Vambe, one of the earliest journalists in the 1950's described this practice as *kubika mapoto* (co-habiting) and today it is called small house. In the 1960's Susan Chenjerayi with Safiriyo Madzikatire sang a song about a man who was caught with a mistress by his wife, a *(kubika mapoto)* wife, the song was called *Mai Mwana Ndanyara* (Mother of my children, I am ashamed).

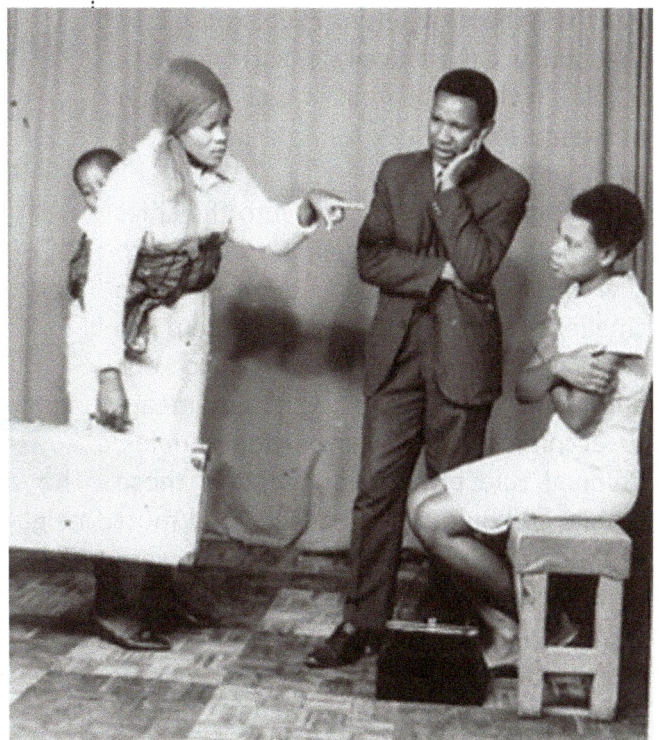

Susan Chenjerayi, Safiriyo Madzikatire and an unidentified actress (1960's)

Women no longer had the 'voice' that used to come naturally through music, as there were now too many forces controlling and suppressing that 'voice'. Urban structures and capitalist economies eroded the women's voice as the custodian of culture. Families hardly sat together to enjoy story telling sessions as the demands of capitalism dictated that the husbands either lived in the cities, farms or worked shift work in factories.

They could no longer pass on the family history to their families through storytelling and music as this was considered to be uncivilised and backward. Introduction of western education meant that children had new 'teachers' to mentor them, who were provided by the new government/ authorities. Traditional wedding songs were now replaced by Christian songs and Western Music; which were seen as 'civilised'. Women, who were once champions in leading traditional gatherings and also playing traditional instruments, saw themselves lost in this new dispensation.

The traditional family set up of black people in the rural setting could not sustain the family economically. Most men as a result left the rural areas to look for better prospects in the city.

The exodus of black people into the cities 'looking for a better life', in the 1930's also saw black women trickling in, although in smaller numbers as compared to men. The city was mainly designed for male workers, and housing provisions were not meant to accommodate black married couples. Colonial rule prescribed that only those employed could live in the city, and most of those working were men. Women were excluded from this arrangement as they were supposed to be at their rural homes looking after the children. Lawrence Vambe a township dweller in the 1950's explains how women were the worst victims of colonial laws in the urban areas.

Women were the most underprivileged members of this community. Originally, Harare was not intended for respectable married people, but for that type of 'native' who kept his wife and kids somewhere in the reserve of his birth. Hence the first section of Harare, MaOld Brikisi, consisted only of single roomed houses and it was hoped that this would prevent the 'native' from having his wife and rows of piccaninnies in the area. But it was not long before the black woman forced herself where she was not officially wanted. (Vambe. 1975, 185, Int. 1995)

Women could no longer use music like in the past as a means of communication in all spheres, especially about their husbands' shortcomings as fathers, and husbands. It became un-Christian and indecent. Anyway, most husbands were not at home most of the time working in the city where they ended up indulging in extramarital relationships, sometimes leaving their wives with a sense of uncertainty and insecurity.

The arrival of immigrants in the city from neighboring countries such as Malawi, Mozambique, South Africa and Zambia to oil the growing industrial machinery of a growing colonial economy, posed a new threat to the housing system. The new immigrants, together with some Zimbabweans who had abandoned their rural life, challenged the colonial government by taking their wives and families to live in the city and stayed with them in the small houses provided for black people. The colonial administration later responded by building more houses and establishing married people's quarters.

From the 1950's white women began to go out and work. This demand by white women sparked off a demand for black nannies (child minders), thereby opening a job market for black women and created opportunities for them to migrate to the cities. It was not considered respectable to be a nanny in the African society but women felt they had no choice but to take up the jobs that were available.

A Childminder (nanny) (c1950's)

Apart from working as child minders, African women also took up jobs as teachers and nurses. These were the first two professions for women that were held in high esteem, as they were associated with being educated. Some of the first female teachers in Harare's townships were Sarah Bakasa, Petronilla Ayema, Victoria Karonga, Ketty Chitumba and Lydia Matiza who taught generations in the townships from the 1950's to the 1970's. Some of the early nurses were Victoria Chingate, Angeline Makwavarara and Grace Mandishona. Women in these two professions were held in high esteem by the society. In the late 1950s black women also took up jobs as journalists. Some of the early women journalists were Angeline Makwavarara (Mrs. Mhlanga), Mavis Moyo and Canaan Jenje (my mother).

However, while there were a few job opportunities for black women, employment regulations were not sensitive to working women's needs. For instance the rules regarding maternity leave were that a woman had to reapply for her job after she had left employment to go and have a baby. In most cases by the time a woman reapplied for her old job she would most likely not get the job or would start again from the bottom of the ladder.

For instance, Canaan (Mateza) Jenje, one of the early female journalists, was a teacher then a secretary before she became a journalist. She said that it was difficult for her to go back to work as a journalist after the birth of her second child (my brother Emmanuel). She had taken maternity leave from The African Daily Newspaper where she was a journalist. She explained that she had to resign and then reapply for the job. When she was ready to go back to work there was another stumbling block, *The African Daily Newspaper* was closed due to political unrests, as it was an independent paper.

As a result it became difficult to go back to journalism. Maternity Leave laws remained

Angeline Makwavarara (Mrs Mhlanga)

Sarah Bakasa

Canaan Jenje (Mateza)

Mavis Moyo

a setback for women until 1980, when Zimbabwe attained its independence. The maternity laws were revised so that a woman could stay at home for three months after the birth of her child, with remuneration, and nursing mothers allowed leaving work earlier than any other employees. This came as a relief to working mothers and enabled more women to consider full-time employment, although the maternity laws need to be further revised.

The taxation laws were also discriminating on women. Women paid more tax than men while at the same time they were paid less in terms of remuneration packages than male counterparts. It was assumed that their husbands looked after married women, which was not necessarily always the case.

Since early urban life, women have worked in the informal sector to supplement their families' income in order to sustain their homes.

Life in the city centre was also expensive, and women took up farming in open spaces and organising themselves into clubs for skills development and money - generating projects.

This eventually saw the emergence of the informal sector. Agnes Jenje (my paternal grandmother), was one of the first women urban dwellers in the 1950s to operate a laundry business by collecting laundry from white people. She was able to live comfortably from this venture and she became one of the first women to buy herself a car, an Austin Cambridge, which she used to collect and process laundry and do other family business.

Another source of income for early women urban settlers was farming in open lands and my grandmother Agnes was also involved in this venture.

Amai Musodzi born Musodzi Chibhaga and married to Frank Kashimbo Ayema, she was involved in this venture from the 1930s

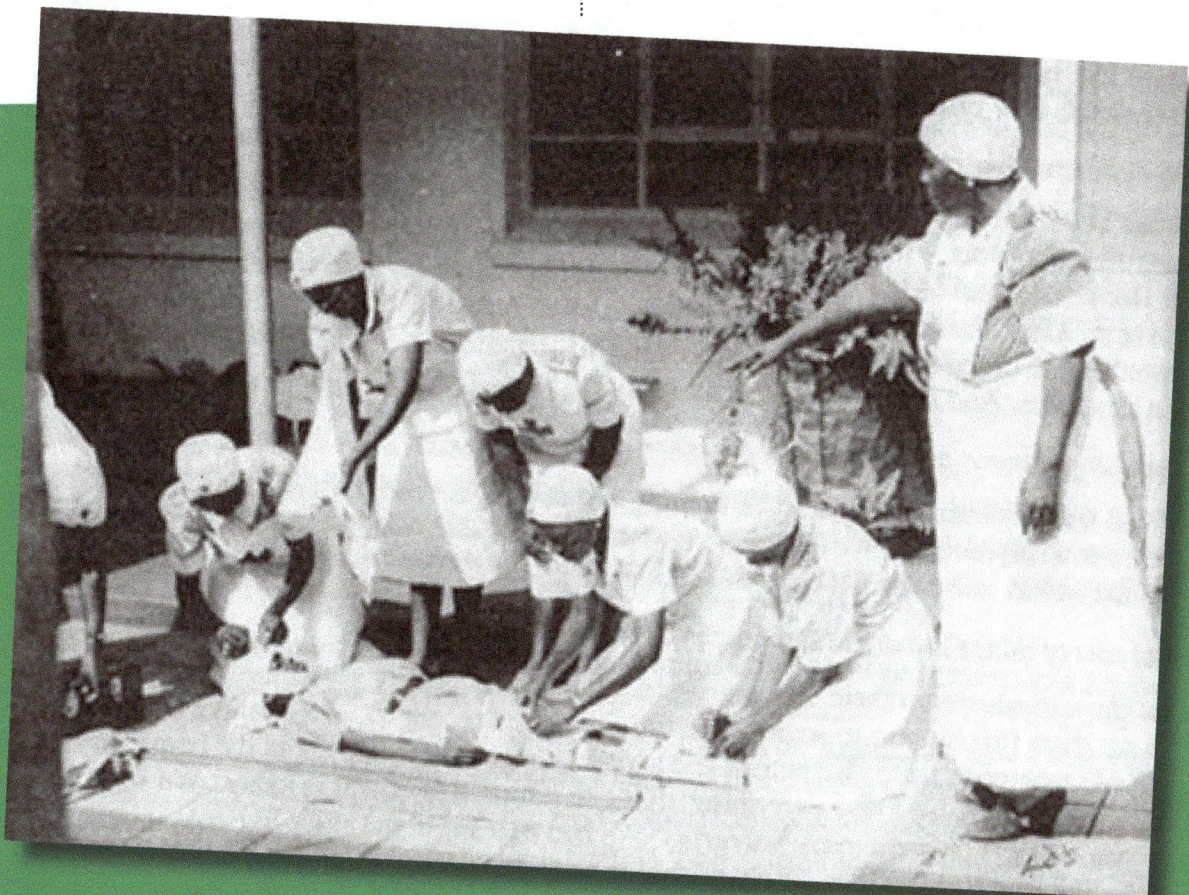

Amai Musodzi (Musodzi Ayema (Chibhaga)

. . . women were the worst victims of colonial laws in the urban areas. W
Harare was not intended for respectable married people, but for that typ
Hence the first section of Harare, MaOld Brikisi, consisted only of sing
having his wife and horo

Early women a

Women in History By Joyce Jenje Makwenda

THE exodus of black people from the countryside into the cities in search of "a better life" (commonly urbanisation) in the 1930s also saw black women trickling in, although in small numbers compared to men.

At that time, the city was mainly designed for men, as housing was not meant to accommodate married couples.

Lawrence Vambe an early journalist and a township dweller in the 1950s in his book From Rhodesia to Zimbabwe and in the interviews that I did with him in the 1990s explains how women were the worst victims of colonial laws in the urban areas.

Women were the most underprivileged members of this community.

Originally, Harare was not intended for respectable married people, but for that type of "native" who kept his wife and kids somewhere in the reserve of his birth.

Hence the first section of Harare, MaOld Brikisi, consisted only of single-roomed houses and it was hoped that this would prevent the "native" from having his wife and hordes of piccaninnies in the area. But it was not long before the black woman forced herself where she was not officially wanted.

The arrival of immigrants in the city from countries such as Malawi, Mozambique and Zambia to oil the growing industrial machinery of a growing colonial economy, posed a new threat to the housing system.

It was their resistance, together with that of some Zimbabweans who had abandoned their rural life, to fight efforts by colonial authorities to deny them the right to live with their families in the city.

My paternal grandparents Marko and Agnes Jenje (Mhembere), were among the first locals who came from Chishawasha who created their own space in the city in 1931.

Our family has been in the city (Mbare) for 75 years and still maintained both our grandparents and our parents' homes in Mbare. My first grandparents' house was in MaOld Brikisi/MaNew Line, then moved to the New Location and then National. My parents' house is in New Location.

The men who decided to take their wives and families to live in the city stayed with them in the matchbox houses provided for black people. It was mostly because the migrant workers and the locals decided to stay with their families in the city that housing was "improved" and the township was expanded.

As time went on, particularly in the 1950s there arose a need by white women to go out and work. This demand by white women sparked off a demand for black nannies (child minders). This was one of the first kinds of jobs open to black women to come to the city. It was not considered respectable to be a nanny in the African society but women felt they had no choice but to take up jobs that were available.

Some of the better jobs that opened the way for women to live in the city were teaching and nursing. These were the first two professions for women that were held in high esteem, as they were associated with being educated.

Some of the first female teachers in Harare's townships were Petronilla Ayema and Ketty Chitumba who taught generations in the townships from the 1950s to the 1970s. Some of the early nurses were Victoria Chingate, Angeline Makwavarara and Grace Mandishona.

As more vacancies that needed women employees began appearing, the numbers of women in the city also started to grow. By the 1950s black women started to be employed as journalists. Some of the early women journalists were Angeline Makwavarara, Mavis Moyo and Canaan Jenje — my mother.

At this stage it could be said that the wheels of urbanisation were now turning at near-full speed. However, the strides that women had made in the 1950s were eroded by the structures that were put in place to control women politically and culturally.

For instance the rules regarding maternity leave were that a woman had to reapply for her job when she left employment to go and have a baby. The laws kept changing that by the time she reapplied the possibility was that she would not get the job she was doing or she would start down the ladder.

For instance Canaan (Matesa) Jenje, one of the early female journalists, said that it was difficult for her to go back to work as a journalist after the birth of her second child (my brother Emmanuel). She had taken maternity leave from journalism. She worked for The African Daily newspaper. She explained that she had to resign and then reapply for the job. When she was ready to go back to work there was another stumbling block, The African Daily newspaper was closed due to political unrests. Bless the souls of those women whose careers were cut short by the only reason that they were women. They passed on the stick to us and guided us.

Maternity leave laws remained a setback for women until 1980 when Zimbabwe attained its independence. The maternity laws were revised so that a woman could stay at home for three months after the birth of her child and also be paid a monthly salary. And when she returned to work she could break early to

KATTY CHITUMBA — an ea teacher.

breastfeed the child and have more time v it. Women celebrated when this law passed.

The taxation law was also a setback working women as they were taxed more paid less than their husbands as it was assu that married women were looked after by th husbands, which was not necessarily the ca

Since early urban life, women have wor in the informal sector to supplement their f ilies' income in order to sustain their homes

The growth of the city meant the increas the cost of living as there arose more and m activities to spend money on.

To meet the growing expenditure, the dwellers, especially women, began to vent into other money-making activities such as tivating on open fields, organising themse into clubs for skills development and mo generating projects. This eventually saw emergence of the informal sector.

My grandmother Agnes Jenje was one of first women to do laundry for white pe since the 1950s. The venture became so cessful that it required a vehicle to cond She then bought an Austin Cambridge that used to collect the laundry and do other fa

en were the most underprivileged members of this community. Originally,
'native' who kept his wife and kids somewhere in the reserve of his birth.
oomed houses and it was hoped that this would prevent the 'native' from
f piccaninnies in the area.

nd urbanisation

business.

In the 1970s women continued collecting laundry from white people and one of the women who was able to send her children to school through this venture was Ebba Nyazema. My brother Newton Nyazema likes to remind me that in Mbare we called it "washeni and not laundry".

Amai Musodzi, a woman who contributed a lot to Mbare's early development, was one of the women who was instrumental in organising women's clubs during the early urban set-up. Another woman who also organised women's clubs in the 1950s was Helen Mangwende who started the Association of Women's Clubs (AWC).

In the 1970s women initiated what today is popularly known as cross-boarder trading. Women's clubs started this idea and one of the first women's clubs was the Mbare St Peters Catholic Women's Club that hired a bus to South Africa to buy goods for re-sale as a way of sustaining families of members.

Some of the women who were in this club were: Easter Masimbe, Pauline Shambare and Josephine Jenje (snr). They would also sell their crotchet-ware in order to be able to buy goods for resale. This has continued up to this day and many women have been able to live a comfortable life with their families and men have joined in the trade but now as "dealers" (madealer).

One of the most thriving but dangerous ways of making a living for early township women in the 1950s was running a shebeen. Among other activities at the shebeens was a musician who would be invited to entertain the patrons.

Bill Saidi, a journalist and musician in the 1950s said it was at these shebeens that township folks would get clear beer and liquor as black people were not allowed to drink clear beer.

Because shebeen queens were streetwise, they got the clear beer. The clear beer was drunk in tea cups or from soft drink bottles to disguise it from the police. Shebeen queens were known to be independent women who enjoyed a certain level of economic power and influence during early urban life.

There were more shebeens in Bulawayo compared to Harare (Salisbury) because in Bulawayo the city's by-laws were more relaxed. Shebeens are still operating today, but they are no longer as vibrant and as popular as they used to be in the 1950s and 1970s.

We will feature in detail women who were involved in all the fields and professions mentioned here as we continue to celebrate women in history.

● Joyce Jenje Makwenda is a Researcher, Archivist, Writer and Producer. She can be contacted on: joycejenje@gmail.com

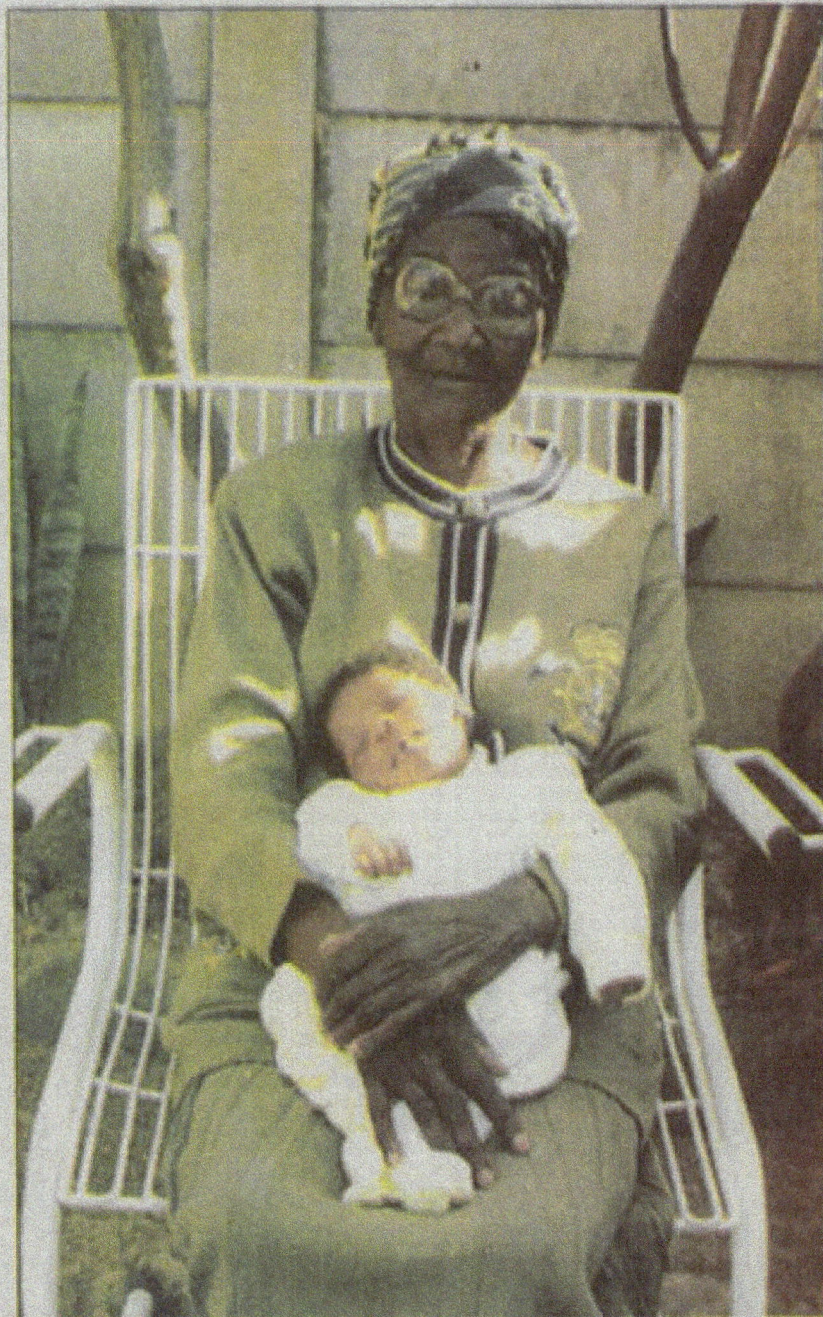

AGNES JENJE with great grandchild Mya in 2000.

and she also introduced clubs to women in the township. (Zimbabwe Township Music Book (2005) page 57). In the 1970s women continued to collect laundry from white people. Ebba Nyazema, the mother of Prof. Norman Nyazema, was able to send her children to school through this venture.

Cross boarder trade has its roots in the 1970s through women's clubs. The Catholic Church ran a Catholic Women's Club (St. Peter's Mbare Women's Club), which hired a bus to South Africa to buy goods for sale, a way of sustaining their families.

They would also sell their crotchet-ware in order to be able to buy goods for resale. This has continued up to this day and many women have been able to support their families through this venture.

The taxation laws were also discriminating on women. Women paid more tax than men while at the same time they were paid less in terms of remuneration packages than male counterparts. It was assumed that their husbands looked after married women, which was not necessarily always the case.

Shabeens were also other means of generating money although they were illegal and risky. In a shebeen women would sell beer illegally without licences, king money for themselves. Musicians

were also invited to entertain the patrons at the shabeens.

Lawrence Vambe, used to be a shebeen patron.

In an interview that I had with him in 1994/95, he said that despite what the general public used to say about shabeens and shebeen queens, he enjoyed being there listening to music and mingling with other township people. Bill Saidi, also an early journalist and musician in the 1950s, also acknowledged that it was at these shabeens that township folks would get clear beer and all sorts of liquor, as black people were not allowed to drink clear but opaque beer.

The shabeen queens were streetwise and managed to smuggle clear beer for their clients, who would in turn drink it from tea cups, mugs or soft drink bottles in order to disguise it from the police. Shebeen queens were known to be independent women who enjoyed a certain level of economic power during early urban life.

Shabeens are still operating today, but they are no longer as vibrant as they used to be in the 1950s-1970s, as other forms of entertainment have taken over. ■

Women and the shabeen business

23 March 2010

By Joyce Jenje Makwenda

WOMEN who ran shabeen were given all sorts of names, and the most popular one was; Shabeen Queen. Whatever one decides to call them, the shabeen business was just like any other business venture; to meet a need and make a profit. Women were able to look after their families through this business enterprise. There were not many jobs available for women as the city was mostly designed for men, who were needed for their labour. Some of the available jobs were being a nanny or house-girl and, for the educated, were teaching and nursing. Some of the women who went into the informal sector did not want to work for other people as they were not happy with the set-up or they did not have the necessary qualifications needed on the job market. The informal sector gave women access to economic power and they became their own bosses.

The emergence of shabeen contributed to the informal sector. One woman who was in this venture was Martha Kuveya (Hanyani). She says, *"Mabasa ainetsa, mwanangu. Asika,vana vaida kuchengetwa. Taida kuriritira mhuri. Kana wanga usina kufunda mabasa ainetsa. Saka ndakazofunga zvekuita shabhini kuti ndiwane mari yekuchengeta mhuri. Mari yaitambirwa nababa yakanga iri ishoma."* (It was difficult to get a job my daughter. Especially if one was not educated, it was not easy. So I thought of coming up with a shabeen in order to get money to look after my children. My husband's salary was not enough to look after the family).

During the time she was growing up families were more interested in educating the boy-child, since the girl-child would get married and the education would then benefit the family of her husband. Ambuya Kuveya, however, had the basic knowledge to read and write, she was taught how to read and write by the young sister of her sister-in-law (muroora).

SHABEEN QUEENS

Martha Kuveya (Hanyani)

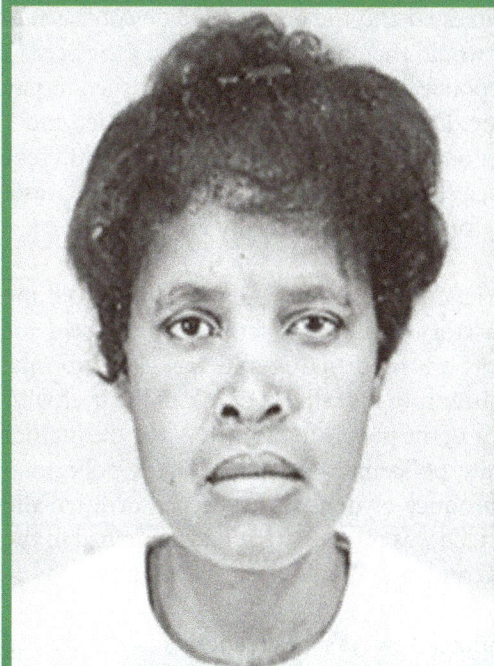

Joyce Hanyani

Now 89, Martha Kuveya is one of the few remaining women in Mbare township who made a leaving through the selling of beer at her home – shabeen - since from the 1950's up to the late 1970's.

She used to sell "7-Days" - a traditional brew, which took 7 days to make. It was not easy to brew this type of beer in the township as the police carried out random house inspections. Since it took time to ferment, one was likely to make a loss, as the brewing could be aborted before the final stage. Ambuya Kuveya had to hide the beer so that the police could not find it during their search. She dug a hole under her bed, where she stored the container of the brew.

When the police came looking for the beer they would search all the rooms including the bedroom were it was hidden in the hole under the bed. They would not find anything, even if they could smell it! They asked Ambuya Kuveya about the smell and asked where the beer was. She would ask them back, *"Riri kupiko, nhai mwanangu?"* (Where is the beer, my child?). "Maybe it is next door".

The policemen, not so sure where the smell of the beer was coming from would then just leave, confused.

There were times when she was not so lucky. The police sometimes raided her home before she could hide the beer or get a tip off. She would be arrested and the brew would be confiscated. She would then be required to carry the beer to the police station as evidence and asked to pay a fine. Despite sometimes being arrested more than once per day by policemen from different police stations, she never gave up, as this was a way for her to be financially viable.

A friend, who also grew up in Mbare, told me of a story of how his father was arrested for beer brewing/drinking and was asked to take the beer into his cell. He drank all the beer with some of the people in the cell. When the mujoni (white policeman) asked the black policemen to produce evidence why he had arrested the man, he was puzzled what had happened to the beer, and all he could do was stammer.

Ambuya Kuveya's shabeen was open during the day and, part of the night, also catering for those who worked night shifts.
When black people were allowed to buy and drink clear beer, she added it to her 7-Days brew. She now had a wide variety for people to choose from. There were times when she would brew what is called chihwani - a brew which takes one day to make. Before black people were allowed to drink clear beer some shabeen were already selling it. They had ways of getting the beer, which would then be drunk from teacups or soft drink bottles.

While Ambuya Kuveya was operating her shabeen she was also raising her children. How did she manage to raise children in a shabeen environment where different types of people frequented the residence? There is a general belief that children who are raised under shabeen environs become social misfits? Martha Kuveya does not subscribe to this school of thought. She said, *"Vandakatorera ndichiri kuita shabeen vakaita chikoro chavo zvakanaka. Vakatoroorwa. Mumwe akaita nurse, akatoita sister in charge.* (The children I raised while I was running a shabeen went to school and did well, and got married.)

When I was operating my shabeen, I used to tell my children that I was doing it for them – so that I could be able to pay for their fees, buy food for them, clothe them – and they understood." She said communicating what she was doing and why she was doing it to her children helped them to understand and appreciate her efforts. It was through this venture that Ambuya Kuveya lived a comfortable life. She was able to look after her family and did not wait for money from her husband. When she looks back at her work she feels proud that she was able to look after herself and her family.

Ambuya Kuveya farmed sorghum, which she used to brew the beer. She had even constructed ruware (drying and processing slab) at her house in Mbare were she processed it. The ruware is now covered with lawn, as she no longer requires it. She used some of the sorghum to brew beer, and sold the remainder. She processed it at night. In the morning people came to collect their orders.

Her field was at what was called *"Kujeri Rembwa"*, now the SPCA in Hatfield. She cycled there from Mbare almost everyday, very early in the morning, so that she would be back in time to sell her brew. She also planted "tsenza" (sour carrot/potato), which was very popular with the coloured community, which lived near her fields. After harvesting the tsenza, she sold it to the coloured community and the money helped her to buy groceries. *"Ndaibva ndauya ndatenga sipo nezvimwe zvakadaro."* (I would then buy soap and other groceries).

Ambuya Kuveya stopped her shabeen venture around the late 1970's, when her children were working and looked after her. One of her daughters who had trained as a nurse was staying with her.

Ambuya Kuveya's sister, Joyce Hanyani, also ran a shabeen in Jerusarema area of Highfields which was very popular. According to her (Ambuya Kuveya), her sister's (Joyces) shabeen was "The" Shabeen. *"Amainini (Joyce) ndivo vakaita shabhini inonzi shabhini. Kana tavakutaura mashabeen, yavo yakanga iri shabhini."* (My young sister's shabeen was "The" shabeen. When we talk of shabeen that was what we called a shabeen). It became the talk of the town, so much so that there was a time when she was declared a prohibited immigrant, (known those days simply as P.I.), because she refused to close down her shabeen. She went to live in Marondera. When the ban was lifted she came back to her house in Highfields, and her shabeen was back on stream. It took off like a rocket.

Different kinds of people came to drink at Joyce's shabeen – white policemen, freedom fighters, you name it. Ambuya Kuveya cannot find words to describe how her young sister had majoni and freedom fighters drinking at the same spot. *"Handizive kuti amanini vaizvifambisa sei. Kwaiti majoni, kwoti magandanga –handizive kuti vaizviiita sei"*. (I don't know how my young sister managed it – white policemen and the freedom fighters drank at her shabeen). Joyce Hanyani's shabeen was an equivalent of a nightclub. There was music playing all night.

Some neigbhours were not happy about it. They complained about their husbands sleeping at Joyce's shabeen, drinking. I asked her whether this did not destroy families. She said, *"Anenge ari murume angorasikawo zvake."* (It will just be one of those men who will have gone astray.)

Joyce, who had three children of her own, also looked after her nephews and nieces and she sent them to school. Despite being brought up in a shabeen environment, they turned out to be responsible people and got educated. One of her nieces trained as nurse and got married to one of the patrons who used to come and drink at the shabeen and she is still married to that man and they are happy.

Joyce made a fortune from this venture and bought business properties in her home area; Njanja. Sadly, she passed on in 2006, leaving a legacy of being one of the most popular shabeen queens.

While most of the informal sectors initiated during the early urban set-up have been legalized, Ambuya Kuveya is worried why the same is not happening with shabeen. In South Africa shabeen have become tourist attractions and they contribute to the GDP. They have gone levels up than they were in the 50's, improving and moving on with the times, just like any other businesses.

Ambuya Kuveya looks back at the work she did

Woman drinking Umqomboti at a shabeen

raising her children, and she feels blessed. On her 89th birthday, her grandchild who lives in South Africa surprised her and, she flew her to South Africa, where she spoiled her and took her for check up. The grandchild was showing appreciation for what her grandmother did for the family.

During early urban life, women had to be innovative in order to be economically viable, and running a shabeen was one of the ways.

Our mothers worked hard to raise us to be what we are today.

Women, continue to strive for economic independence, so that you can be able to celebrate life and womanhood with confidence. ▪

Chapter 3

Women Penetrate the music Industry

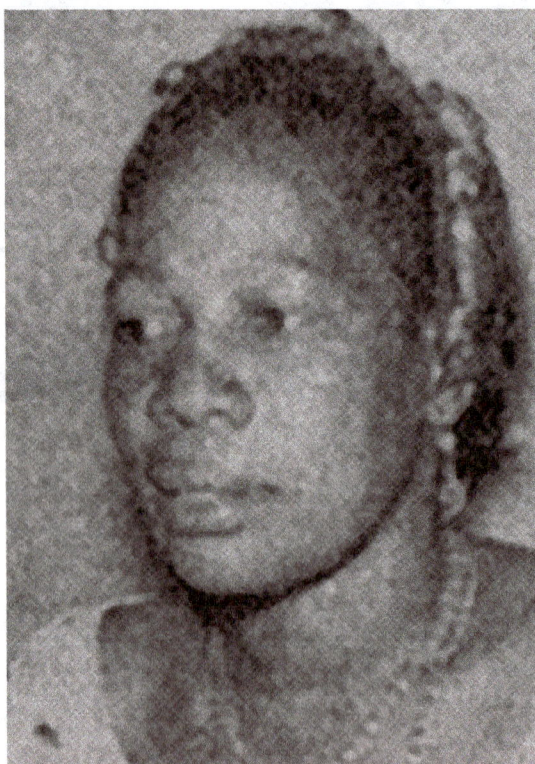

Lina Mattaka (50s)

Lina Mattaka (2000s)

AS the cities grew bigger, so too did the demand for entertainment, which was influenced by the media; films and other forms of media. This gave rise to the emergence of public entertainment, as artists sought to fill the demand by organising themselves in a more professional way. This development saw women seizing the opportunity to achieve fame and fortune and becoming part of the urban culture entertainment scene. Prior to this, women could sing only in church and at funerals during early urban life from 1930's. When they started singing in the public domain they were not easily accepted, as people were used to seeing women singing in the more traditional arrangements and in conventional environments. But because they brought in unexpectedly wonderful performances, society found itself reeling with excitement from their voices and dancing. To add to their greatness, women were also associated with the supposed 'civilised' culture. Women usually sang and performed in jazz, which was seen as sophisticated. Lina Mattaka and Evelyn Juba were some of the earliest Black women musicians in the 1930s. They were reported as the pioneers of township jazz music by the *African Daily News*.

When the Bantu Actors toured Northern Rhodesia and the Congo border four years ago, audiences everywhere mobbed and heaped praises on the troupe's slim, vivacious and elegant looking leading female singer-Lina Mattaka. To them she was all and all that showbiz could give Southern Rhodesia troupes that had visited the Copper belt before. Many had received thunderous welcome, but none of their stars had been so warmly received as Lina Mattaka. As the old MaShona proverb aptly puts it, "It was the sound of a drum about to crack". And indeed it was, for that was the last Northern Rhodesia saw of Lina and what a fitting finale to life so full of gaiety and splendour. On returning to Salisbury Lina quit the stage for her family of four.

Lina Mattaka's singing career is perhaps the longest on record. She very well deserves being termed the greatest of the women pioneer; for it is Lina in those stale curtain-laced years, the late thirties who alone championed the women's cause. In the larger cities, there were times, so she tells me, when a woman was not so readily welcome on stage. But Lina and jazz came rolling and was among the first few women who joined to set the Ball of Jazz Rolling the Jazz-O-Africa Townships rolling'(4, February 1958 – Socialite).

The African Daily News paper also reported

on Evelyn Juba:

"Concert goers of the early 1936 would focus on the name; Evelyn Juba. Eve, as fans in showbiz knew her, held sway in musical showbiz until 1952, long after the advent of the old jazz era. She soon retired from active stage work to give more attention to her growing family, having been active for more than 16 years. Such an achievement is her singular honour and memorable contribution. Evelyn Juba made her debut in Bulawayo during 1936, at the newly built Stanley Hall with the Merry Makers." (8 March 1958- Socialite).

Evelyn Juba (50s)

Evelyn Juba (late 1990s)

THE two early women musicians sang mostly Negro Spirituals, church songs, slow jazz, and mixed the music with their traditional music or simply changed a popular tune into vernacular (Shona and Ndebele). Their groups comprised family members, including their husbands. Lina's husband was Kenneth Mattaka and Evelyn's was Simon Juba. Singing with their husbands gave them a certain status in society. They were seen as good role models and they were also respected.

They were accepted by the society because they were operating within the confines of social structures: they performed with their husbands; there were seen to be what the society perceived as 'descent' when performing on stage; and the type of music they played did not require them to dance, or to move their bodies extensively. They were therefore seen as role models of a decent society.

Lina and Evelyn recruited and trained young women to join the music industry in the 1940's-1960's. This created a gradual increase of women musicians in the cities.

Public perception of Women Musicians

IN the 1940's a woman musician Reni Nyamundanda came into the music scene, with the De Black Evening Follies. Then the 50's saw a large number of women taking their place in the music scene, women like Faith Dauti with the Milton Brothers, the **Gay Gaieties** (an all female band that was composed of nurses who were the first trainees at the Harare Hospital) and Dorothy Masuka who became very popular during the 1950's, and is still popular today.

The 1950's saw popular music in Zimbabwe reaching its peak and women also finding their place in the entertainment arena.

In the 1950's music flourished particularly

THE GAY GAETIES - From left standing: Tetiwe Solani, Dorcas Fry, Tabeth Kanyowa, Ruth Jero, Martha Mabhena and seated: Grace Mandishona

during the Federation of Rhodesia and Nyasaland as many people from around the world were investing in the country. There was money to spend on entertainment. It is also during this time that **Dorothy Masuka** gave her first press conference. *The African News (Weekend Edition)* December 13, 1958, reported that:

Dorothy Masuka, the Rhodesian Star arrived in Salisbury this morning to take part in the Music Festival. She was introduced to reporters at a press conference called by Dan Madzimbamuto this morning, the first press conference ever called by an African in Harare. S.A.P.A. and African Press were represented.

Lara Allen explains how the media promoted women musicians.
'The rise of the mass media also provided sites of emergent consciousness in other ways: notably it created new opportunities for women musicians, opportunities

Dorothy Masuka (50s)

Dorohty Masuka (2000s)

that contributed to recognition of gender roles and, ultimately, gender relations. Examining the roles played by women musicians in Sophiatown culture, I agree that they became the primary female icons of this world, simultaneously creating a new kind of female performance artist, the Hollywood-style star. (Allen 2000, 74)

At the festival Dorothy Masuka played to a wide spectrum of people. Her audience included diplomatic and consular corps, the business community, educationists and the general public. The media was presenting opportunities to women to launch their careers and to encourage them. As Lara Allen also observed, in the 50's, the media opened doors for women:

It was during these years that the establishment of the mass media provided spaces for women to professionalize fully their musical activities, and establish themselves as stars with a fan base extending beyond local audiences. (Allen 2000,1).

Institutions and people from around the world came to invest and settle in the Federation of Rhodesia and Nyasaland, particularly in Salisbury, which was its capital city. The British promoted the Federation of Rhodesia and Nyasaland with the understanding that it was going to encourage the Policy of Partnership amongst its citizens (Bill Saidi 1992-int. Muriel Rosin int. 1995) although the patnership later proved to be that of a horse and rider, the white person being the rider and the black person being the horse (Eileen Haddon 1992-int.) Haddon was to challenge the Federation of Rhodesia and Nyasaland through music and journalism.

Eileen Haddon also used to visit political detainees in prison at Gonakudzingwa and made their plight known to the world. Amongst some of the politicians who

Eileen Haddon

Barbara Tedgold

were arrested during her time was **Ruth Chinamano**, the first woman political detainee. Eileen used music as a tool to fight colour bar (racial discrimination), as she would organize multiracial musical shows.

Another woman who also used music to bring together the devided nation during the Federation of Rhodesia and Nyasaland was Sister **Barbara Tredgold** she was in charge of the Anglican Church, and was a keen patron of township entertainment. Sister Barbara as she was affectionately known often organized trips for the young performing artists, with one such outing during Rhodes and Founders Holiday in Zvishavane in the 50's, during the Federation of Rhodesia and Nyasaland. It still lingers as a memorable event to those who participated in it.

The Federation of Rhodesia and Nyasaland was dissolved in 1963 when Zambia and Malawi were granted independence by the British government, with Southern Rhodesia now becoming Rhodesia (Vambe

int 92,93; Hove int. 93) The political situation became unstable, a state of emergency was introduced, and in 1963 musicians were not allowed to sing for more than one person (Moses Mpahlo Mafusire 1992 int.)

This saw many musicians leaving the country. Dorothy Masuka was one of them. She went into exile in Zambia, which had achieved its independence in 1964. Eileen Haddon was also to find sanctuary in Zambia. Like other exiles, they only came back when Zimbabwe gained its independence.

The return of Dorothy Masuka and other township jazz musicians in the 1980's saw township music coming back to life. Young musicians became part of this revitalisation, musicians like **Virginia Sillah, Pinky Mseleku, Biddy Patridge, Penny Yon, Ava Rogers, Kundisai Mutero**, and later **Prudence Katomeni, Dudu Manhenga, Kudzai Sevenzo,** and many others.

Virginia Sillah

Ava Rodgers

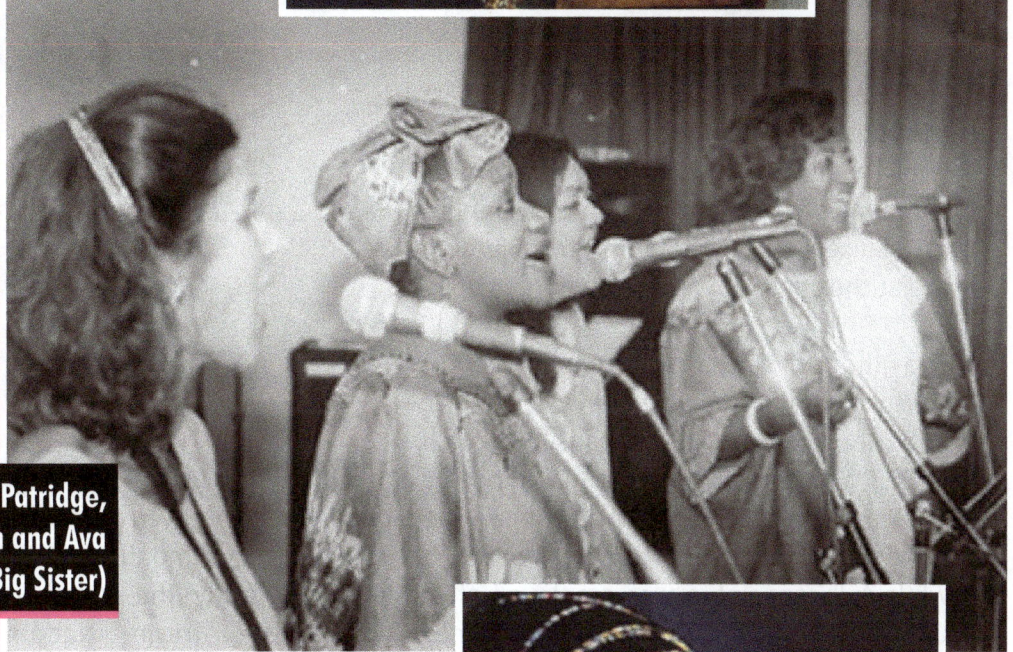
From left to right: Biddy Patridge, Kundisai Mtero, Penny Yon and Ava Rodgers (Big Sister)

Prudence Katomene-Mbofana

Dudu Manhenga

Women Musicians and Politics

When township music was "forced to go under" from the Zimbabwean music scene in the early 1960's, new forms of music dominated the airwaves as well as music venues; rhumba from Zaire and mbaqanga from South Africa. There was not much of local music going on, except for musicians who were copying mbaqanga styles and using Shona or Ndebele lyrics. Then in the late 1960's, Susan Chenjerayi emerged on the local scene as part of a duo with Safirio Madzikatire. She sang songs as a social commentary. Her music was widely accepted and received a fair amount of airplay.

Susan was a great composer and, amongst her music she composed a political song *"Hondo YechiNdunduma"*. But recording companies would not publish the song, as it was likely to get them into trouble with the authorities.

The Rhodesian Censorship Board (RCB) censored media, including news and music as a way of oppressing Africans. Windrich (1979), argues that censorship in Rhodesia existed in one form or another when the Rhodesian Front came to power in 1963, while full censorship was employed after UDI in 1965. Despite the difficult times from the 1960's to the 1970's, which did not allow artists to fully express themselves, women musicians continued to play a role on the music scene.

The 1970's saw **Susan Mapfumo** coming onto the local scene. She sang songs which depicted the plight of women, and also political songs. Her political songs were in riddles, like most of the musicians did during the UDI period.

The controversial UDI (Unilateral Declaration of Independence) by Ian Smith on November 11, 1965, saw the political situation deteriorating further. Black

Songs with a message

As a woman, Susan composes songs whose words are of social importance not only to women but to our whole society. In her song **"Baba vaBhoyi Maita Sei?"** we see the problems faced by families with irresponsible fathers. The wife asks her husband how he expects her and the children to survive when he brings home only half of his pay and left overs from the kitchen where he works.

"Composing songs is easy – but you must compose something which will be evergreen." "Baba vaBhoyi Maita Sei" with a message on an actual social problem is definitely an example of an "evergreen."

"Although I only play the keyboard and do the vocals, I play the rest of the instruments with my mouth because I show the boys what to do!"

Susan is alive and well!

On the issue of women's rights Susan said, "My message to women is: Be STRONG! We must be like men and do things for ourselves. If I could, I would love to tour the whole of Zimbabwe for women, to give this message in my music and my songs".

Susan Mapfumo

people became even more disgruntled. In 1966 ZANLA (Zimbabwe African National Liberation Army) the armed wing of ZANU (Zimbabwe African National Union), started what was to be called the Second Chimurenga. Seven ZANLA forces died in an encounter with Rhodesian forces at the Battle of Sinoia (Chinhoyi). In that same year ZAPU (Zimbabwe African People's Union), formed the ZIPRA (Zimbabwe People's Revolutionary Army).

As a way of consolidating his rule, in 1972 Ian Smith signed a settlement with Britain that had to be ratified by the whole country. But the British Commission headed by Lord Pearce declared a resounding rejection of the settlement from the black population.

ZANU and ZAPU united as the Patriotic Front (PF) and waged the Second Chimurenga war against Rhodesia from 1972-1979, through their respective armed wings (ZANLA and ZIPRA respectively). With the independence of Mozambique in 1975, the war intensified and PF started gaining political ground in Zimbabwe as ZANLA combatants could now be trained in Mozambique, unlike before when ZANLA and ZIPRA were trained in Zambia.

The events leading from 1963-1979 saw the position of women deteriorating even further, politically, socially, professionally and economically. As the war intensified women also joined the struggle. They brought moral support through music and would also carry guns on their backs as they also fought the enemy.

Margaret Dongo who joined the struggle at an early age of 15 said, "Women carried weapons as if they were carrying babies because the enemy could not imagine a woman fighting, and the women would either pass the weapons to other comrades or used them to fight the enemy themselves."

Margaret also argues that the liberation struggle started in earnest when women joined the struggle as they provided moral support through music and various other ways. According to Margaret Dongo, the song *Mbuya Nehanda* was composed by a female freedom fighter who is now late *(Muchazosiya maBhunu)*, and it became like the National anthem for the freedom fighters before and after independence.

There were also women musicians who later became popular in the 1980's who used to play mbira music for the comrades (freedom fighters) in order to boost their morale; these were Francisca Muchena and Irene Chigamba, Elizabeth Ncube, who used to do praise poetry for freedom fighters and became the first female imbongi.

Zimbabwe's liberation war was another form of authority structure that was able to partially override petty patriarchal rules and opened doors for women musicians.

Women Soldiers going to a training session

A New Era – Women Musicians finding their feet

In 1980, Zimbabwe gained its independence from the British, and Zimbabwe music was to flourish and women found their niche, and many opportunities opened up for women. Women traditional popular musicians were free to play mbira in public, which was once 'banned' and they travelled abroad, gaining fame at home and internationally. Beaulah Dyoko, Stella Chiweshe, Elizabeth Ncube, Francisca Muchena and younger women like Irene Chigamba, Taruwona Mushore and Chiwoniso Maraire are some of the women who play traditional mbira music, some who have won accolades internationally.

"Mbira music had been banned from the airwaves, and so were people from playing the music by the Rhodesian regime because it was believed to also evoke ancestral spirits to lead the struggle" (Amai Muchena int. 1993).

Beular Dyoko

Elizabeth Ncube

Irene Chigamba

Stella Chiweshe

Chiwoniso Maraire

Taruwona Mushore

However; women in the 1980's continued to provide moral support in the political arena. Women through the Zanu PF's Women's League sang for the heads of state, and also would welcome the president at the airport from his visits. This seems to be practiced not only in Zimbabwe, but also in a number of countries in Africa. Kelly Askew's research in Tanzania revealed that women's groups performed at state functions and also welcoming state guests. In Zimbabwe men and the youth have also become part of the musicians who sing for the heads of the states and welcome the presidents, and sing at other state functions.

One group that fused the Women's League vibe and popular music was the Murombedzi Women's Group. They recorded their music and found their way into the mainstream of popular music. Their songs became hits and they were played on the radio and television. They usually performed in their Women's League regalia. One of their songs that became very popular was Samora Ayenda (Samora has gone), which they composed after the tragic death of Samora Machel in 1986.

Although women musicians made strides in general during the 1980's, there were still some shortcomings in the way the structures of the country related to women across the board, which also affected women musicians.

In October 1983 women were rounded up by the police for being in the city centre after 6.00pm. This affected the entertainment industry as a whole and women in particular. Women musicians were the hardest hit, as this move instilled fear in women across the board. This resulted in the emergence of more pro-active women's groups coming on board to rescue the situation. The Women's Action Group was the most vocal pressure group. Many women became part of the Women's Action Group, I also became part

of this group during its formation. Like other concerned women, I wanted to exercise my freedom. The rounding up of women in 1983 confirmed society's attitudes that the public space is not for women.

While women were celebrating their achievements, the society was disillusioned by women's newfound freedom which was a threat to the establishment.

Women have since realised that they are not benefiting from the domestication and, like their male counterparts, they also want their place in the public sphere. Women no longer want to oil the engine that oppresses them; the predominantly patriarchal structures of the society. This attitude by women frightens society, but women want to live a normal life just as any other human being.

Joyce Mujuru also known by her Chimurenga name of *Teurai Ropa Nhongo*, when she was Minister of Women's Affairs, also encouraged women to press for their rights. On the Women's Day rally in Harare on 8 March 1983, she told the meeting:

> *The goal of Zimbabwe as a developing socialist state was equality for all citizens before the law. ...Women participated in the national liberation struggle for human rights, and their resources must be made full use of in a mutually complementary manner rather than in a master-servant relationship which smacks off exploitation of one group by the other? (Weiss 1983)*

The demand for women's rights from almost all quarters of the society including the highest echelons did not go down well with the society. Violence became common practice. In October 1983 women were rounded up and sent to some remote place as punishment for using and enjoying the public space and wanting to exercise their rights.

In the past, women would have protested in

song. Unfortunately the 1983 environment did not give women the platform to articulate their concerns, as their voice had been silenced.

There are few women musicians whose music has challenged the status quo; Dorothy Masuka, Susan Chenjerayi, The Two Singing Nuns, Susan Mapfumo amongst others. Not many women musicians were brave enough to challenge the status quo in as much a manner as their male counterparts would have done if they had similarly been rounded up and refused rights to public space.

Women mostly focused on songs of praise or music which did not have any political connotations and did not challenge societal structures, especially in the 80's. They hadinitially thought they were part of the new Zimbabwe as equals and part of the Independence, only to find out that gender equality had not yet been attained in the new acclaimed free Zimbabwe.

Unlike women during pasichigare when women could challenge any structure of the society through song, from their homes (grassroots) to the highest echelons (politicians). Women in recent times were weakened by events, which took place from the 18th century to today. They prefer or seem to want to toe the line in order to remain with dignity and not to rock the boat, as this is what seems to be civilization.

Two Singing Nuns

Susan Mapfumo

Dorothy Masuka

Dorothy Masuka composed and sang a song about Malan, *uDr. Malan Unomthetho onzima* (Dr. Malan's government is harsh), which challenged the oppressive Malan's government during apartheid in South Africa. Dorothy also sang another song challenging the apartheid system called *"Mhlaba"* (This World), with one of the lines as follows:

Kulomhlaba siyahlupeka, abamnyama basosizini (In this world we are having problems, black people are in sorrow).

Susan Chenjerayi composed a song called *Hondo Yechindunduma* in the 60s but recording companies refused to record the song. (War of Chindunduma-was a war were people were killed and the bodies bursted (*vakawanda vakabva vatanga kuputika*). Susan Mapfumo sang a song which ridiculed Muzorewa's government, which came as a result of the internal settlement in 1979, and another song proposing to a man, *Mukoma Ticha ndinokudai* ('Brother' Ticha I love you). It is not usual for a black Zimbabwean woman to directly propose love to a man; and Susan's song can be seen as a direct challenge to cultural oppression. Susan Mapfumo also sang songs to do with the plight of women like *Baba vaBhoyi Maita Seiko (munowuya ne-half ye-pay)* (What is wrong with you the father of my child? You bring half of your pay).

The **Two Singing Nuns** also sang political songs in the 70s in support of the liberation struggle. One of their songs, which became quite popular was *Tatetereka*, (We have wandered). They also sang songs to do with the plight of women, like *Kundenderedzana*, (a husband wandering aimlessly, with other women). The song *Tatetereka* asked the Almighty (divine powers) to intervene during the liberation struggle.

The **Chataika sisters** (Edna and Molly) who sang mostly gospel music also made a name for themselves singing with their brother **Jordan Chataika**. One of their songs with their brother Jordan that became popular in the 70s was *Ndopatigere Pano* (This is where we live) depicting the plight of internal refuges living in squatter camps like *Chirambahuyo* as people fled the war from the villages and lived in squatter camps in the peripheries of urban areas. This was also a political and social commentary to do with the plight of black people during the 70s who were forcibly removed from their homes and put up in "keeps", guarded camps, so that they could not be in contact with the freedom fighters.

Standing: Jordan Chataika. Sitting: Edna, Joyce and Molly Chataika

According to Pongweni (Pongweni 1997), this song became a national anthem of the homeless who were displaced by the war.

Despite the difficult times, the 1970s produced exceptional women musicians, of the likes of Susan Mapfumo and **Jane Chenjerayi.** There was also Susan Chejerayi who had joined the music scene in the 50s and **Virginia Sillah** who joined the music scene in the 60s era. Some of the musicians who shaped the 1970s musical terrain were **Rivonia Khumalo, Eva Melusi and Margaret Mbele.** In the 70s just like in the 50s, Zimbabwe popular music reached its peak, with the fusion of pop and traditional music. Some women musicians who started singing in the 1970s carried on up to the 1980s, and some to the early 1990s.

Jane Chenjerayi

The 1980s continued to see women taking their place in the music scene in all genres of music, pop, traditional pop, township jazz, gospel and rave music which was mainly for the youth.

Township jazz which had taken a break in the early 60s, emerged in the 80s, slowly taking its place in the music arena and becoming the music to identify with on the music scene for both the young and the old. It was popularised by such musicians as Dorothy Masuka, Sara Mabhokela and Virginia Sillah among other jazz musicians. Gospel music also started to find its place in the hearts of Zimbabweans, and **Shuvai Wutaunashe** made her mark in the 80's as a gospel musician and she became the queen of gospel music in Zimbabwe. She became popular with her song *MuKristu* (Christian) which topped the charts.

Shuvai Wutaunashe

During this period Zimbabwe produced a diva to reckon with **Busi Ncube** who teamed up with Ilanga up to the 1990's. She went solo and led her own ensemble, Band Rain. She is now based in Norway.

The 80s also saw the emergence of the Queen of Rave, **Rozalla Miller** who made her mark on the music scene with her album; *Everyone is Free.* She is still rocking the world with her music. When Rozalla Miller left the country rave music slowly died down, and it was replaced by urban

Busi Ncube

grooves in the late 1990s.

Charlene Robertson was another popular musician in the 80s featuring gospel and pop music. She became popular with her album, Liberty, which featured a popular tune *Happy Land (Tinofarira Nyika)*.

Some of the women who took to urban grooves are Memory Zaranyika, Plaxedes Wenyika, Betty Makaya, Pauline Gundidza, Portia Njazi aka Tia,Tambudzayi Hwaramba and Kudzai Sevenzo whose music sways between Urban Grooves, Gospel and Jazz

music. A young vibrant woman Ammara Brown also came onto the scene in 2005 although her musical career had started while she was very young. Her music is more than one genre; rave, urban grooves and pop. The urban grooves era brought out talent from young women musicians. The 75% local content government directive to local stations helped to bring out women's talent as more of their music was played on the radio and television.

This is what **Selmor Mtukudzi** had to say about the 75% local content government directive to local stations. "Through the 75% local content introduced by Prof. Jonathan Moyo, meant that we could get to listen to my music, people would get to hear of me, even though I hadn't recorded then it gave me hope that in the event that I want to record and do something I would have a listenership because then our music was not played much, we used to hear musicians like Beyonce and everyone else but ours was not played."

Almost all the genres benefited from the 75%, and women took this chance to have their voices heard, and began to take music seriously, as a profession and business; even employing managers. Some of these managers were their husbands or boyfriends, which also created some problems. Some women became managers in their own right.

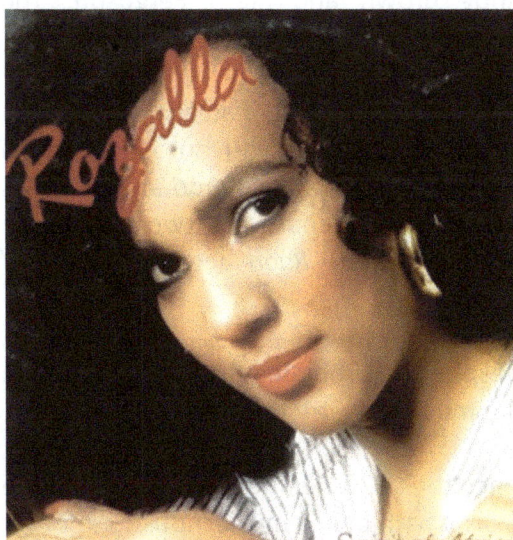
Rozalla Milla

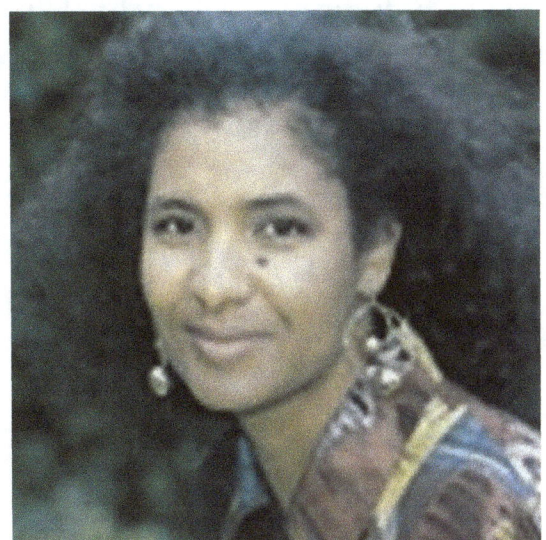
Charlene Robertson

Some of the women who made their mark in the Zimbabwean music landscape are Benita Tarupiwa, Patricia Matongo and Fortunate Matenga. Benita Tarupiwa a mbira player, has played with different groups since 1987 to 1996 when she formed her group Negombwe Mbira group.

In 1997 she went to Switzerland by herself and recorded her first CD titled *Ndotamba Ndega.* In 1998 Benita toured Europe together with her group – Negombwe Mbira Group, on this tour together with her group recorded her second CD *'Shirikadzi'* which is a live-recording of one of the concerts.

Patricia came onto the music scene and made her mark as one of the few women solo guitarists – a one woman band. Her music is between *Jiti* and some country style influence. The way she blends her guitar playing and her voice is mesmerizing.

From an early age Patricia was fascinated by music and in 1998, she enrolled at the Zimbabwe College of Music; Saturday Pop Workshops and her tutor was the renowned guitarist – the late Andrew Chakanyuka. It took her a year to become an accomplished guitarist/musician and in 1999 she came up with an album *Musarovane.*

A versatile musician, Fortunate Matenga is one musician whose music is difficult

Patricia Matongo

Sister Flame

to classify, her music is between reggae and blues she has performed with several bands; Imbongi (Albert Nyathi), Andy Brown. She was the lead vocalist for most of the songs on the album produced by Andy Brown and Kieth Ferguson. The project launched her as a solo artist.

In 2003 she was part of an all female group which was called Ruvhuvhuto Sisters with Ivy Kombo, Jackie Madondo and Plaxedes Hwenyika. Fortunate has two albums on her sleeve; *The Road* and *The Flame of House.*

Despite the problems that women face in the music industry they are not giving up.

Since the 1930s women have travelled the thorny path of the music industry in order to be accepted and recognised.

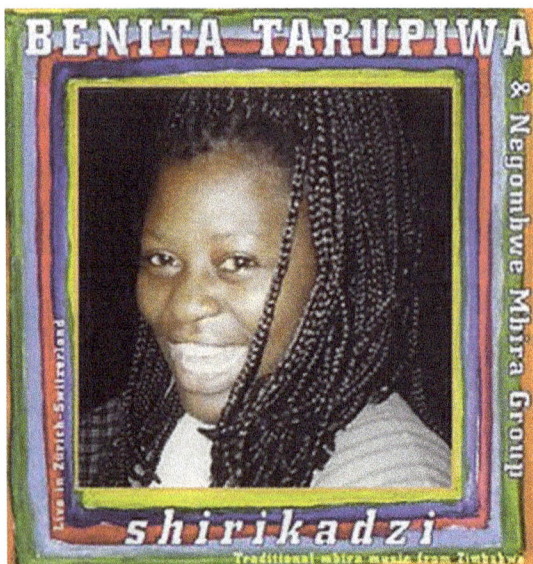

Benita Tarupiwa

Chapter 4

An outline of the contribution of women to the evolution of musical genres; pre-colonial era to the present

MUSIC is generally shaped and influenced by various situations including the political, social and economic environment. It is also influenced by external factors such as influences of other cultures. During Pasichigare (pre-colonial) period women's music was shaped by the work they did, their status in the society, the language that they spoke and the environment in which they lived.

During pasichigare women spent most of their time at home, looking after children, the elderly, their husbands. Women as nurturers managed the affairs of the home and did not seek employment outside or engage in most outdoor work unlike today. They also ploughed in the fields and did most of the house work, making them to be educators of children. As stated earlier, women also performed music at different cultural events and for different life cycles; for initiation, weddings, for death etc. Therefore the music during that time was shaped by what we can term as traditional life style and it varied with tribes or cultural groups. There was usually less external influence although inter-tribal influence was common. They would compose music for when they were working in the fields, at home, grinding, pounding, working in the fields, looking after children - lullabies, and communicating with children.

Earlier on I explained how and why music was composed in pasichigare (the time before colonialism) and explored how music was shaped by various lifestyles. Some of the traditional songs and musical styles have survived till the 1930's when it could not withstand external pressure caused by colonialism and migration (both internal and external). Traditional music begun to be diluted and also influenced by various factors such as the environment, venue, how it was recorded etc, and these influenced production and the outcome of the final product. However, some of the traditional music styles or rhythms

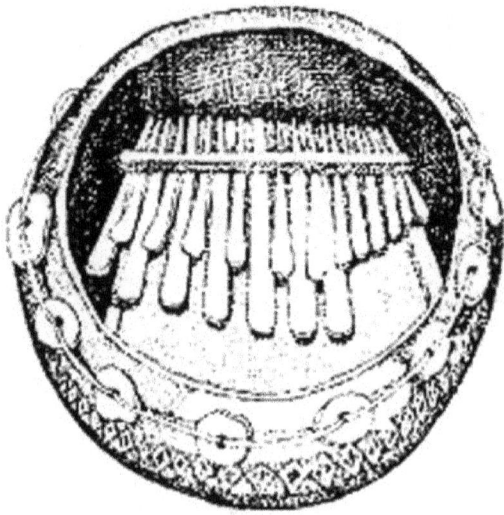

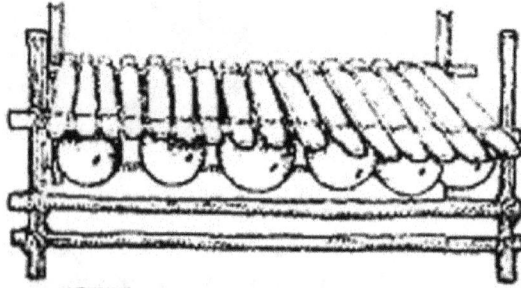

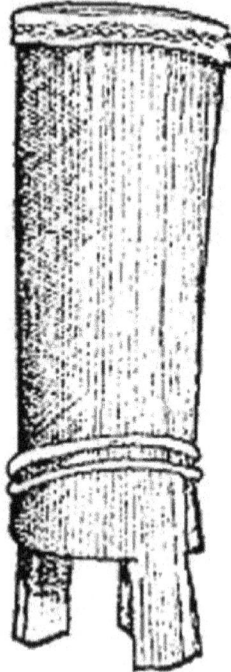

have survived up to this day although they have been rearranged. This trend of using traditional music as the basis for fusion started in the 1930s and became very popular in the 1950s when Zimbabwean popular music reached its peak and has continued to this day. This has helped to pass on traditional music to today's generation.

During *pasichigare* the music was sung in the musicians languages, which in Zimbabwe are mainly Shona and Ndebele. Although the languages shaped the music, however, since music is a level up for the spoken language, it takes a different form and it blends with everything that is fused in the music; instruments, dance etc. Their languages shaped the final product of their songs, which would have been influenced by other factors that we have already discussed. The audiences also influenced the final production of the music, most who were their relatives or were part of the community who would either participate or encourage the musician in whatever they were singing about. Their costumes were also determined by a particular occasion. Instruments which accompanied some of the music were: *ngoma* (drum), *mbira* (xylophone), *amahlwayi* (leg rattles), *marimba* and many other instruments.

Some women musicians carried on with the traditional music or fused it in their repertoire. Women musicians in Zimbabwe continued with the mbira music much later when other types of music had dominated the music scene. As mentioned in chapter one, the late **Miriam Makeba**, a township

Miriam Makeba

jazz musician made popular the Nguni traditional lullaby *Thula Sana Lwami* into a Jazz standard tune, which became very popular.

Post-colonial

Music changed from being "traditional" when Africans migrated to cities. Those who remained in the villages also witnessed pressure from the influence of Christianity which introduced new Christian songs. Women sang in church choirs. Those who did not convert to Christianity also experienced heavy encroachment from the Christian movement. Some forms of traditional music performances were regarded as demonic.

Jerusarema, a music dance performed by the Zezuru people of eastern Zimbabwe especially Murehwa, is one such dance which was regarded as demonic by the missionaries because of its acrobatic sexual movements. *Jerusarema* was originally known as *Mbende* dance and was regarded as a symbol of fertility, sexuality and family, but the dancers had to change the name to *Jerusarema* (Jerusalem in the Bible) due to the new name's religious connotation (UNESCO, 2009: Representative List of the Intangible Cultural Heritage of Humanity available online).

Among the Tumbuka people of northern Malawi, the Vimbuza Healing Dance was criticized by the missionaries and suppressed as it was seen as associated with demons. In the dance, people are possessed with spirit mediums and are able to tell people's ills and cure them.

New musical styles and genres fused from the cities by town dwellers into the rural areas emerged. The music was introduced in the form of records (vinyl) which were played on gramophones while in the cities both gramophones and radios were used.

Traditional Dancers

Music was played through loudspeakers for the town dwellers, and it was played for the whole day up until midnight.

The African-American Jazz influence on local music

The type of music which was played on the radio in the township through loud-speakers was later fused with other music to form the early urban hybrid styles, which was loosely known as township music/jazz. The music was composed of American Jazz, South African music and other types of music. Musicians then fused traditional styles with American Jazz Music, jazz music became the most popular base for fusion as black people in the townships identified with African Americans.

The African Americans music which had a major influence on local music was that of the Negro Spirituals, since a number of people had then been converted to Christianity. Negro spirituals fused well with Christian and a little bit of traditional music. According to Gibson Mandishona, "Zimbabwe Township Music evolved on a parallel trend as the 19th century slave work songs, hymns and spirituals; with melodic elements borrowed from African traditional lyrics."

The similarities between the African American and black Zimbabweans contributed to, and encouraged Zimbabweans to use Negro Spirituals jazz in their repertoire during the 1930s early urban music. The music's lyrics were changed into Shona or Ndebele to give it a local flavor. Jazz music was also associated with decent women and women who were part of this genre were seen as being able to maintain their dignity.

Lina Mattaka and Evelyn Juba

Women musicians who were associated with this type of music were **Lina Mattaka** and **Evelyn Juba** and had a strong church background. When Lina Joined the Bantu Actors, their opening song was a Christian song, *Idiko Zita raTenzi* (It is true the name of the Lord).

At the time women were viewed as having morals if they sang in churches and choirs *(makwaya/amakwaya)*. The *makwaya* music took after church music although choirs were mostly associated with entertainment. Lina and Evelyn became

The Mattaka Family

Bertha (Mattaka) Msora and brother Eddison Mattaka

the first women to be associated with jazz music in the 1930s. Their type of jazz was slow jazz which was influenced by Negro spirituals, slow jazz, Christian songs and traditional music.

When Lina Mattaka worked at the Stanely Hall, she decided to have a big choir, resulting in her being named the Queen of Soprano, and she taught other musicians this type of dance. In 1958 the *Central Daily News* reported that:

> "For a decade tape dancing was chic, it really dominated the music scene to be replaced by jazz music in the 40's and who was at the forefront? No other than Lina Mattaka and those women who had followed in her footsteps."

Lina Mattaka groomed and influenced her daughter Bertha, who became the youngest musician in the 1950s, and carried on with township music as pass time until her death in 2005.

Evelyn Juba came on the music scene immediately after Lina and in the 1930's they were the only notable women in the popular music scene. Evelyn Juba also sang with her husband Simon Juba, and her brother Remmington Mazabane. Their group was called the Merry Makers. They sang *makwaya*, swing and jazz music. Evelyn Juba became very popular during her time that when the Merry Makers travelled to Botswana (Bechuanaland) in Serowe, people wanted to see Evelyn Juba.

> "A story is told of how some Bamangwato concert fans, wishing to attend the Merry Makers show at Serowe, journeyed for days on foot and horse backs to catch a glimpse of the very popular singer." (the Daily News in 1958).

With time, other music styles came on board, some of them were *tsaba, tsaba* and *amarabi,* these early musical urban hybrids were also loosely known as township music. The fast beat of *tsaba tsaba, marabi* and jazz of the 1950s was faster than the 1930s jazz music and the three brought in a unique township sound.

The Merry Makers

The 1950s saw a number of women musicians coming onto the scene, with notable groups and solo acts as Dorothy Masuka, **Victoria Chingate**'s Gay Gaieties, **Faith Dauti, Sylvia Sondo, Sarah Mabhokela, Joyce Ndoro, Christine Dube, Margaret Pazarangu, Flora Dick, Tabeth Kapuya, Una Chipere, Mabel Bingwa, Ruth Mpisaunga, Mabel Pindurayi, Miriam Yafele**, and one of the best musicians who is still in the music scene up to this day who came from the 1950s is Dorothy Masuka.

Flora Dick

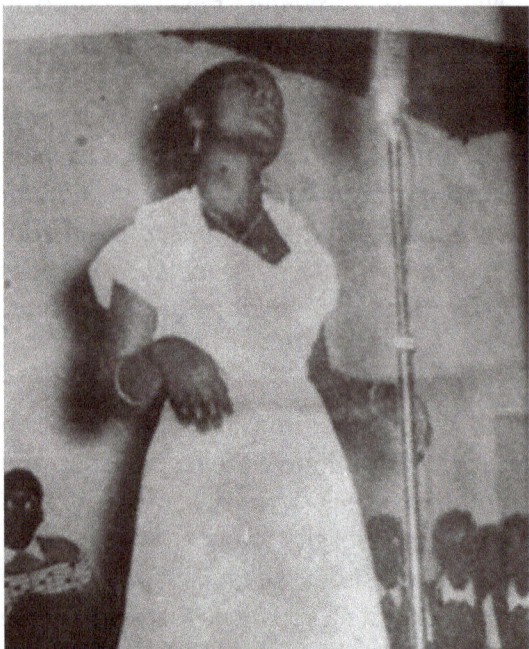

Faith Dauti

Mary Mabhena

Joyce Jenje-Makwenda

The music of the 1950s varied from jazz, *amarabi, tsaba tsaba, calypso, cha cha* now known as *Rhumba* music. Traditional music was fused with other types of music from neibghouring countries and abroad. The music can still be classified as an early urban hybrid music, but had changed from the one sung by women like Lina Mattaka and Evelyn Juba.

Women musicians then, brought a fresh and new sound of the 1950s and 1960s. Some of the women recorded songs which they composed, which were part of their repertoire.

Dorothy Masuka composed and recorded more than any artist in the 1950s. She introduced new lyrics, new dressing, and new stage work. Dorothy sang about shabeens, about fashion, about politics. Her lyrics reflected what was happening in the society in the 1950s. She did not toe the line; her lyrics reflected her feelings and not what the society wanted or expected to hear. She was not apologetic and did not want to play the 'moral' woman that the society expected so that she could be allowed to use the public sphere without ridicule; she used the public space in any way without asking for 'permission'. Her free spirit shaped her musical style and she came up with a Dorothy Masuka beat/style which was, and is still very unique. Her music sold in numbers, this could have been due to the fact that the society either bought the records out of curiosity or just chose to go along with her.

Dorothy brought a new era and her carefree lyrics resembled the way women in pre-colonial era who expressed themselves through music. Dorothy Masuka did not allow anything to come between her voice and artistic expression. She also wrote songs for the late international township jazz musician – Miriam Makeba.

Dorothy Masuka challenged the society's perception of women who wore trousers, known as bogarts. Another song which was controversial was *Pata Pata* (touch

Who can this be – none other than Dorothy Masuka – Southern Africa 50s

Dorothy Masuka 3rd from left with singer of the Tandi 2nd from left and far left Rose

touch) this song raised society's eyebrows as the dance was about touching ones's breasts and buttocks; it was sexual. She was bringing sexuality to the fore which was considered un-Christian and uncivilized.

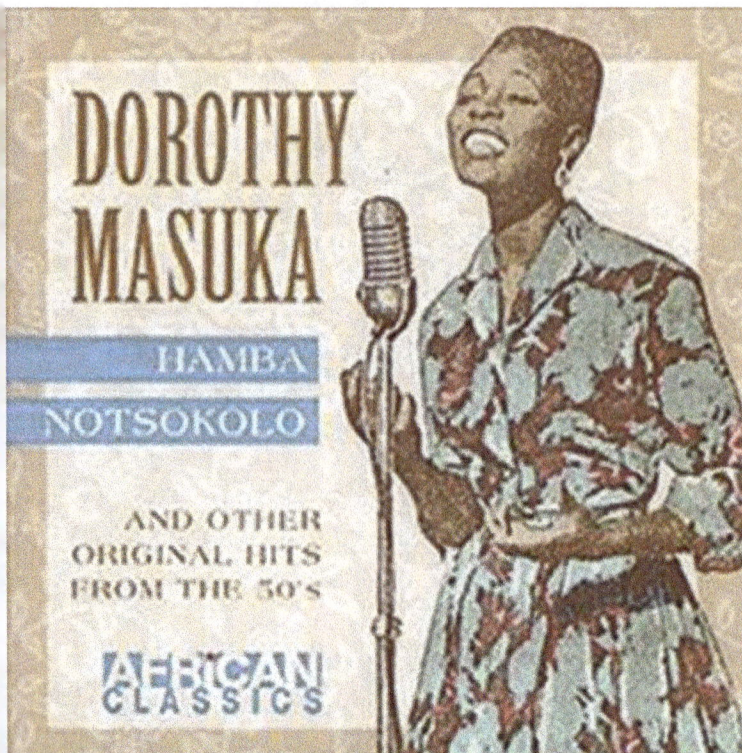

December 2 1997

May 14 2002

She used music as a platform to challenge the concept of women and sexuality. She also sang and composed political songs, with her most popular political song as *UMalan (UMalan Ulomthetho Onzima* –'Malan rules with an iron fist'). This song got her into trouble and she was banned from South Africa. She could not live in Zimbabwe then Rhodesia either, as she was considered security threat in both countries.

She went to live in Zambia in exile and only came back to Zimbabwe and South Africa when the two countries had gained independence. Dorothy composed and recorded more than 20 songs with Troubador in the 50s and the most popular song was *Hamba Nontsokolo*.

One other woman who was a brilliant composer and arranger was **Faith Dauti,** who was at times mistaken for Dorothy Masuka's sister because of the similarities of their voices. Some of the songs she composed and arranged were: *Rosvika Zuva,* (The Day has come) *Hama neva Bereki.*

(Relatives and friends) (from the tune *Hamba noNsokolo* by Dorothy Masuka),

Ngatipemberei, (Lets rejoice) *Shoko rasvika* (The Word has Come), and many others. *Rosvika Zuva* was played on General Service which was not usually the case as Shona songs were only played on the African Service and the General Service was meant for Europeans. This was during the General strike of the 1950's, the song was about love and the authorities used it to persuade Black workers to abandon the strike and go back to work.

Rosvika Zuva

Shona
Rosvika zuva rekuti ini newe
tigare tose zvedu tidanane
hona nyika nhasi yoziva uri wangu.

Rudo rwangu nepfungwa dzangu
hona tigare tose zvedu tidanane
hona nyika zvino yoziva uriwangu

English
The day has come for me and you
To live together
See the world
now know you are mine

My love, my soul
If we can live together
The world knows that you are mine

Euna Chipere

Euna Chipere did not stay for long in the music scene in the 1950s, but she will be remembered for her song Kana Usingandide (If you do not love me), which she composed in 1956 and was later to be recorded by Thomas Mapfumo in the 1970s. The song Kana Usingandide is one of Thomas Mupfumo popular songs although it was composed by Euna Chipere.

Sarah Mabhokela

She started singing and performing in the 1950s era although **Sarah Mabhokela** made an impact in the 1960s when she returned to her country of birth, South Africa,

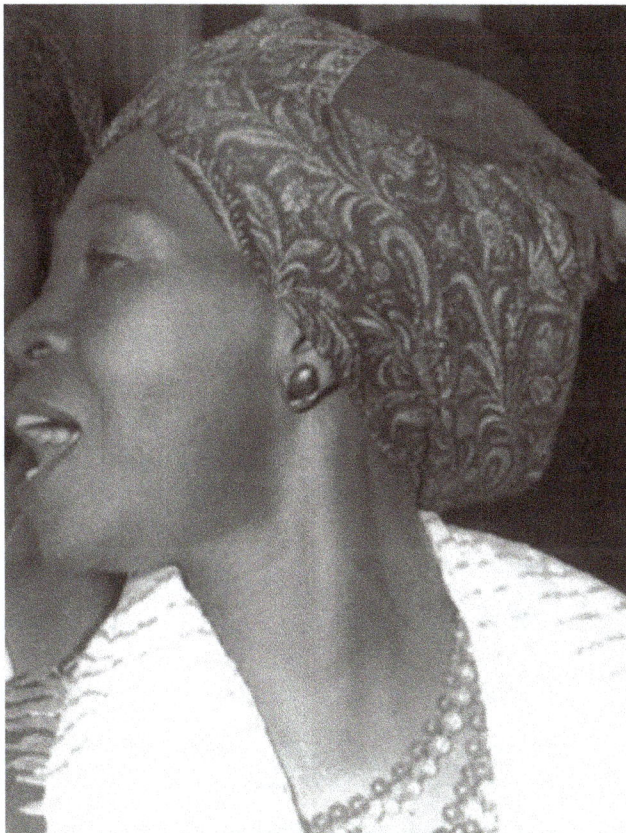

Sarah Mabhokela

where she performed with the Mahotella Queens. Sarah Mabhokela rearranged Jeremiah Kainga's song *Imi Munosara Nani Ndaenda* which Jeremiah had recorded with the Menton and Sisters and one of the Menton and Sisters was, **Ruth Mpisaunga**. Sara rearranged the song very well with a mixture of the 1960s *Mbaqanga* music; she recorded the song with the Mahotella

Queens, a Mbaqanga South African outfit. The fusing of Shona with *mbaqanga* music became a hit and Sarah Mabhokela went on to write more Shona songs for the group. When the Mahotella Queens, who had a large following in Zimbabwe, toured the country to perform; the fusing of Shona and South African languages, earned them popularity and an even larger crowd than before. It also became a marketing strategy for them.

The late **Ruth Mpisaunga** (Muchawaya) was a multi talented artist besides music she was also into acting, and writing. She grew up in the surburb of Mbare and her parents stayed near the Mai Musodzi Hall

Ruth Mpisaunga

which was then the hub of entertainement. She belonged to a musical group led by Jeremiah Kainga the "Menton and Sisters", she was one of the backing vocalists on the hit song "*Imi Munosara Nani Ndaenda*".

Joyce Ndoro

Joyce Ndoro fronted the De Black Evening, and became the only female musician who

Joyce Ndoro

was 16. The Masholand Melodians, just like the De Black Evening Follies, became a stable for a number of women musicians and one of them was Flora Dick (Zonk Girl), who was popularly known for her dancing skills. She was also known by the listeners of the African Broadcasting Corporation for her song *"Sesse-ture"* which was ranked highly as it captured the minds of many Zimbabweans.

Tabeth Kapuya's musical talent was nurtured by the Gay Gaeties, she was a contemporary of Faith Dauti and Flora Dick. Mabel Pindurayi had her stint in township music but her career was cut short by an automobile accident. Miriam Yafele, following the footsteps of Lina Mattaka and Evelyn Juba, started her musical career with her husband who was the leader of

stayed the longest with the group. She sang and performed the song *Goli Goli*, an Indian song which she was taught at a cultural festival in Harare. Joyce was one of the most popular women musicians of the 1950s-1960s, she also won the Miss Harare beauty title.

There were quiet a number of female musicians in the 1950s and 1960s although some of them did not stay for a long time. These include **Christine Dube** who used to sing with the **Milton Brothers. Margaret Pazarangu** popularly known as Sugar Brown Baby, and was discovered by the De Black Evening Follies as they searched for talented people in the townships. Pazarangu proceeded to join the African Mashonaland Melodians. Margaret was popular with her song; *'Andidi Kuenda Tanganyika'* (I don't want to go to Tanganyika [Tanzania]).

During their talent search the De Black Evening Follies also discovered Mabel Bingwa who made her name during the Cecil Rhodes centenary in 1953 when she

Tabeth Kapuya and Victoria Chingate who was the leader of the Gay Gaeties (1991)

the Mubvumbi Brothers. When the De Black Evening Follies started their group in 1943, the first woman they brought into their group was Rennie Jones who was later to be known as Mrs. Nyamundanda. Rennie Jones' career did not last for long but she was one of the early women musicians as reported by the African Daily News (8 February 1958); 'It is Fancy and Rennie who made that wonderful two-some. Together they tapped, danced and crooned the music of the African setting.

They mixed ancient with new, and sang in the mines, schools as well as in towns. Whenever they sang they were packed houses.'

FEMALE MUSICIANS AND POLITICS

BESIDES performing music, some of

Mabel Bingwa

the women were also involved in the promotion of music. **Eileen Haddon** was a promoter of township music. She belonged to an organisation which promoted multi-culturalism and she used music to send this message. When the Rhodesian government introduced the state of emergency, she left the country and went into exile in Zambia. Like Haddon, Dorothy Masuka found sanctuary in Zambia.

The mid 60's saw some women in jazz taking a break or disappearing from music altogether because of the political situation which had become unbearable.

The early hybrid township jazz music which had disappeared for almost 15 years, was to resurface when Zimbabwe gained its independence in 1980 when most of the people who were at the helm of the music came back, including Dorothy Masuka and Eileen Haddon. Although Eileen was no longer active in the music scene she supported the music from the sidelines, and she has been documented in the Zimbabwe Township Music Documentary (Joyce Jenje Makwenda, 1992).

Returning Exiles

The coming back of musicians from exile also saw young female musicians becoming part of the early urban music and playing the early urban hybrid that most of them had roots in the townships. Although other genres of music had taken over, a township jazz movement was slowly born and today township music competes with other music genres.

Some of the musicians who revived township music were Sarah Mabhokela, Virginia Sillah, Pinkie Williams-Mseleku, Eva Melusi, Prudence Katomeni, Penny Yon, Ava Rodgers, Biddy Patridge, Kundisai Mutero.

Virginia Sillah made her mark in the 1970s although she had started in the 1960s, she recorded a 1950s tune *Ndafuna Funa* a Nyanja fast jazz tune, originally by the City Quads and it became very popular. She

Pinky Mseleku

was part of the Harare Mambos an outfit which was resident in the Monomotapa Hotel.

Eva Melusi also was popular in the 1970s and she was resident at the Federal Hotel and she did mostly copyrights of the popular songs which dominated the airwaves, like soul and pop mostly from the USA. She also sang cover versions by such musicians as Diana Ross, Gladys Night, Candy Stanton and many others, the international women musicians had a great influence on many women musicians in the 1970s just like some women jazz musicians of the 1950s; the likes of Ella Fitzgerald.

In a career spanning almost 30 years **Anjii** has fronted some of Zimbabwe's well-loved soul, jazz, and rock bands.

She began her career singing lead

Angie Greenland

professionally at the age of 16 with "Boykie" Moore and the band Colour. Performing Soul and R 'n B in venues all over Zimbabwe and opening at Rufaro Stadium for the Incomparable Staple Singers.

Eileen Haddon was a promoter of township music. She belonged to an organisation which promoted multi-culturalism and she used music to send this message.

Anji has been recently involved in the project FLAME (Female Literary Arts & Music Enterprise) which is led by Penny Yon. Flame is a Pamberi Trust Gender Mainstreaming project, which is designed to provide a special platform for emerging women artists, to play their music in the safety of daytime performances. Anji has been part of the "SISTAZ OPEN MIC" to give support to the young women by performing and sharing the stage with them.

Township music is growing and new performers include **Prudence Katomene, Dudu Manhenga, Patience Musa, Rute Mbangwa, Chengetayi Razemba, Nomsa Mhlanga, Hope Masike, Angie Greenland, Dadirayi Manase, Vicky Zimuwandeyi,** among many others. Dadirayi Manase and Vicky Zimuwandei are part of the Maita Jazz Women's band.

Rute Mbangwa

Patience Musa

Chengetayi Razemba

ALTHOUGH they have gone quite, the group will go down in the history of Zimbabwe as one of the few women musicians who were serious about playing musical instruments. An all-female group, the Maita Jazz Women's band, was a novel outfit which spelt out its own niche in the jazz circles during 2000-2006. The group was always raring to go, with all members of the band playing instruments.

The group's artists qualified from the Zimbabwe College of Music, in a special programme funded by the Swedish International Development Agency. Ultimately, the group fine-tuned their expertise during their spare time, at their own cost. The saxophonists continued with their studies as individual students at the College.

Dedication and sacrifice ultimately paid off - Maita was a smart group and a force to reckon with during their time. They were masters with experience several years'

more than how long they had been in the business.

The band consisted of: Susan Ndawi – drums/rhythm guitar; Shamiso Chitsinde – bass; Stella Mkundu (Mamvura) – lead guitar, Sophia Madzivanyika (J.B) – bass guitar/voice; Anna Matondo Sharai/ Saru – rhythm; Marita Tafirenyika (Seby) – keyboard/voice; the youngest, Victoria Zimuwandeyi (Nakai) – saxophone/voice; and Dadirayi Manase (Choks) – saxophone/ percussion, who is also the leader of the band.

One of the members of the groups Victoria Zimuwandeyi participated in the CD/ album – Women's Voices of Zimbabwe and she did three songs ('Baba Va Boyi', 'Tatetereka' and 'Kundenderedzana'), her voice is captivating. She also holds a Degree in Music from the Zimbabwe College Of Music and this album represents her first work as a vocalist. The group used to perform at different venues and also played at private functions and clubs.

1960s-1970s (UDI Rhodesian era)

DURING the mid 1960s to the mid 1970s,

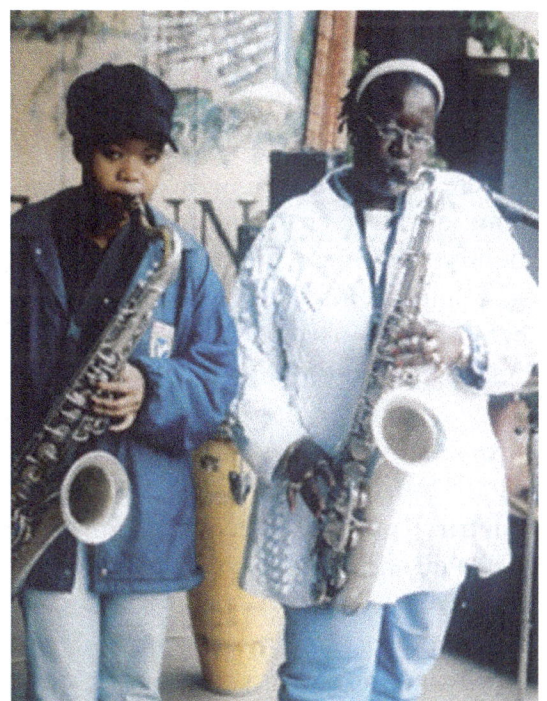

Victoria Zimuwandeyi and Dadirai Manatse

Maita Women's Ensemble, Sophia Madzivanyika – Lead Vocals, Anna Matondo – guitar, Marita Tafirenyika – keyboard,

other forms of music took center stage mainly because of how Zimbabwean musicians' creativity was controlled by the authorities. There was not much of the local music genre produced, except for musicians who were copying music mostly from South Africa, USA, UK, and Zaire (now DRC).

The mid 1970s experienced the peak of Zimbabwe popular music which was a mixture of traditional music with other forms of music that had dominated the country. Although other forms of music were infused into the 1970s mix, but – rhythmically, harmonically, melodically and linguistically – the music remained firmly within the Zimbabwean confines. Further, music in the 1960s and 1970s got influences from abroad and neighbouring countries; mostly, *Mbaqanga, Rhumba,* Rock, Pop and Soul.

The influences from abroad and neighbouring countries brought new forms of music that would dominate the airwaves as well as music venues; *Mbaqanga* from South Africa, which was then popularly known as *Simanje manje* music. *Rhumba* came from Zaire, soul, pop and rock music from the USA and reggae from the UK, there was also reggae from Jamaica but very few Jamaican artists were promoted in the 1970s. Reggae music by Bob Marley was not allowed and was actually smuggled into the country as it was seen as revolutionary music which would encourage people to rise up against the Rhodesian Front government. Reggae artists who were promoted then were Jonny Nash and Jimmy Cliff. There were no women reggae artists known in the country at the time. If Bob Marleys music was allowed in the country then women could have been influenced by women like Rita Marley and the female musicians who backed Bob Marley

The types of music that was played in Zimbabwe in the 1960s-1970s featured women musicians from other countries and this also influenced women musicians in Zimbabwe who copied the music, like mbaqanga and rhumba. The music from neighbouring countries was given enough coverage on air by the media, which had a major influence on both the local musicians and the general public. The music was promoted because it did not have any political messages as it was pure entertainment.

Some musicians who had come to the country to promote their music decided to make Zimbabwe their permanent home, and one of these groups was the Limpopo Jazz Band, a DRC group. The group recruited some female musicians to add on to their repertoire, amongst them was Virginia Sillah and Faith Dauti a township musician of the 1950's who performed in rhumba outfits towards the end of her career, and some of her music was influenced by rhumba.

The women in the Rhumba groups provided dance and vocals. They did not lead the groups like the jazz groups of the 1950's, which gave women some power and control of the jazz genre. Most Rhumba women musicians lived at the mercy of their male band leaders, because there were mostly backing vocals. The 1960's displaced women as far as music was concerned. The political situation did not allow them to be creative, and they did not own their creativity on stage as was with women like Lina Mattaka and Evelyn Juba. Most of 50's women musicians might not have owned the groups they were involved with but they at least owned their creativity on stage. They were accountable to society at large by the way they carried themselves on stage but they had some kind of ownership.

Besides being involved in Rhumba,

The types of music that was played in Zimbabwe in the 1960s-1970s featured women musicians from other countries and this also influenced women musicians in Zimbabwe who copied the music, like mbaqanga and rhumba.

Virginia Sillah in the 1960s also got involved in *Simanje-Manje* known today as *Mbaqanga.* She joined the Sunrise Kwela Kings Band, which performed versions of the mbaqanga music. The Sun-Rise Kwela Kings was a group based in Bulawayo and was owned by the Jairos Jiri Association; an association for the disabled, although some of the members of the musical group were not disabled like Virginia Sillah. She was an exception in the group because it was her aunt who was blind who made it possible for her to join the group.

Virginia Sillah is one of the few musicians in the 1960s who continued with township music, whose influence she had had from her father who was a jazz pianist. After performing with the OK Success Jazz Band, she joined the Harare Mambos, which drew their inspiration from the 1950s and 1960s music. The Harare Mambos

also became very popular in the 1970s and they continued up to the late 1990s. Most of their music was based on cover versions and Virginia Sillah was the lead singer and drew a big audience, although her name was not acknowledged in the group's name, which remained the Harare Mambos.

Virginia later married the leader of the group, Green Jangano. Besides cover versions of the 50's, 60's, 70's and 80's, Virginia Sillah and Harare Mambos recorded original songs but their breakthrough came when Sillah recorded Mbuya Nehanda with the Harare Mambos, which became like a national anthem. Mbuya Nehanda was written by a female freedom fighter during the struggle and when Zimbabwe attained its independence Virginia did her own version of the song. Having spent 25 years in music, Virginia Sillah decided to retire, disgruntled by the lack of visible proceeds from her 25 years in music. However, her wish has been to be able to record some of her original music on her own.

Virginia Sillah Jangano and the OK Success Band

Influence of South African Music in Zimbabwe

A NUMBER of *mbaqanga* groups mushroomed in the 1960s particularly in Bulawayo, mostly because of its proximity to South Africa, and because of the same language, Ndebele a dialect of Zulu which is widely spoken in South Africa. The Mtwakazi Sisters or Izintombi ZikaMthwakazi was a local *mbaqanga* group which made an impact in the 1960s music arena. It was led by Japhet Masuka and based in Bulawayo. Eva Melusi who was to become popular in the 70s and the 80's also belonged to some *mbaqanga* outfits of the 60's.

Izintombi ZakaMtwkazi from I-R; Maureen Maphosa, Mimi Hleza, Attalia Dube, Melina Ntomisa and Lulu Khoza

Sakaza Sisters - Bulawayo – Pildah Tazman, Attilia Dube and Joyce Banda

Some of the South African groups which had an influence on local mbaqanga groups were the Izintombi Zesi Manje-Manje and the Mahotela Queens. These groups visited Zimbabwe in the mid 1960's to promote their music, which enjoyed a considerable amount of air-time on the radio (as stated earlier). Both groups sang most of their songs in Zulu, which has a dialect spoken in Bulawayo, but as music knows no boundaries, they were received well in the whole of Zimbabwe.

As mentioned earlier, they also sang some of their songs in the Shona language, which is the first language in Zimbabwe. As stated earlier the Mahotela Queens sang in Shona because of one of their members, Sarah Mabhokela, who had lived in Zimbabwe for a long time with her sister, Mrs. Agnes Sekie Mhlanga (Kekana); Louis Mhlanga's mother. Louis Mhlanga is a renowned jazz guitarist/artist. Some of the Shona songs composed by Sarah Mabhokela were *Zvekumusha, Dai Kurikwedu Machembere,* and *Imi Munosara Nani Ndaenda* by Jeremiah Kainga (which she rearranged) and which became very popular. Most of her songs have been re-arranged by her nephew Louis Mhlanga and has given them a new feel by singing them. Louis Mhlanga's daughter (Nomsa) has also done her own rendition of the songs on the Women's Voices Album entitled Women's Voices of Zimbabwe and produced by Joyce Jenje Makwenda. Sarah Mabhokela came back to Zimbabwe in the 1980's and continued with her musical career, sometimes singing with Dorothy Masuka or her nephew Louis Mhlanga. She passed away in 1988 at the age of 57.

Dorothy Masuka and Sara Mabokela

Nomsa Mhlanga

Joyce Jenje-Makwenda

-1990's with her song *Zai Regondo*. Her youngest daughter Petronilla, who is now late, rose to prominence as an actor and she worked with her mother in her radio and TV productions. Her granddaughter Meylene Chenjerayi has also taken after her grandmother and mother Jane Chenjerayi, and she has featured some of her mother and her grandmother's songs on the Women's Voices CD; Pagedhi and Mwedzi Muchena. Meylene is also a dancer.

Most local musical groups during the 1960's -1970's used to sing popular cover versions. With time, they had their own versions of Rhumba, Mbaqanga, soul, rock and pop which had the Zimbabwe feel and in the mid 1970's the music was either a fusion of the music from the region or abroad.

While people were still excited by music from outside Zimbabwe in the 1960s, Susan Chenjerayi emerged on the local scene with a new genre that changed the musical terrain, which had a strong Zimbabwean rhythm. She was a part of a duo with Safirio Madzikatire. Chenjerayi was one of the best composers and musician. Some of her songs include *Isaac Hawuchandida Here? Mwedzi Muchena, Dali Iwe Ndosara Nani.* She also composed *Vana Amai Vanerugare* (Mothers have a good life) which she unfortunately did not record, but was later recorded by Thomas Mapfumo. Regrettably she did not retain copyright to this song. Her music varied from what can be called mellow music to jiti.

Susan Chenjerayi influenced her children who were to be popular in the 1970's up to 1990's. Jane Chenjerayi rose to fame with her song *Usandimirire Pagedhi* which was a fusion of jiti and pop. Her other daughter, Daisy Chenjerayi, made it in the 1980's

Susan Chenjerayi with her 2 children in the 70s

Meylene Chenjerayi

Susan Chenjerayi's fame started to fade in the 1970s although she continued as a recording artist and an actor on an on-and-off basis in the 1980s. Younger female musicians had entered the 1970s scene, one of them being her daughter and they had brought in a new sound of mixing pop and traditional music.

Jane Chenjerayi's hit song *Usandimirire Pagedhi* was a rearrangement of an old traditional song that she fused with pop and it gave the song a new feel which identified with the youth then, an Afro pop feel.

The song itself was taken from a traditional song which was sung during *jenaguru* (when the moon had set), when young people were searching for their life partners. The other song on the same album of *Usandimirire Pagedhi* also became very popular. It was called *Kuwomesa Mutambo*, which was also a fusion of pop and traditional music. The music dominated the music scene. Musicians became quite experimental mixing all sorts of rhythms/styles from outside the country and creating a Zimbabwean brewed music.

Women as Hotel Resident artists

It had become fashionable that hotels had resident bands and most of these bands had a woman fronting them. Rivonia Khumalo belonged to an outfit called Champ, a band which was mainly based at Mushandira Pamwe. Rivonia had a following of patrons who came to the hotel wanting to see her perform, she was a good singer and she did cover versions of the 1970s.

The Hotel Elizabeth had also a resident band the Pied Pipers which was fronted by Margaret Mbele, who had been with the Tutankhamen Band and she was the female voice behind their first LP, I *Wish You Were Mine.* Margaret, like many

women musicians, also did cover versions of the popular music which was going on, including South African music mostly by Letta Mbuli, whose music was very popular in the 1970's. Margaret had been originally from South Africa.

MARGARET MBELE AND THE TUTENKHAMEN 1975

Other than just Black African women singing and performing in hotels, a white young woman, **Laura Bezuidenhout** who belonged to an outfit called the Movement, was seen in the black townships with Movement Band, visiting their homes and even playing at Mushandira Pamwe which was a nightclub in the black township of Highfields. Laura played almost anywhere the band was invited. She played the piano. The Movement Band became one of the multiracial bands which had a composition of almost all the ethnic groups in Zimbabwe, and because of that it got a wide following.

Laura is one of the few women who can be accredited to having been involved in rock music.

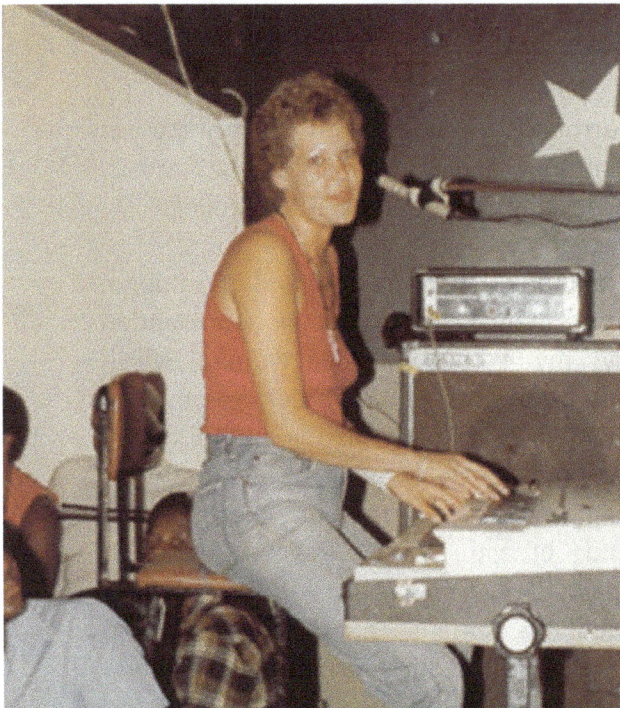
Laura Bezuidenhout

Susan Mapfumo, took the music industry by surprise in the late 1970s with her song *Baba Va Bhoyi*, which was a mixture of Rhumba, Mbaqanga, Pop and traditional music and a bit of rock music. It was well received by the audience as it heralded a new era of a new fusion and also the strong message about the problems that women were facing. Susan was then based at Simba Night Sport. Susan Mapfumo composed more than 25 songs and most of them were hits and most of her songs are still popular today.

Susan Mapfumo

Joyce Jenje-Makwenda

The **Two Singing Nuns** also took the music industry by surprise as they also sang songs about the emancipation of women and political music in riddles. The Two Singing Nuns were the now late Sister Tendayi Helen Maminimini and Gertrude Matsika now Mrs Mushayabasa. Their most popular songs were *Tatetereka* (We have wondered [in the bush]), this was during the war, *Kundenderedzana* (a married man wondering aimlessly with other women). Their songs went on to top ten and up until now they are still popular. They recorded eight singles with Teal Recording Company. Their songs were accompanied by two guitars bass and lead and they sang in Shona.

The Two Singing Nuns Getrude Mushayabasa and Tendayi Maminimini

Women also sang political songs to give moral support to freedom fighters in the bush during the war of independence. The music was influenced by traditional music or instruments. Some of these musicians resurfaced when Zimbabwe gained its independence in 1980 and they became musicians in their own right fusing traditional music with pop creating a traditional/pop sound. Some of them were Stella Chiweshe, Irene Chigamba, Francisca Muchena and Elizabeth Ncube. It was not easy to penetrate the traditional music genre as it was not only a male domain but had myths which were attached to it.

These myths made it difficult for women to learn how to play traditional instruments as there were no people who were willing to teach them. Some men, for instance imbongi (praise poets), felt threatened by women who wanted to venture into traditional music. However, women found ways to penetrate the traditional music and performance sphere and created a unique Zimbabwe traditional/pop music and performance.

Stella Chiweshe

Influence of the Spritual World on Women and Traditional Music: Ancestors versus Patriarchy

Although it was difficult for women to penetrate the traditional music genre, some women feel that they were inspired to do so through dreams. It is important to understand the mystification that surrounds gender and patriarchy in Zimbabwean Traditional/Popular Music, especially gender and spiritual beliefs.

Traditional instruments and traditional performance have been surrounded by myths that excluded women, which has been used by some cultures to stop women from participating in traditional music because women are supposedly unclean — because of menstruation and breastfeeding. However, through spirituality and spirit mediums, some spirit mediums demand that they want women to play mbira. Such incidents exemplify a struggle between the spiritual world and patriarchal society.

Women musicians overcame patriarchal rule using the strengths that comes from the spirit world. The ancestors provided an open door for some women.

Women have entered the sphere of traditional/popular music using various channels and guides. Dreams have been a particularly strong force of inspiration for most women who play traditional instruments. Dreams are a strong force in the spiritual world as they are seen as the ways ancestors communicate with the living.

According to Veit Erlman a renowned international ethnomusicologist, music is thought to be a product of the ancestors, which they use to communicate with those they like. Ambuya **Rena Chitombo** who at the age of 83 in 1998, was still active in music, made sure to go to bed with a book and pen that she put under the pillow and would write songs that mostly came to her in dreams.

She said "Dreams are very powerful because that is the way one communicates with the spiritual world."

Like in Shona and Ndebele cultures, the Zulu culture also passes music to the living through dreams. Joseph Shabalala who

Ambuya Rena Chitombo

Joyce Jenje-Makwenda

During 1950s, **Beaulah Dyoko**, a popular mbira player, said she had been very sick for over a year when she was taken to a traditional healer, who told them that her sickness was due to a spirit medium (ancestor) that possessed her and wanted Beulah to play the *mbira* instrument. The ancestor had been a *mbira* player before he died. Because women were forbidden to play the mbira instrument, these instructions were not followed and Dyoko remained sick for another year until she herself dreamt of playing the mbira. This time her mother, believing it was a further sign, agreed to buy her one. In 1996 Dyoko told me how she was initiated by the ancestors into playing mbira. The day her mother brought her the mbira she dreamt playing a song called *'Bhuka Tiende'*, (Wake up and go). "When I told my mother I had dreamt this song she asked me to play it and when I did it was as if I had been playing mbira for a long time, because I played it so well that day."

is known world over for his Isicathamiya believes that all dreams are ultimately encounters with the ancestors. He says "To dream and compose Isicathamiya songs are parallel strategies at creating continuity with the past."

When Beulah Dyoko started playing the *mbira* she was healed. As a result, those in her community near Zimbabwe's border with Mozambique grudgingly accepted that in fact a woman could play the mbira. During the 1960s, Dyoko became the first woman to record *mbira* music. She believed that she had been chosen by the ancestors.

"If it is true that the mbira instrument was supposed to be played by men only, then... [the spirit] could have gone to Beaulah's brother or could have waited for Beaulah to have sons which she has anyway," said Dumisani Maraire (ethnomusicologist) in an interview before he passed on. "But the spirit chose to possess Beaulah."

Ambuya Rena Chitombo who at the age of 83 in 1998, was still active in music, made sure to go to bed with a book and pen that she put under the pillow and would write songs that mostly came to her in dreams.

Beulah Dyoko

Beaulah Dyoko and her son

Stella Chiweshe

Stella Chiweshe

WHEN Zimbabwe attained its independence in 1980, so did *mbira* playing. Dyoko returned to the studio and Stella Chiweshe, now known internationally as the Mbira Queen of Zimbabwe came onto the scene. Chiweshe had also learned to play mbira after a dream. She said her mother had dreamt being told that she had to teach all her children to play mbira. But while her brothers easily found people to teach them, no one wanted to teach Stella until an uncle Gwanzura Gumboreshumba volunteered and she excelled far beyond her siblings.

This was in keeping with the Shona belief that not everyone can learn to play the mbira; some are simply born to play, while others are not.

In 1974, Chiweshe recorded her first single, "Kasahwa." It became a hit and was followed by 24 singles over the next six years. In 1985, she formed her highly successful band, Earthquake. In early 1998 Chiweshe was one of three women showcased on the Global Divas tour, which toured all over the U.S. In the early 1980's, Chiweshe and Dyoko made the mbira popular by adding guitars and taking it beyond the biras, (night vigils). Soon they were no longer just considered women who played the mbira, but among the best African musicians worldwide. Their powerful female influence on this instrument laid the path for the next generation of women to make their own mark on the *mbira*.

Elizabeth Ncube

Elizabeth Ncube, the first *imbongi* (Praise Poet) in Zimbabwe, says she was inspired to become an *imbongi* through a dream. She says she became sick from an incurable illness, when, after a dream, she was shown how to become an *Imbongi*. It was through her grandfather's spirit that Elizabeth became an *imbongi* when she was eleven (11) in 1974. Her grandfather Mtetwa had been an imbongi for Mzilikazi,

Elizabeth Ncube

Joyce Jenje-Makwenda

Before she passed on, Elizabeth performed in public places - even going to beer halls. She also performed internationally including Chicago, Milwaukee, Boston, Detroit, Toronto and Holland.

The use of praise poetry in the Ndebele/ Nguni culture was fundamentally political, to sing praises or to warn the head of state, and also to praise those who went out fighting and when they returned from war. Albert Nyathi, a famous Zimbabwean Imbongi attributes the lack of female Imbongi to the limitations that women face because they had children and therefore could not go to war. It was the duty of the Imbongi to go to war and to give moral support to the soldiers through praise poetry.

However, since women were also involved in the Zimbabwe liberation struggle in the 1970's, it became appropriate for them also to be involved in the art of imbongi. Elizabeth Ncube started her imbongi performance at political gatherings, and she performed to give the freedom

Elizabeth Ncube, the first imbongi (Praise Poet) in Zimbabwe, says she was inspired to become an imbongi through a dream. She says she became sick from an incurable illness, when, after a dream, she was shown how to become an Imbongi.

the king of the Ndebele people, who led the Ndebele people into Zimbabwe after battles with Shaka the Zulu king in South Africa. Elizabeth dreamt that she was wearing the clothes which her grandfather used to wear, and it was these clothes that she used when performing.

Elizabeth Ncube was nearly killed at a competition which was held in Harare by a male Imbongi. The male Imbongi tried to attack Elizabeth with a spear as she was performing, but Elizabeth overpowered the man. She attributed the overpowering of this man to the warrior spirit that guides her. She won the competition, beating the two men whom she was competing with. As stated earlier, when Elizabeth met the man some months later and confronted him on why he had wanted to beat her, the man said (*Wake wabona ngaphi umfazi otanyula inyawo pambili kwabantu!*) "Were did you see a woman who opens her legs in front of people!"

fighters moral support in the camps.
The war of liberation (1970s) also changed gender perceptions of female roles. Although in the 1890's women like Nehanda and Lozikeyi had played significant roles in fighting with the European settlers, the contributions of women to any wars had been downplayed for decades. However, women fought alongside men as freedom fighters during the liberation struggle, arguably reclaiming their position in the political sphere. Nehanda's spirit played an important role in guiding the freedom fighters.

Irene Chigamba

Irene Chigamba played mbira for freedom fighters during the 1970's, as did Stella Chiweshe. Irene Chigamba plays mbira with her father, which has not gone down well with hard core traditionalists. Chigamba, learned the instrument from her father who had found it hard to acknowledge that he had learnt to play mbira from his wife.

When Chigamba started playing mbira she was discouraged by relatives. In an interview that I had with her she said, "They would say that I would never get married because I had ventured into a man's world. They would also try to convince my mother to try and stop me as this was going to bring bad spirits to me, but my mother stood by me," Irene also plays drums.

Dumisani Maraire, who introduced *mbira* to the American West Coast in the 1960s strongly disputed the notion that women should not, and could not play the mbira instrument; he himself having been influenced to play mbira because of his great grandmother. During an interview I had with him in 1999, he disputed the general belief that women were not allowed to play mbira in *pasichigare* (the pre-colonial period) since his grandmother played the instrument. Maraire taught and encouraged his daughter, Chiwoniso, to play mbira, and today Chiwonsio is known in Zimbabwe and internationally as one of the best mbira players.

Chiwoniso Mararire

Chiwoniso Maraire revolutionized *mbira* music by adding English lyrics and church songs. It was a natural choice for Chii, as she is affectionately known. She was born in Washington State, the United States, where her Zimbabwean parents were studying and teaching *mbira*.

Chiwoniso started playing mbira at the age of 4, and at 12 she was performing with her parents on stage. She wrote music for the sound track to the Zimbabwean hit film; *Everyone's Child*. Chiwoniso has won many musical awards.

Laina Gumboreshumba, a mbira player/ teacher was also encouraged by her father Gwanzura Gumboreshumba to play mbira. Gwanzura Gumboreshumba recorded a mbira video with Andrew Tracy in 1975. Laina, like Irene Chigamba and Chiwoniso Maraire, performed with her father at biras and concerts. She has taken mbira music to another level, as she is working on a PhD at

Laina Gumboreshumba

the Rhodes University in Ethnomusicology.

Despite their success, even today female mbira musicians receive mixed reactions from the society. Some male musicians are angry that women are taking their place, while traditionalists continue to assert that women musicians offend the spirits.

Irene Chigamba's response is very simple "...now that women can play traditional instruments much better than the men, they are the ones who feel offended."

Although they are spirits speaking to the patriarchy as well, I am sure they are patriarchy spirits up there otherwise were did all those men go. But the spirits of those representing all human beings regardless of sex won the battle as women musicians have made a name for themselves as far as traditional performance is concerned. It is the wish of these spirits that every child (human being) is given the right to shine and continue with the tradition of the ancestors.

Music sounds, rhythms of 1980s -1990s – 'Everything Goes'...

THE 1980s to the 1990s is an era which we can refer to as 'Everything goes', a lot of music styles and genres were either new and were being introduced, or revived to come back on scene. The independence of Zimbabwe in 1980 led to an influx of new genres through international musicians

Joyce Jenje-Makwenda

who saw a new market to perform in this new state.

Recording companies, as a marketing strategy gave free music to the mainstream media to play on air. Some recording companies were scouting for talent both from abroad and local, and this had a major influence on both musicians and the music of the time. As much as it was an era of 'everything goes', there were musicians who stood out with particular music styles and genres.

As stated earlier, Susan Mapfumo's music continued in the 1980s and she rose to prominence, but in the late 1980s her popularity started dwindling until her death in 1991.

The 1980s saw Busi Ncube coming up with

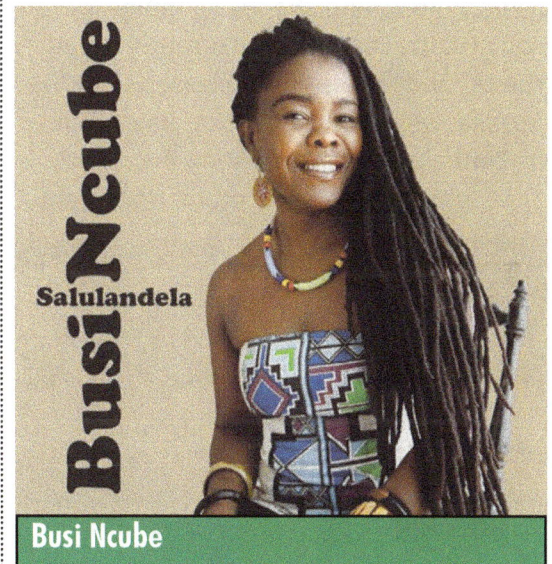

Busi Ncube

a different kind of sound, which did not really belong to a particular genre although it could be classified as Afro pop music. It was a fusion of different rhythms, and she sung mostly in Ndebele and English.

Busi was a member of the group Ilanga and she made her name with a song called *I want True Love*, based on the tune *Imi Munosara Nani Ndaenda* tune.

When Ilanga broke up she continued on her own and she is one of the few women in charge of a band, and she owns her own instruments. Her new group is called Band

Rain. Busi has been involved in a number of projects in the music scene.

Charlene Robertson was another young

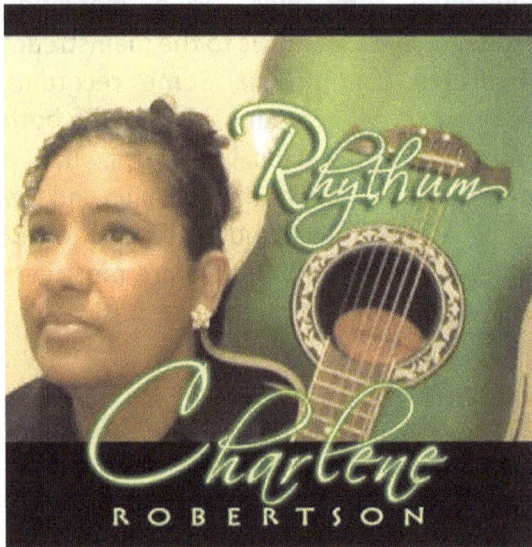

Charlene Robertson

woman musician who came onto the scene in the 1980s. Her music could be classified as pop music and she was popular for her song Happy Land. She is currently based in the UK and she has just released two CDs. Rozalla Miller became the Rave Queen in Zimbabwe with her song *Everybody is Free*, which earned her international fame.

Rozalla Miller's CD

Rave music was amongst the music which dominated the local scene and it was more aligned with the youth.

The 1980s mood was that of freedom and this song was celebrating that mood; the coming of independence in Zimbabwe.

The Murombedzi Women's Choir came on the music scene in the 1980's. The group comprised women singers, mostly in their 50's-60's. Their genre was aligned to the women's league kind of music mixed with a little bit of pop and the addition of instruments like guitars and drums

brought out a unique style of the music. Although short lived, they made their mark as one of the few women to come from a rural/women's league (the ZANU PF women's wing) background and to make an impact in the mainstream music scene. Their music got airplay and also good reviews. One of their most popular song was *Samora Waenda* (Samora has gone). Shuvai Wutaunashe brought in a refreshing kind of gospel music, which was a mixture of pop, jazz and traditional music. She had started her music career in 1979 and her music was influenced by the 70's and 80's music to create her own type of gospel music. Her song *MuKristu* went on the top of the charts and it got good coverage on air.

Elizabeth Taderera, popularly known as Katarina, hit the dancing floor with her energetic dance, in a duo with Safiriyo Madzikatire in a group called Seaside Band.

Shuvai Wutaunashe

In the group Safiriyo also brought in other women musicians as backing vocalists, and some of them had come before Elizabeth Taderera and provided female vocals and dancing, but Katarina attracted more attention than the rest of the group.

When Safiriyo Madzikatire's musical career came to an end and he eventually died, so did Elizabeth Taderera's musical career, she started having financial problems and she eventually died a broke woman.

A young woman musician Sandra Ndebele has also made a name for herself as a

Elizabeth Taderera (Katarina)

dancing Queen.

The trend of having women musicians as backing vocalists had started in the 1950s and continued in the 1960s with the Mambaqanga bands and the Rhumba groups. Zakes Manatsa whose music was heavily influenced by South African music, also had women backing vocalists and he continued with them to the 1980s/90s.

Sandra Ndebele. Sandra enjoys her independence as the leader of her group.

Daisy Chenjerayi became popular in the 1980s-1990s with her music which was dominated by *jiti* and one of her popular tunes was *Zai Regondo*.

While new genres were introduced, the early township music hybrid was reappearing and making inroads in the music scene slowly, especially with the coming back of musicians like Dorothy Masuka at independence in the early 1980s.

Township Music slowly penetrated in the music scene and was to gain momentum in the 90's. Today township music competes with almost all genres of music in the music arena in Zimbabwe. Township music regained popularity due to the coverage it was getting on air. It was later to become a movement in the 90s up to today. Township music has a large following among both the young and the old, and there are clubs specifically for this genre although other types of music are played. The late 1990s saw other music gaining ground, such as urban grooves and gospel music.

URBAN GROOVES

A new genre called the Urban Grooves started in the 1990s although it finally took off in 2000. It is mainly associated with young people. The urban grooves music came at a time (in 2000) when the 75% local content was introduced and it enjoyed considerable amount of airtime. This saw musicians involved in the genre producing music at a large scale, but most of this type of music is done through the computer, which did not go down very well with some listeners, particularly the older generation. The young musicians who most of them did not have enough resources to hire a band to play for them saw this as an opportunity (of recording using a computer) to be able to produce their music and have it played on air. This music is still dominating the airwaves. Most of the urban grooves songs were sung in English, and very close to the American R&B, but with time they now sing in Shona and Ndebele which gave it a local feel. Women musicians like **Plaxedes Wenyika, Betty Makaya, Tia (Portia Njazi), Memory Zaranyika, Pauline Gundidza, and Tambudzayi Hwaramba** have made names for themselves in the urban grooves genre

GOSPEL

Gospel music is also dominating the music scene. It remains the main genre which is dominated by women than any other music genre. It is easier for women to be involved in gospel music and also a passport to get into popular music with respect. Many female musicians have been involved in this genre since the late 1990s, although

Portia Njazi(Tia)

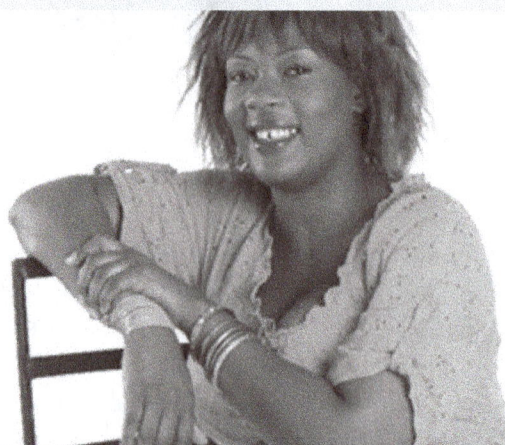

Plaxedes Wenyika

Tambudzai Hwaramba

Pauline Gundidza

Betty Makaya

the early women musicians from the 1930s used to sing church music it was not their main genre. The 75% local content introduced by the government in 2000 also helped Gospel music to grow by giving it airtime and write-ups just like all the other genres of music. The music borrows from a diverse of music styles and genres; church music, jazz, traditional music, rhumba. The fusion is diverse depending on the musician, but church music is more dominant and is the base for fusion. Some of the musicians simply add instruments to hymn book tunes, which has become like the norm.

Some of the popular women musicians in this genre include **Shingisai Suluma, Shuvai Wutaunashe, Bonnie Duschle, Ivy Kombo, Fungisayi Zvakavapano – Mashavave, Carol Chiwenga (Mujokoro), Olivia Charamba, Mercy Mutsvene** and

Gospel music is also dominating the music scene. It remains the main genre which is dominated by women than any other music genre.

the late **Jackie Madondo.**

Why women may not be associated with certain types of music

Women musicians could not be associated with certain genres like rock, sungura

Olivia Charamba

Fungisai Zvakavapano-Mashavave

Bonnie Deuschle

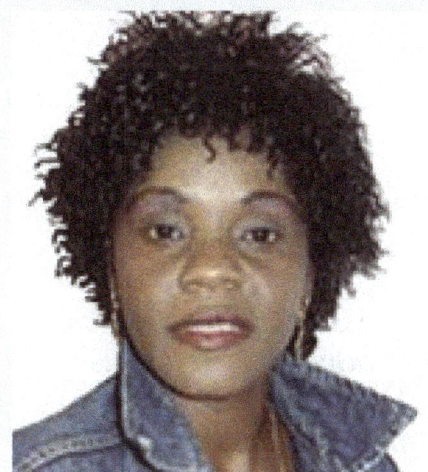
Shingisai Suluma

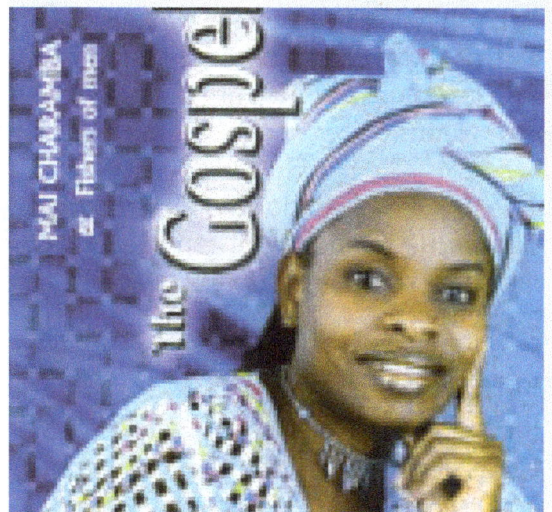
Ivy Kombo

(growth point) music, pennywhistle music, as they did with music styles and genres like, jazz, pop, rhumba, urban grooves and gospel music.

This was largely to do with how the music was formed and what it represented, for instance jazz music, which was started by the slaves taken from Africa during the infamous trans-Atlantic slave trade. Although most of the slaves did not understand each other's language as they came from different parts of Africa, they were united by a common language; jazz music. The music was used to protest in a 'quiet' way and also at the same time praying to the Almighty Creator to free them.

They had to be careful the way they sang the songs as they did not want to anger their masters, so they sang in a subdued manner but bringing out their anger and also praying. The music was to find its way in the mainstream of music and it became associated with sophistication. When it was transported back to Africa through different mediums; radio, records and film it found its way in the hearts of Africans who had settled in the urban centers. Gibson Mandishona who grew up in Mbare township, wrote in the foreword for the Zimbabwe Township Music Book, that;

"Over the years, Zimbabwe Township Music artists have experimented, improvised and sung their way with ecstatic tunes that proved irresistible and unforgettable. The music nurtured a new identity which outwitted urban boredom, ushered in family entertainment, and finally bridged the middle passage between the generations of jazz/blues lovers.

Alike politicians during the colonial period, Zimbabwean musicians braved their way forward, despite being subjected to overt and covert racism, which was then a grim reality, but which nevertheless created an innovative and sleek idiom-jazz expression."

Women musicians in the 1930's started to copy other women jazz musicians especially the Negro Spirituals, and came up with their own form of jazz; township jazz music. The women who performed jazz music were seen as decent and they became accepted by the society as civilized. Jazz music was also used to air their grievances; it became the symbol of identity. Musicians like Dorothy Masuka and Miriam Makeba sang township jazz music as protest music which resulted in them living in exile.

Women and Rock Music

Rock music was and it is still not associated with women musicians in Zimbabwe because of how it was formed. Very few women could be said to have been associated with rock music, and these include Susan Mapfumo, Laura Bezuidenhout, Anji Greenland and Virginia Phiri. Virginia Phiri was with the 70s rock outfit High Chord later to be known as Well Fargo, she left the band to go and join the liberation struggle in Zambia. Rock music became popular in the 1970s, although it can be traced from the 1950s-60s under different styles.

In the 1970s the popular music was hard rock and was mostly challenging the status quo, from religion, education, dressing etc. It was also protest music which did not observe society's structures. It was radical music, and women found it difficult

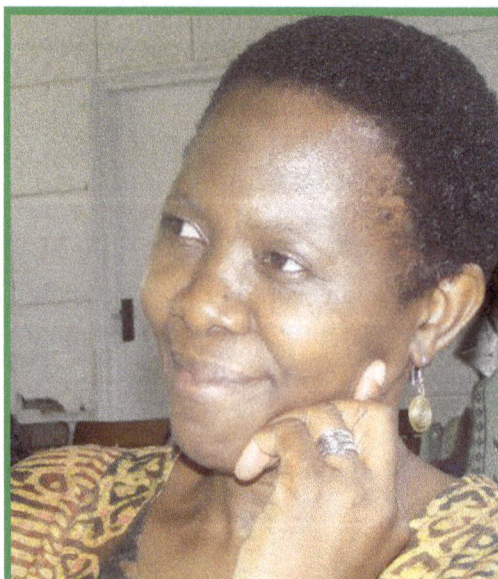

Virginia Phiri

to be associated with this kind of music as this could make it even more difficult for them to be accepted by the community/society.

Women and Sungura music

Sungura is also one genre which seems not to attract female musicians. This could be largely due to where the music originated. Sungura music originated in the mines and growth points, which were associated and dominated by men. Sungura music was popularised at growth points, which are less frequented by women. The lyrics belittle women and portray them as objects which must be kept under the control of men. This may have deterred women from venturing into this kind of genre and restrict themselves to jazz, soul, gospel etc, which were considered more civilized or sophisticated. Edna Makanda bassist for Mulunguti naMakanda Express becomes the first woman to lead a Sungura outfit. Some of the members of her band are her two sons.

When Sungura music eventually managed to penetrate the urban mainstream music, it was dominated by male musicians and the backing vocalists were also men. However, lately we now see some women dancing groups such as Amavithikazi,

Edna Makanda (left) and her sons Archvon Makanda (centre) and Washinton Lungu.

Mambokadzi and Girls La Musica, who base their repertoire on rhumba, kanindo and sungura music, but they perform just as women or they are hired by some sungura bands to accompany them. The women dancing groups enjoy their autonomy and do not necessarily belong to any male groups.

Pennywhilstle

Pennywhilstle (Kwela) is one genre of music which has not really been associated with women playing the instrument except

Mambokadzi

providing dancing as backing. The way the music started also makes it not attractive to women playing the pennywhistle.

"Kwela" music once had a big following in Zimbabwe from the 1950s-1960s, it was originally played on penny whistles, (wind instrument) and it can be traced from the black South African Townships. The pioneers of Kwela would play in city street corners attracting both black and white passersby. The police disliked such gatherings in the city, which soon put the audience on the alert. The sight of police automatically triggered the dispersal of the audience.

"Kwela" was originally associated with social outcasts who played cards on street corners, where crowds would gather around. At the sight of police people shouted "Kwela - Kwela", which in Zulu means "climb" since the police would order those arrested to "climb" into police trucks, shouting "Kwela - Kwela." The word subsequently became a warning signal at the sight of police vans, for people to flee to safety.

"Kwela" music did not initially appeal to township jazz musicians, who felt superior to penny-whistlers. That may also have influenced how women perceived Kwela music as unsophisticated music which they would not want to be part of. Kwela music was revived in the 1980s just like jazz music but it still remained a male domain, with Kwela musicians performing on a small scale.

A project is underway to encourage young women musicians to play the pennywhistle (kwela music) and other wind instruments. Despite not being part of some of the music genres, women musicians in Zimbabwe have done well in the music that they have decided to be associated or be part of. ■

Chapter 5

Limited public persona and space

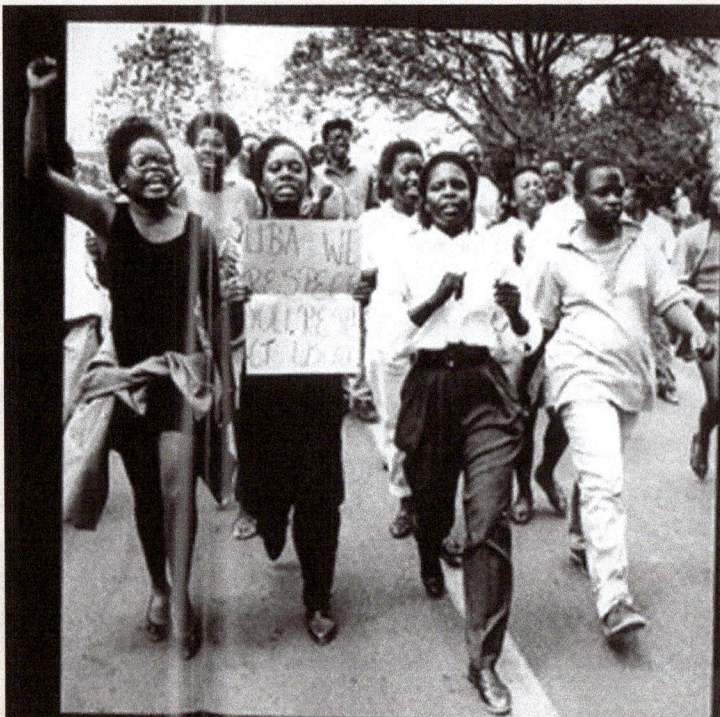

University of Zimbabwe students protesting, 1992

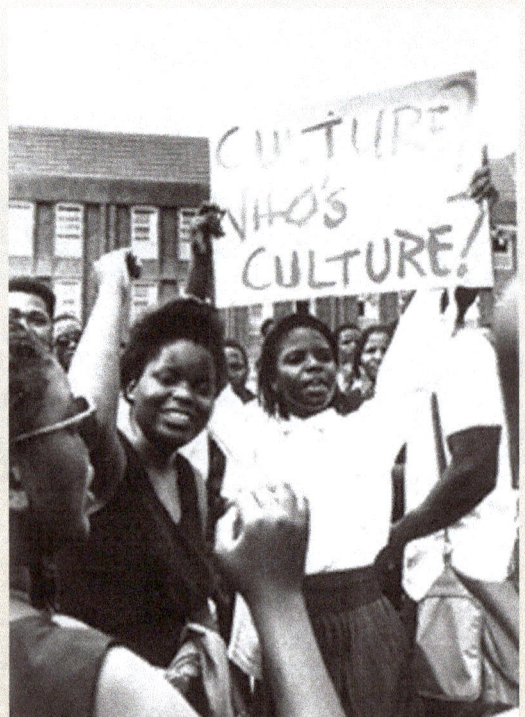

Female students at the University of Zimbabwe, 1992

IN many patriarchal societies women are supposed to confine themselves to the domestic sphere. Their access to public space is very limited. They are not supposed to develop a public persona. Persona is defined as "the versions of self that all individuals possess" (wikipedia on-line) and "persona presented to other people vary according to the social environment the person is engaged in" (ibid). For most African women, this persona is something dictated by culture. From a tender age most African women are discouraged from developing a public persona. Their personality is inhibited in order to benefit society. The way they are raised does not instil confidence in them. They are not encouraged to venture into the outside world. This has affected women musicians in terms of how they interact with public space.

A *mbira* performer and teacher, Laina Gumboreshumba, observes that there are certain behavioural patterns expected of the boy and girl child because they are raised differently in the Zimbabwean Shona culture: "I would say yes, obviously in our traditional Shona culture there are certain things, behaviour, conduct, expectations for boys and for girls". Boys are brought up to venture out and try new things outside the home while the girl child is domesticated in order to prepare her for motherly and wifely duties.

The girl child is discouraged from even having adventurous thoughts. For instance, musician Thembelihle Ngwenya was asked by her teacher what she wanted to be when she grew up, when she said she wanted to be an actress she was reproached just for wishing to be an actress. Nevertheless, Thembelihle has learnt bass guitar and played for the group, Amakhosi. She does not regret becoming a full-time actress and musician.

Negotiating public space has not been easy for women as patriarchy aims to confine women to the home where they do unacknowledged or unpaid work. Further, this results in the women having limited personal time. Their personal time is determined by their family and by society.

Often, they combine the responsibilities of working to earn a wage, and doing domestic work. The unfair division of labour as girls are growing up, and when they finally have their "own homes" (get married), means that they do not have much time to spend on developing themselves and their talents. The lack of personal time has made it difficult for women to fully develop their persona. The little personal time they have to themselves has not made it possible for them to be able to understand how they function as human beings and, most importantly, as women.

Women become vulnerable by not understanding their own functionality, which further contributes to patriarchal society being in an advantageous position to exploit and allocate women the personality that patriarchy sees fit. The patriarchal approach dictates that women should confine themselves to the domestic sphere. Women's private persona contributes to the way they approach public space. Not understanding public space also contributes to women's financial ignorance and financial insecurity, and limited access to economic power makes it difficult for women to challenge structures. This cycles back to how they function in public space, and in turn, their ability to bring out their persona. The fact that women do not have access to economic power makes it difficult for them to function effectively in the music sphere as band leaders, managers, promoters, venue owners or producers. As a result they mostly end up as backing vocalists and dancers, at the mercy of their male bosses. Women who have taken up music management and promotion in recent times include Barbara Chikosi, Jackie Cahi, Derby Metcalf, Tsungi Zvobgo, Nomsa Mwamuka, Rhoda Mandaza, Sheila Cameron, Priscilla Sithole and Irene Gwaze who used to own the musical venue – The Red Fox Hotel.

Debbie Metcalfe

Tsungirirai Zvobgo

Rhodha Mandaza

Irene Gwaze

Jackie Cahi

In the 1950s there were women like **Eileen Haddon**, **Barbara Tredgold** and **Monica Marsden** who also took the challenging roles of promoing music. Amongst the notable women who have made it as band leaders are Victoria Chingate, who was the leader of the Gay Gaeities (Zimbabwe's first all-female group) in 1954; and Sylvia Sondo, who led the group Yellow Blues in the late 50s. In 1976, Susan Mapfumo started and led the group Susan Mapfumo and the Boogaloos, and was the first woman to own musical instruments.

In the 1980s, Busi Ncube formed Band Rain, which she still leads. Portia Gwanzura was very popular in the 1990s as the leader/manager of the group Hohodza. Some of the women who have been at the helm of their musical groups in recent times are Ava Rogers, Kundisai Mutero, Biddy Patridge, Prudence Katomeni-Mbofana, Charlene Robertson, Shuvai Wutaunashe, Dudu Manhenga and Hope Masike.

Nomsa Mwamuka

Portia Gwanzura

Hope Masike

Some of the women musicians who have managed to traverse public space and create their own persona have either had encouragement from their families, associations or connections, communities and societies, or they have bulldozed their way through. Regardless of women musician's entry point into public space, the treatment they get once they are in this space is the same. However, their background and support system makes it easier or harder to survive problems and times of uncertainty.

Venues Determine Create Women's Persona - 'Private Public' and 'Outside Public'

Public space and public persona of women during *Pasichigare* the (pre-colonial era) was protected by the social order whose

structures made it possible for women to sing and perform in a protected environment. Women who became well known musicians, singers or performers were not seen as putting the community or society at risk as they were controlled by the social order that acknowledged patriarchal structures. There was an era when African society was more matriarchal than patriarchal but this time was not properly documented; when, how and why it came to an end.

Matriarchy still has a place in the African society, since mothers are the ones who raise children. In a way children get values through mostly their mothers. To some extent the matriarchal society still exists and it still has some influence in the African society, socially and culturally, but not politically. The patriarchal society seems to have been documented both through oral traditions and through modern ways of documenting, as a way of passing and strengthening on patriarchal values.

Music, which, women performed, was for particular purposes that served the particular society, helped patriarchy run smoothly without being disturbed. Women were acceptable because they were fulfilling a service required by society. Therefore, women's public persona was not compromised, because they were not singing in a popular culture environment which would see them become products, resulting in them being packaged. The traditional belief system seemed to protect them but, at the same time, controlling them using the patriarchal structures. When women's music left the traditional dictates to become part of a popular culture; the way women were viewed by society changed. Their public personality also changed. The 'new woman musician' no longer fully contributed to strengthening the patriarchal structures, and her character was to be scrutinised by the new order which the men had put in place; laws of the country, the media, the church, and other institutions or instruments which controlled or policed society.

As pointed out in the first chapter, before Zimbabwe was colonised (pasichigare), women's role in performing music was centred mainly on singing: lullabies, for calming and putting children to sleep; songs which helped them to carry on their work efficiently; and protest songs – about issues in the family, the community or against the authorities.

The public they performed to could be termed 'private public', hence their public persona was not compromised. The space they performed within was contained – as part of the family, community or societal structures. It was a 'private public' in that women rarely performed for complete strangers because communities were smaller. The public persona of women came under scrutiny in the 1930s, when they crossed the 'private public' boundary to an 'outside public' or 'unprotected public' space due to fragmentation of social structures.

African social structures were fragmented by a number of factors and it was difficult for women to continue operating in the disintegrated structures. Society has been forcing or sacrificing women to piece up these structures so that they can continue to operate, despite being obvious that it is not practical.

Like everyone else, most women also left the Tribal Trust Lands that, at least, still had some of the pre-colonial structures struggling to be functional. Caleb Dube (1996:100) argues that "urbanisation and industrialisation as consequences of European colonisation produced new urban lifestyles, social networks and gender relations, which were in many respects different from those in indigenous rural societies."

In the new dispensation, women's music had to be performed not only in their homes, but also as part of public entertainment, as the concept of community had been broadened. It had been broadened in the sense that, although people in the townships lived communally like most African (black) societies used to during the pre-colonial era, in this new community people were from different tribes and different nationalities. They were also influenced by western culture, which was transported through the media, and this affected their way of living. The fusion of all these elements created a popular culture that in turn created popular music. This music had to be performed in a public place, that is, in the streets, the community hall or the township hall. Since the 1930s women musicians, like their male counterparts had to move to an even more public space with patronage from different nationalities; black, white, etc. Women musicians then progressed to an international public. All this has affected their public persona and how they are perceived by society.

The structures of public space that is not in the confines of 'traditional' space is defined by or shaped by the infrastructure that is designed by men, who have been fortunate enough to be in that space long before women. Men designed public space in the 1930s during the early urban drift. Men created these structures for their own benefit, and women still find it difficult to work in the provided environments. Most of the music venues operate within these set structures, those of drinking, smoking and where women are treated as sexually available, which has a negative bearing on women musicians/performers and women patrons. While the traditional public space the 'private public' arrangement was also set up by men, it was, at least, 'user friendly' in that a woman was free to express herself and was not viewed as a sexual object. Today's public space can be termed as 'outside public' and was designed in a way that it is not 'user friendly', as it does not allow women to fully express themselves and the treatment of women as sexual objects.

Kudzai Sevenzo

Kudzai Sevenzo a jazz/gospel musician is not happy with the way a female musician is viewed in some of these venues. "Sometimes you need to make a statement that I'm here because of me. I find that with a female musician you always need to remind people that I'm not here to do a strip tease on stage, I'm here to sing music, fine you want to see me as that, that's your problem. I'm here to sing music, you always need to sort of draw those boundaries that this is who I am and this is where I stand but as a guy you never have to."

Women patrons and women musicians prefer an arrangement/venue that suits them, their lives and where they would even want to bring their children and families. Taruwona Mushore is a musician who finds it difficult to perform in the venues that were structured mostly to suit men, and she would like to create a friendlier environment for women and children. This is what she had to say:

"My future plans, I think, are to perform more and more. Maybe to embark on challenging the present music venues that is typically the jamming sessions, the boozing sessions the typical hotel sessions. You either have to have a hit on radio or hit to be accepted. No. But you can be sure that you get there

and find the majority of people are men. Unless its Saturday or Sunday, there is no family or, women can't feel free to go there on their own, or feel that there are going to listen to good music. I'm talking about the hotels where in essence there is got to be alcohol and it's sort of a male binding session where, whichever woman is there, is easily available. So I feel why can't the entertainment speak for itself? and have family gathering where it maybe on lunch time but they can make money out of soft drinks, meals, even alcohol, but get the family together, like an audience - people who are going to appreciate your music" (Taruwona Mushore 1994)

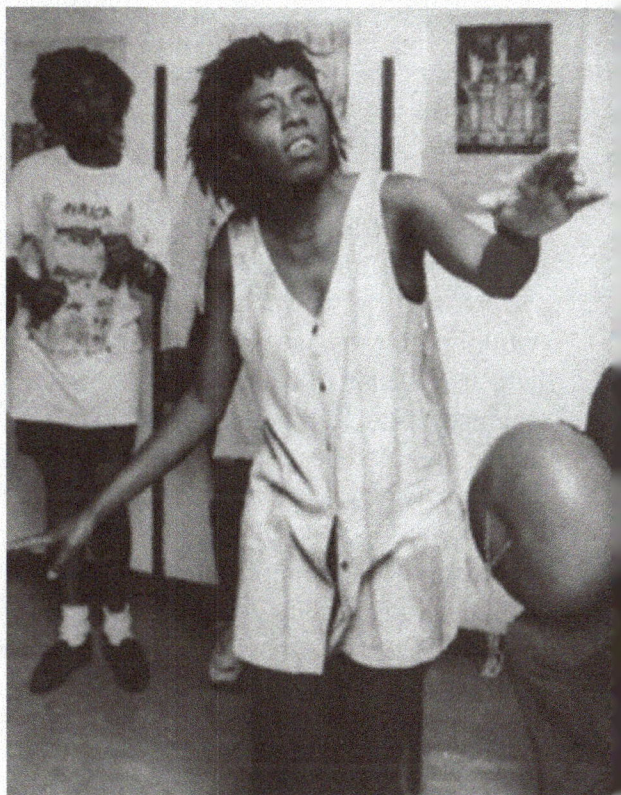

Taruwona Mushore 1993

Although it is important to change establishments from within; like performing within the set structures of 'outside public' and women celebrating that they have made it, women can also stand up and be counted as having challenged and become part of the structures set by men in recent times. While this can be seen as a milestone, it has, in many ways, worked against women, as they have to toe the line of this 'unprotected public' unconsciously. That is why women musicians have been going back and forth, not registering real progress. They may think they have made it, only to discover they have not, because they do not understand the dynamics of how the public is structured. They have, as a result not had much success in their careers and professions.

These structures are set to make women fail, perform below men. Women in public space are seen as objects and they are expected to provide a service that is supposed to make men happy, which is predominantly, sexual. When a woman musician comes into this space she is also required, among other things, to be sexually available just like all women around her in that public space. Male patrons frequent public space more than the women patrons because of where these venues are situated, and also the times that they operate.

Another contributing factor to why women cannot fully participate in the setting up or creating these venues is the way they would prefer to use their limited resources which, because of circumstances they find themselves in, they are forced to share with many people, particularly their children. Women were raised not to believe that entertainment is important for their personal development. This perception has resulted in the few numbers of women patrons who go to watch and listen to music. That, in turn, has an impact on women musicians as this affects the way they interact with the crowd.

It is important for women musicians to get support from their fans, more so other women. Guitarist Penny Yon was encouraged by female patrons to continue playing the guitar at the nightclub she was playing:

"I can say in Zimbabwe I have been respected as a woman musician and honoured and encouraged. You know you will find women in the ladies bathroom at the end of the gig, they are the ones who will say, 'go my girl – go and show them you can do it, we can also play'. So there was so much

Penny Yon

support from even the women I did not know" (Penny Yon int. 2003)

Failing to put structures in place, that benefit women musicians and women in general in public space has been a disadvantage in the development of women across the board as it affects women performers and audience members. Women, in general, are misrepresented in music. The purpose of music in the society, as a vehicle for change and tool for communication, is not realized, this end up benefiting men, who set these structures.

Penny Yon and other established musicians have gone on to help create space for young and upcoming musicians. Women musicians have expressed displeasure at being given negative names when they are in the public space, some have been called sex combatants according to Penny Yon who with other established women has helped women in this situation by providing them a protected public space to feel safe when performing. For young musicians it can be intimidating and may not continue with music.

FLAME (Female Literary Arts and Music Enterprises) which houses Sisters' Open Mike gives platform to women musicians to be able to perform and grow in the

Joyce Jenje-Makwenda

process and establish a good fan base.

According to one woman musician Taruwona Mushore, because of the defined structures in public sphere women musicians end up acquiring a certain persona or faking a certain persona in order for them to fit, be accepted, or to be able to survive. She changed her persona in order to survive in public space.

"I think I managed to get confidence, but I think to the detriment of my performance, because here is what I was doing: I would go and give my soul and then, immediately, I would become another image. I would become sort of a hardened person where if anyone wanted to approach me in any way I would immediately cut them and defend myself, but that's not the way I feel. As a performer I feel that you portray your performances. You become what you are performing, but I don't think you should separate. You shouldn't be another person. I don't think you have to recondition yourself to do something else. I feel it's a reflection of me, that's how it should be. So, immediately I was assuming another persona which was not what I wanted to be, the hardened woman who is going to be more liberated than liberated" (Taruwona int. 1994).

In the process of women trying to recondition themselves, acquiring a more hardened persona and overprotecting themselves it is not only their persona that is affected, but also their voice and self expression.

PUBLIC SPACE BECOMES A WAY OF LIFE THROUGH FAMILY SUPPORT - PERSONA PROTECTED

The public persona that women acquire as musicians is, to a large extent, determined by how they get into music and what they do as performers and as instrumentalists. The way a woman comes onto the music scene creates or puts her into a certain category or grouping, and this is the way she will be viewed by the public and her band members who usually then either respect her or exploit her because of the category that she falls in. The group that women operate in within the music industry determines how they are viewed. This, in turn, creates their status and also constructs their public persona.

Lina Mattaka and Evenly Juba who entered the music scene in the 1930's were initially part of musical family groups and then went on to sing with their husbands. They were respected by society as they did not threaten the set structures of society, and they were seen as role models for upholding the institution of marriage and family values. The way they also behaved on stage was restricted by the fact that they were married women who were supposed to carry themselves in a 'respectable' manner in public. The protection of their public persona, in a way, compromised their freedom of expression, as they were not supposed to cross certain parameters either through their lyrics or through their body language. Although they had control of their musical groups together with their husbands, the husbands understood the music business more than the women, who were more concerned with performing and taking care of immediate issues like looking after the group. Generally, the women were more confined to the stage.

They also had a certain way of carrying themselves in public that did not seem to undermine their husbands' authority. In an interview that I did with both the couples for the documentary that I produced, Zimbabwe Township Music 1930's-1960's, the two women (Lina Mattaka and Evelyn Juba) did not do much talking. Their husbands offered most of the comments and besides being knowledgeable regarding public space, were obviously supposed to be seen as the heads of their families.

Kenneth and Lina Mattaka

Evelyn and Simon Juba

The confinement of women from childhood follows them throughout their lives into their adulthood and being in public space may not necessarily change their perception of how they view public space and themselves. Lina Mattaka and Evelyn Juba's other public space that they were accustomed to was the church; a 'protected public' which did not contribute much to their popular music growth, as this was another form of being 'domesticated'. Women at church instead looked up to

them as role models, and at the same time, Lina and Evelyn had to prove to the church and the community that the 'unprotected public' had not changed them. They had a duty, as public figures, to uphold patriarchy and ensure that Christian family values (which are centred on patriarchy) do not collapse. It is in the church that women are constantly reminded of being 'good women', and how their behaviour is always under scrutiny. In this 'protected public', Evelyn and Lina did not get much help regarding their musical profession as they were seen as idols that despite being in the unprotected public space, remained 'good women'. Their social status in the church was way above most women, who looked up to them. So they did not gain much other than being seen as women who had made it in the entertainment world, and still remained 'real women'.

The domestication of women has made it not easy to understand the music business other than on the stage. Men have better 'access' to public space and this becomes an advantage when dealing with issues to do with the public, like music. For instance, Kenneth Mattaka had connections in the business world as he worked for the *Rhodesia Herald Newspaper,* and he met many people who advised him on what to do as regards the music business.

This was the same with Simon Juba who was a teacher, and, through his work, he gained information regarding the music business. It was because of these contacts that the Merry Makers, the group that Simon Juba led, became the first black group to sing as a curtain raiser for a multi-racial group and an all white audience in Bulawayo. (Simon Juba int.1992). By virtue of being a teacher, Simon Juba also managed to clinch some deals to perform in certain halls. The public space that Lina and Evelyn were familiar with did not add sufficient value to their work as musicians for them to understand music as serious business the way their husbands did. Most of their associations were actually at a lower level in terms of knowledge and understanding the public.

Lina and Evelyn's husbands were in public domains with access to information, contacts, networks and influential people who added value and growth to their understanding of the music business.

Despite not being fully conversant with public space, being in music with members of their families, particularly their husbands gave Lina Mattaka and Evelyn Juba dignity on stage, which saved their public persona from being scrutinized by the media, society and their patrons.

Most women who sing with their husbands met them through music circles. For this kind of couple music is seen as just any other job or hobby. For instance, Francisca (Mai) Muchena met her late husband Mondereki through their families who were involved in mbira playing at traditional ceremonies, or biras in Shona. They continued to sing as a couple, and with their children. Couples who meet through family musical groups tend to take music as a way of life, and being in public space for the woman is nothing new.

Mai Muchena, as she is affectionately known, is a confident woman. I attended performances where she was singing with her husband in the 1990's, and she would just take over the stage and perform. Her husband was not worried: rather, he would support his wife. Watching their show one could see and feel a positive energy around them. In such a situation, inhibiting public space is not heavy for the women involved and they can show their musical talents without inhibitions. As Mai Muchena recounts:

"I got married in 1963, it did not bother him [my husband] that I was a mbira player because we met at a bira. He was a mbira player. I was also good at singing. He also got attracted to me because of that. From there on we sang together with my husband and family. I do not play mbira that much, but the talent that I have is in playing drums, I can also

play rattles, I can dance, sing even when we have gone overseas. I am the one, who usually does most of the stuff, playing drums is my specialty."

Amai Francisca Muchena, Mondereki Muchena and Erica Azim

There are times when Mai Muchena would be invited to perform on her own without her husband, and the husband did not see any problem with that. However, most couples that perform together end up fighting for attention and fame and, in cases where Mai Muchena was invited to perform alone; it could have caused problems in their marriage. Fighting for fame and limelight amongst singing couples seems to be an international problem; Ike and Tina Turner, the once famous American couple, are an example of how a husband might get threatened by his wife's success and fame. It is generally believed that Ike ended up physically and sexually abusing Tina Turner, until she moved out of the marriage. Mai Muchena thinks it is a misunderstanding on the part of the husband:

"I have my own way the spirits come to me, and my husband's come in a different way. So the way we work is different. It's not like if I sing on stage I totally forget about my children (family). I will also be helping my husband buying food and paying debts with that money I get from the stage.

I would like to advise them (women) not to be scared, to talk about their careers with their husbands. Find a way of telling him that you are going to do it no matter what he thinks. Your husband might not allow you but you simply ignore him. There is no one to stop me to go wherever I want to go. The love for my music gives me the energy to go."

Some of the other women who also shared or share the stage with their husbands are Virginia Sillah, Shuvai Wutaunashe and Dudu Manhenga. Although some of these women started before they met their husbands whom they met through music. Singing with their husbands has been seen as carrying on with society's moral values. Prudence Katomeni-Mbofana also falls into this category although she does not share the stage with her husband, Comfort Mbofana, who is/has been her manager, but because of his busy schedule he will not be managing her full time.

"We are both looking for a manager, I do the picking and he scrutinizes. My experiences whilst working with the Cool Crooners and their French Manager, I have picked up the characteristics that make a good manager. It's got to be somebody who truly, truly believes in your music and what you do. It is not about the money factor at all times, that was Comfort; the fact that he took me out of the cooperate world and said that - because your spirit has died and that's not what you are meant to do, it's somebody who believes in me. (Prudence Katomene –Mbofana 2012 int.)

Prudence Katomene Mbofana

Dudu Manhenga finds it an advantage to have a husband who is a musician. Her husband is the drummer for the group she leads; Colour Blu. She explains how it is a benefit working with her husband, "I think it's much better to have someone in the industry if you come home at 2am and he will understand when you wake up at 12 in the afternoon and you still haven't cooked and will say she was working last night. Whilst if you were married to a bank teller who works from 8am to 5pm, and then at 8pm you are bathing telling him you are going out for a show, so it's easier to have a partner who is an artist who will understand the procedure that an artist has to go through"

Dudu Manhenga

I asked Selmor Mtukudzi how she is managing to sing with her husband Tendai Manatsa and manage not to fight for limelight like other couples who sing together have done for instance Ike and Tina Turner.

She said; *The thing with me and Tendayi is that we were very good friends before we even dated, we connected very much and we have got similar backgrounds so we are always hoping for the best for each other. He is always saying I want you to succeed; I want you to do that.*

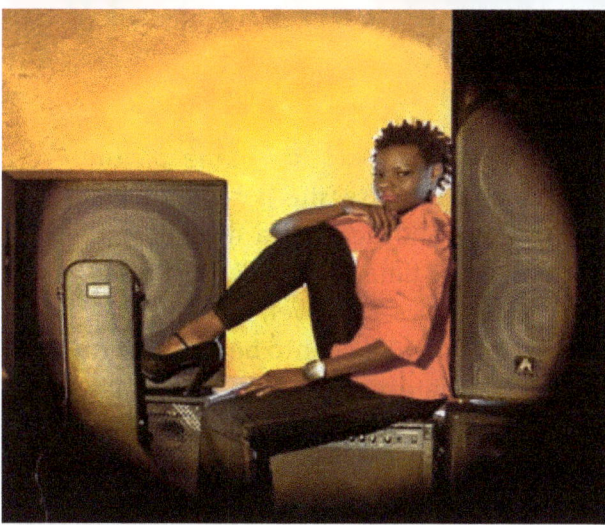

Selmor Mtukudzi

Singing or sharing the stage with a partner has its dark side as Virginia Sillah observes. She feels it is more about understanding one's partner than being in the same field.

"I don't think it's the field that really matters. It's the consciousness of the other partner. You might even get married to a clerk when you are a musician, but men don't want to be over-ridden, others might think 'Ah may be if she gets too popular, she will be too pompous or something' - maybe they get jealous. It's someone's mentality that counts."

Louis Mhlanga, a musician and producer, attributes the lack of support from some male partners to insecurity and jealous on their part.

"They (men) think of how the audience responds to them when they are on stage particularly women patrons and they are not settled on the same happening to their wives who are musicians/performers. It's jealousy because they (women) become exposed to handsome guys out there. When singing it brings out your voice - brings out your artistic expression that might be termed sexual as the whole body has to move. Those who are watching your body and your voice and expression might get attracted in a sexual way just like they (women) do when it's a male musician. Men who are musicians may not like it, but it will depend on the woman's level of musicianship whether she continues with music or she is controlled by the husband, and leaves music altogether" (Louis

Mhlanga int. 2007)

For women to get to a higher and conscious level of musicianship, many factors come into play. Confidence is a crucial component that helps women to rise to a higher level but, all too often, before they can get anywhere, their confidence is shattered. One of the reasons that contribute to women dropping out of music is mostly how generally society associates them with prostitution, or viewing then as loose, sexually available women. Many women musicians have had to prove that music is just like any other profession and build their public persona to convince people that being a musician is work like any other, and this is the profession they want to be in. Virginia Sillah, who started her musical career in the 1960's, explains how women were not taken seriously in the music industry:

"Music was taken as like a ..., if you became a musician as a woman you were like a prostitute. People took you to be something funny you know. I cannot even describe it. And the women thought the exposure was like also... it wasn't something decent, people preferred women to be in offices. I can even remember my father asking me: I sent you to school to just sing like that? Is this the profession you have chosen my daughter – you know – why can't you be a teacher or a nurse? You're going to sing like this for the rest of your life? And then I said this is what I like, I like singing and in the end he was convinced. He was very happy because it didn't go like what he thought, I don't know. Yes, he thought maybe I was going to be a loose type maybe because of exposure to the world. May be he thought I was going to be drinking – smoking. No I didn't. I tried but I don't know something just said – No. I don't love the taste of beer. I was just sober."

Despite her father's fears and lack of support, Virginia's aunt opened and facilitated her path into music. She had started music at an early age and was encouraged by her aunt (her father's sister)

who raised her after her mother passed away when she was only three. Virginia's aunt was blind but played a guitar and a cello . She also worked as a teacher for the Jairos Jiri Association, an organization for physically challenged people. The Jairos Jiri Association had a musical group called The Sunrise Kwela Kings that was very popular in the 1960s and 1970s. When she was at Mzilikazi Primary School, Mr. Jiri noticed Virginia's talent, and asked her aunt if she (Virginia) could sing for the band. Because she was encouraged by her aunt and a family associate, Jairos Jiri, Virginia discovered that she had a talent that was appreciated and also that she did not have stage fright.

She drew her strength and inspiration

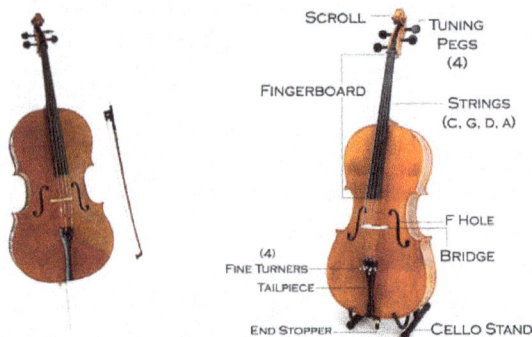

from her aunt, who was a strong woman. She had an idol to look up to in her family. From then on, she did not look back. When she completed her secondary school, Virginia moved to the capital city, Harare, and joined several bands and sang at various venues. When she joined the Harare Mambos she met her husband Green Jangano.

Therefore, family structures are important, in terms of encouraging and supporting women musicians. Such support gives them the confidence that it is acceptable to go out there to sing and perform. Family support has helped some women to be able to become musicians and to see music as any other normal profession.

A family outfit in the 1950s produced the youngest musician of that time, Bertha Mattaka Msora. She was introduced to music and acting at the early age of five.

She did not stay for a long time on the music scene because she got married at an early age and became a mother and, at the same time she was furthering her education. However, her family background moulded her to be a confident person in whatever she did. Specifically, the fact that she was allowed into public space at an early age built her confidence. She became educated and she knew the meaning of education in the development of a person.

In my research in music I have observed that women who have support from their families have had better opportunities in the industry than those who do not have any support from their families. For them, music can easily become a way of life, because they are grounded in music. However, some of them may fall into the laid-back trap of the privileged, thereby letting some opportunities slip through, as some of them end up not as much of real go-getters as those who discover the industry by themselves. On the other extreme the go-getters might end up doing it in a very ruthless way, instead of just being firm to get what they want, they end up going to extremes – just to prove a point.

While Bertha Mattaka Msora was young, she featured in dramas and films in which her parents took a leading role. She continued with her acting career in her adult life, and she wrote a very popular television drama (series) on adoption in the Zimbabwean African context, titled Nyasha. She also wrote an award winning play; I Will Wait. Her upbringing gave her the confidence to go for what she wanted. This was demonstrated by how she went back to school after getting married and having children. She also continued with her artistic work by writing, singing and acting. Just before she passed away in 2005, Bertha wanted to record some of the music she used to sing with her parents. Unfortunately, she did not. The only recording that she did was when I interviewed her and she sang with her parents and her young sister Dolly Vengesai who also passed on.

Family groups continued to have an

Bertha (Mattaka) Msora

impact on the music scene in the 1950s. As a way of protecting women musicians, parents felt at peace when their daughters (women musicians) were in family groups. For example, Faith Dauti, popularly known as the 'Shot Gun Boogie', came from such a group, The Milton Brothers, which comprised her brother and two cousins. Although Faith was the lead singer and the crowd puller, the group did not include her name as Faith Dauti and the Milton Brothers, it was just The Milton Brothers. Faith and the Milton Brothers held their rehearsals at the home of Faith's parents, who were supportive of the group. When she went out to sing, her parents would feel at peace that she was with her brother and cousins, who looked out for her and protected her. Moving in music circles, Faith married a musician, called Timothy Selani, and they had two children. Unfortunately, the marriage did not last for a long time. According to Faith's cousin, Bill Saidi, the end of the marriage caused Faith to break down and she died a very heart broken woman.

Faith was a brilliant composer and arranger.

Some of the songs she composed and arranged are: *"Rosvika Zuva [rekuti iwe neni tigare tose, tidanane]",* (The Day is approaching for me and you to be in love and stay together), *Hama Neva Bereki* (Relatives and Parents) the song is from the tune *Hamba noNsokolo* by Dorothy Masuka, *Ngatipemberei*, (Let's rejoice) *Shoko Rasvika* (The Word has Come), and many others. *Rosvika Zuva* was played on FBC (Federal Broadcasting Corporation) General Service of the radio, which catered for the white community, and was not usually the case, as Shona songs were only played on the African Service. This was during the general strike of the 1950s. Even though the direct translation of the song was about love, the authorities used it to persuade black workers to abandon the strike and go back to work.

Another star musician who came from a musical family is **Chiwoniso Maraire**. Her parents were music teachers, and were amongst the first to introduce mbira music in America. Chiwoniso started playing mbira at a very early age. She was in public space at an early age because of encouragement from her parents and later in life; she got support from friends and the band she was

Chiwoniso Maraire

playing with. She was able to negotiate public space because of the confidence that she gained from her childhood. This confidence helped her to approach the band that she later performed with before she went solo. She explained;

"So what could happen from the time that I was very young, my father - like I told you - would let us play (instruments), we started playing marimba. I remember we were so short, that we would have to stand on small boxes, one could barely see our eyes, so mbira came about later. The way that we were playing was a very closed- in type of a situation. At the most you could have me playing mbira with my father at the same time, never more than two and so it tends to be a very personal experience and I think for my parents they just wanted to know that, not only was I ready but also my sister because my sister sings as well she plays hosho.

First of all playing mbira in the nightclubs ah, there has been the most amazing support. I think also because, I was lucky when I played mbira for the first time at the night club. I was playing with Andy Brown and the Storm and in that sense already, I was in a very supportive circle of friends because, not only did people work together, but we also had many friendships amongst us. Okay we were friends, we were a little family unity, so there was already that support. Mwendi the woman that I was working with was up there playing with me hosho and singing just because you know they wanted to say look this is what you do. This is what you shine at, get up and do it we are with you. My father would come to see me you know what. So already I think if there hadn't been that warm reception from the audience, the people that mattered to me most were giving me that you just feel this confidence, okay: Alright I have to do what I can do. My people are here with me, but besides that, people were so receptive so warm, so wanting to just ah, so receptive,......, 'kamusikana ako,

makawona, kamusikana ako kanoridza mbira wena, ah ridza iwe shamwari' (have you seen that girl (Chiwoniso) she is good at playing mbira. Play.) You know that type of situation and find yourself playing and the next week someone will come back and ask you for a specific song and realise 'saka vanhu vanga varikuto terera, zveshuwa' (so people are really listening). You know I just thought they are sitting there drinking their beers and yet they are actually listening."

Similarly, Jane Chenjerayi, who was popular in the 1970's, was introduced to the public by her mother, Susan Chenjerayi who was a musician. As a result, Jane was not intimidated by public space. She used to tour with her mother. Jane had access to public space because of her early childhood, in which her mother had paved the way and given her confidence. Jane Chenjerayi recounted:

"I joined Wagon Wheels, this time it was me, Oliver Mutukudzi, my mother and the Wagon Wheels. We would do our shows, touring as well all over the country. The three of us were up front. I had compositions that we ended up all singing live on stage.

An unusual combination of father and daughter came on the music scene in the 1980's in the traditional/popular music gatherings and shows. Irene Chigamba and her father Tute Chigamba. Tute behaved as if he was giving his daughter away to the public – which was his social right since it is the same practice as at weddings and is therefore acceptable. Even though traditionalists in society complained at first, they later accepted this combination as the man; particularly a father has some authority, which society respects. Also, in this way, society is assured that the father would always be there to keep her in line in case she decides to be wayward. Irene's father, Tute, did not see introducing his daughter into public space of music as problematic as he viewed music like any other job. Irene played almost all kinds of mbira as she performed with her family at traditional gatherings:

"We would sleep over at the ceremonies. The kind of mbira that

Irene Chigamba   Tute Chigamba

I used to play that time was called 'Nyamaropa tune'- which consisted of 22 keys that was the kind of mbira that I started learning. But now I'm playing 28 keys, it's kind of discorded because it takes all the mbira keys. But it's all up to a person to choose which key to start with, it be 22 keys or 24" (Irene Chigamba).

Irene's mother stopped playing mbira to become a fulltime housewife, while her daughters Irene and Julia joined their father and travelled and performed around the world. Julia Chigamba is now resident in Califonia were she perfoms and teaches traditional dance.

However, Irene's mother had prepared the public space for her daughters. She was among the first women to play mbira in public. Irene remembers her mother being one of the first women to play mbira for traditional gatherings.

The support Irene got from her parents has made her proud of her identity, and she has continued to use her maiden name. She likes to carry the flag of her surname, Chigamba, unlike many women, who feel

Julia Chigamba
Charity Maness Pho

that in order to be accepted in the public space one has to use their husband's name and giving up their first surname (maiden name) as a way of confirming that she is married and upholding society's principles.

Prudence Katomeni-Mbofana has also kept her first surname (maiden name), because the public already knew her as Katomeni. When she got married she used her husband's name, Mbofana, and the public became confused about who she was.

Nomsa Mhlanga, a young woman musician made her debut on Women's Day on the 8th August 2008. Her father, Louis Mhlanga who played the guitar, accompanied her. She started her musical career when she was only four years old. Her first musical project was with her father Louis Mhlanga, when they worked on a project with abused children for the South African Broadcasting

Nomsa Mhlanga and her father Louis Mhlanga 8 August 2008

Corporation SABC.

Similarly, Ammara Brown is also one of the few women musicians who started singing at a very tender age with her father, Andy Brown, who was at that time married to Chiwoniso Maraire. Amara was introduced to the public when she was young, and

Ammara Brown

Chiwoniso Maraire, Ammara Brown

that helped her to be a confident musician. She was in the top ten of the 2008 Idols Competition that was held in Kenya.

Women have also managed to get into music through family connections. Prominent family names are a ticket for women musicians to be able to carry themselves confidently and in an informed manner in the music industry. For example, Taruwona Mushore's family associations helped her to gain confidence in the music industry as a new comer. It was easy for her to be accepted by the male band that helped her to get started in the music business, particularly Simangaliso Tutani, Chris Chabuka and Jonny Papas, who were respected township jazz musicians. They accepted her and gave her guidance, as they knew her family and were friends with her brothers.

WOMEN HERALD NEW ERA: ALL FEMALE GROUPS

Surviving in public space has also to do with a number of factors, with confidence playing a major role in contributing to creating personality and the understanding of the complexities of public space. Education also plays a significant role in boosting the confidence of women. In 1954, for instance, Victoria Chingate, who was working at the Harare Hospital as a Senior Nursing Sister after having been trained at Baragwanath Hospital in South Africa, formed the Gay Gaieties. She came to work in Harare after marrying Scotting Chingate, who she met while he was training to be a social worker in Johannesburg.

Victoria revolutionised the music industry in Zimbabwe by establishing the first all-female group, which consisted some of the first female trainees at the Harare Hospital. An "all female group" was a new phenomenon, and some people attended the Gay Gaeities shows out of curiosity just to see an all-female group. I interviewed Bill Saidi in 1992, a musician in the 1950's one of the early township musicians and a long time serving journalist, who said that the formation of the Gay Gaeties was really a new trend (Zimbabwe Township Music documentary 1992).

Victoria formed the Gay Gaeties as a way of creating entertainment particularly around Christmas time, as the white nurses had their own separate entertainment. She said that when the Gay Gaeties were formed it brought the two races together as the Gay Gaeties' parties became more popular because of their music. During

The Gay Gaeties

Christmas time, the hospital authorities would give the Gay Gaeties the task of organizing a Christmas show for the hospital, which was attended by all races. This demonstrates that music crosses racial boundaries and can bring people together.

Victoria was able to manage the Gay Gaeties partly because her country of origin, South Africa, was more advanced in the music and entertainment industry than Zimbabwe. Victoria's education could have been an added advantage. She could stand public space pressures and she had a better chance of negotiating well on behalf of the group as compared to some of her counterparts, who were not familiar with the outside world or the business world. Victoria's public space was much broader, and stretched far beyond the stage compared to that of Lina Mattaka and Evelyn Juba. Furthermore, being a nursing sister, she met prominent people through her work and also while socialising. She was also able to tap in her husband's network and to talk to them herself, and not relying on her husband to do so on her

behalf.

Although Victoria's husband helped her with the promotion of the group, she was fully in charge of the group together with other members. She was also involved in making major decisions about the group. The Gay Gaeties' fan base was composed of a wide spectrum of society and

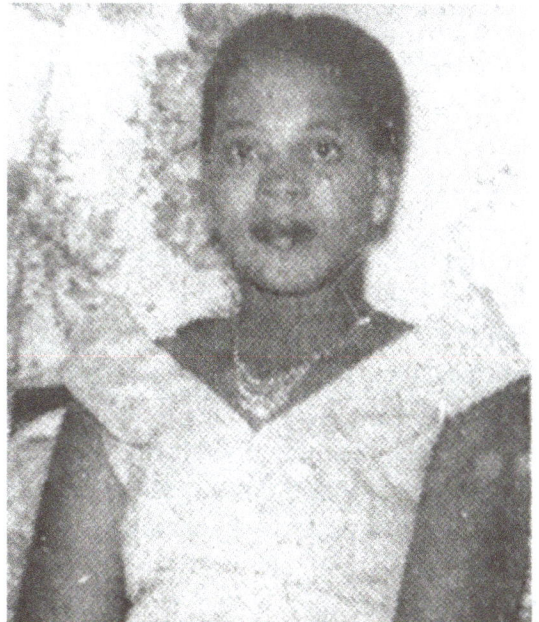

Victoria Chingate (50s)

Victoria Chingate (90s)

amongst them political leaders who were mostly brought by Victoria's husband, Scotting Chingate, who was a politician and an MP for the Federation of Rhodesia and Nyasaland. This attracted patrons of significant status in society.

The other advantage for the group was that its members were employed, most of them were still student nurses on salaries. This may have enabled the group to finance itself. During the 1950s, not many women were empowered economically. The Gay Gaieties could buy their own musical costumes, could pay backing vocalists, and were even able to pay for the venues. This made music a viable venture for them.

While earlier women musicians had not been viewed as a threat to the cultural expectations (they were seen as role models of a descent marriage and home), the Gay Gaeties on the other hand gained their respect because they were educated formally. The Gay Gaieties destroyed the myth that music was for the so-called 'social misfits' including the uneducated women. Initially some people were surprised to see educated women like Victoria and the nurses taking to music, more so being an all female group.

One female teacher asked Victoria why a woman would choose to perform in the public. She said, " when I came to the show I wanted to see what a woman can do in a public like this, but the music was good and I had fun." The teaching profession itself was associated with new values that were, to a large extent, influenced by Christianity.

Despite their mindset being for moral correctness, professional women also wanted to have time out and to see other women perform on stage as it was refreshing. Tutu Malamufumu, a female actor, says that it is important for women performers to have women in the audience as they become their cheerleaders and influence a positive performance by encouraging fellow women. It is important for women to be economically empowered across the board. It gives them independence, allows them to pay for their own entertainment and, in this way, are able to support other women. The Gay Gaeities also produced plays that were educational. One of their

famous plays was about a woman who was refusing to have surgery. The message was to allay the woman's fears. The play could also have been influenced by their professional background as nurses, and it went down very well with the hospital authorities. Their involvement in music and drama raised their status at the hospital as black nurses.

Sylvia Sondo

Also originally from South Africa, she was a nursing sister by profession. Sylvia led the group The Yellow Blues in the 1950s. She revolutionarised the music scene by the way she danced to *Chachacha* music which is known as *Rhumba* today, compared to the soft dance performed by other women musicians.

Sylvia came to settle in Harare after marrying Sonny Sondo, who was the leader of the 1950s City Quads band. Sylvia graced the music scene in the 1950s with an all female troupe called The Yellow Blues. They combined township jazz music

Slyvia Sondo

with dance music mostly Rhumba music. Sylvia's shows became popular because of her unique dance unlike other women who were careful about the way they carried themselves in the public.

The African Daily News under the column:

"Women Set The Ball of Jazz Rolling" reported:

"There was a moment, brief though it may be, in the history of Jazz-O-African Townships when women led the men. We can fix this period somewhere during 1954 to 1955. There was a memorable occasion when Vic Chingate's Gay Gaieties jointly staged a concert with another female troupe. It all happened at the Runyararo Hall. Young women leapt and wriggled in fantastic dance-styles. The Yellow Blues, although short - lived, owe their existence to the untiring energy of Mrs. Sylvia Sondo." (11 January 1958).

To a larger extent the two nursing sisters enjoyed a certain level of financial independence, which enabled them to establish and finance their musical groups.

Financial independence has been another means that women musicians have used to fight for and negotiate public space. There were more female only groups to follow these two groups, but they were mainly backing vocalists in *Simanje-manje* or Rhumba groups.

The late 1990s witnessed all-female groups such as Maita Women's Ensemble, which came out of the Saturday Workshops held by the Zimbabwe College of Music. All the women in this group played instruments.

The Amakhosi Women's group was also an all-female group and their members also played instruments, just like the Maita Women's Ensemble. Groups like Mambokadzi and Amavitikazi have made their names as some of the best dancing all-female ensembles.

Other all-female groups were Amakhosikazi which was founded by Priscilla Sithole and she natured the group. Through her guidance the group rose to stardom and gave birth to one of the celebrated female guitarist Edith weUtonga. Big Sister was founded by Ava Rogers, and African Voices – Women's Acapella founded by Kundisai Mutero who is the leader of the band.

Establishing women-only groups demonstrates that women have reached a certain level of independence in the music industry, that of not leaning on or depending on men. While women musicians have been brave enough to traverse the musical terrain, it has been a nightmare for those who do not have a support base. ◼

Priscilla Sithole

Edith WeUtonga

Chapter 6

Voice, artistic expression and public space

zimbojan

Dudu Manhenga traversing the public space

THE voice and artistic expression of any musician is the cornerstone of good performance. What makes music to have meaning is the way it is expressed, without any hindrance. The confidence that a musician exudes is portrayed in the way s/he expresses themselves, and the way their voice is projected to the audience. The level of musicianship is judged by the way musicians assert themselves in voice and artistic expression. Unfortunately not many women musicians have been able to reach the highest pinnacles of musicianship, as their voice is disturbed by a number of factors. The way women are raised and, also, the structures of the society that shape them, has had a significant impact on how their voice and artistic expression is moulded. Women have not been able to fully assert themselves in voice and artistic expression. The freedom of expression is something that is built from within, and nurtured for a long time but not many women have had the freedom of expression cultivated in them as they grew up.

From a tender age, a lot of women have not been encouraged to be open about their feelings. An observation of boys and girls playing can reveal the independence or freedom that boys have/enjoy. The way the girl-child is brought up (with a lot of monitoring)– in a way affects her ability to exercise her right to freedom of speech/expression and choice later in life; which can continue to be a stumbling block in later life, including career choice. The same does not apply to boys, who are in most cases groomed to be risk takers. This socio-cultural gap bestowed on the upbringing of boys and girls makes men to be confident musicians, allowing them to do whatever they can to mersimerise the audience.

The words that create the voice are also determined by one's gender. Men are free to sing whatever they want and, if women do the same, they would be stepping out of line. Men can sing about sex, and the crowd applauds them, and it is seen to be normal. Although there are exceptional women who behave the same way as the male musicians, it is because most of these women have not, or do not function in the mainstream structures of the society. Most of these exceptional women have operated from the periphery of the societal structures in order to rise to the highest levels of musicianship.

They have had control of their voice and artistic expression, which many women have not. It is because the exceptional women are not a 'real part of the society'. Women who are real part of the society have not been able to stand pressure from the general public, because they would like to belong to the society. Because they want to belong, they usually abandon music so that they can fit in the mainstream structures of the society, and become 'real women'. If they continue in the music industry, then they have to behave according to the unwritten rules set by the society: that of being a woman or face being ostracised; not necessarily on the stage, but in the various structures of the society. A large percentage of the world is shaped in such a way that women have to behave in a particular way, different to

Young girls playing

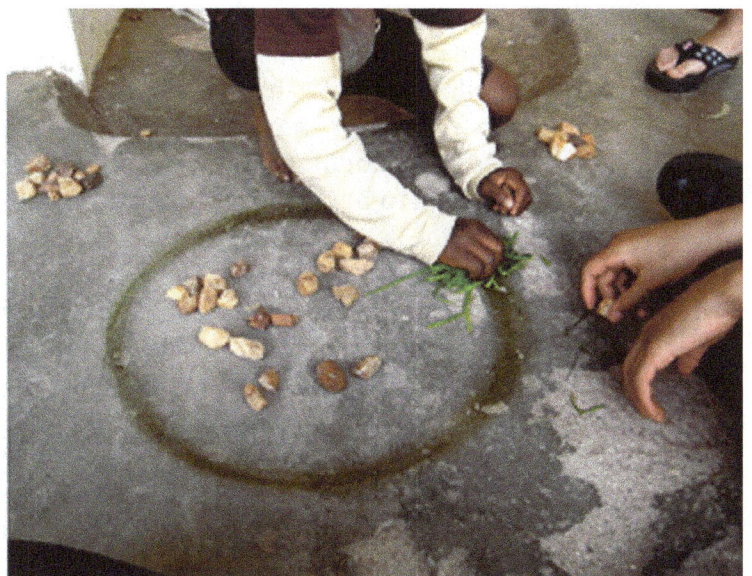

that of men. The world is predominantly a male centered planet. This has affected the voice and artistic expression of a Zimbabwean woman musician, which has been shaped, from childhood, by the structures that govern the Zimbabwean society, which is controlled by patriarchal structures.

Many families do not celebrate the arrival of a girl child as they would if it were a boy –child. The girl child does not carry on the family name, more so if the girl is born into a family were the boy child is anticipated. The fact that not so much value is placed on her as she is not seen to carry on the family name, but as a person who will be married off to another family, affects her from the onset. She grows up feeling that she is a second-class citizen.

There are rules that she must abide by, that result in her being passive, as she cannot challenge these constructed structures. When she gets married, she is not accepted as a full member of the family, which means a woman does not belong anywhere. This is deliberately meant to confuse her so that she may not take control of herself so that society can do whatever they want to/and with her by confusing her into having no sense of belonging.

A girl is seen as an asset for the family who, when married, will bring wealth; money and cows in the family through lobola (bride price). Therefore, for her to be 'marketable' when she becomes a woman, since she is a commodity, the family has to bring her up in such a way that she does not become an embarrassment to the family where she is going to be an in-law. She is reminded that, for her to be loved and accepted by that other family, she has to carry herself in a certain way.

This has to start from when she is a child. She works towards that and she does not develop her true self, for fear of ending up as a single woman. Women have spent all their lives working on how they can be loved by men, and they will do almost anything in order for them to be loved. From an early age, a woman is too careful about what she says, and how she behaves, which also results in controlling her voice. In a family set up, the girl -child is brought up to be more careful about what she says compared to the boy-child. The girl does not enjoy the freedom of speech as compared to the boy. In most cases the girl child's opinion is not respected as compared to that of a boy-child.

Even when family issues are being discussed at places like padare/enkundleni (family forum), it is the sons of the family who should be present, and a mature tete (sister of their father) considered "honorary male". In many cases, the sister of the father tete is "overridden" by men who usually pass family laws without necessarily getting her approval. Many tetes at these forums (padare/enkundleni) just rubber stamp what the males will have said save for a few who are said to be 'women who are like men'.

When a woman is getting married it is also the males of the family who gather and decide the amount of her lobola (bride price). The family usually brings the tete (who is, again, the father's sister), but the woman getting married and her sisters are not supposed to be part of this discussion except for the tete, they just sit and are told what to do. The voice of a woman who is getting married is very important, since this is her future that is being decided on this day, but because she is not supposed to have a voice, others have to determine her life.

Consequently, her voice and the way she expresses herself, is controlled in such a way that she is not free to say what she wants, and her confidence is shattered.

The country's institutions are also designed in such a way that they enforce this control of the woman, from childhood to adulthood, in order to shape her voice and how she expresses herself. Institutions like the community, the church, school and the workplace: all these are patriarchal structures and have to strengthen patriarchy, in order for them to function without hindrance.

Joyce Jenje-Makwenda

The Church as strengthening Patriarchal Societies

The church is one of the first institutions that a woman is introduced to besides her family. It reinforces most of the values that the family introduces or exerts on the girl child, that of being submissive, so that she can always remember that she is a 'girl', and she will be a 'woman'.

The Church – a vital establishment in society, has also been used as an instrument to curtail women's voice. This has been done, not only by emphasizing the family position, but also sometimes using the verse in the Bible which says; "As in all the congregations of the saints, women should remain silent in the churches. They are not allowed to speak, but must be in submission, as the Law says. If they want to inquire about something, they should ask their own husbands at home; for it is disgraceful for a woman to speak in the church." Taken from 1 Corinthians 14:33-35, : The verse has been translated to strengthen patriarchal structures in the church.

Despite women constituting a large number of the congregation, the leaders of the church are men, who are ministers, pastors, reverends and priests. Not many churches have women leaders in the highest echelons. Many churches still do not believe that a woman can stand in front of the congregation and deliver a ministry. The recent introduction of women as ministers in some churches has seen some of these churches splitting. The introduction of women priests in the Anglican Church saw some male priests resigning in protest.

The Roman Catholic Church, which is considered to be one of the oldest churches in the world, although it glorifies the Virgin Mary, has not introduced any women priests. The church finds it difficult to have a woman stand in front of the congregation and preach. Instead she has to be preached to, which means that the voice of women is not heard. How women would like to translate verses in the Bible, and how they would like to shape their destiny in church, is suppressed. Even though women can preach to other women especially at Mother's Union gatherings, most of the time is spent advising each other on how to look after the home, the husband and the children in order to strengthen patriarchal structures.

Women are, however, needed for their singing services in the church. In most churches they constitute the majority, and they may even end up singing bass because of the shortage of male attendants. This is the only voice they provide in the church, and it is already controlled by the mere fact that men control the church.

It is the church that upholds family values, more than any other institution in the world. It is in the church that women are structured to be 'good women'. That is why going into the public space and singing church songs known as Gospel music is, in a way, seen as a way of ministering, not entertaining. Since the congregation is usually made up of the community that one lives in, the church arguably manages to put some checks and balances; - monitoring systems as far as how women live their lives, and continue to whip them in line.

This does not provide the freedom that is needed in women's self–expression, as this

A church Building

comes with a lot of deception that makes it difficult for women to be themselves. The church can be argued to be one of the structures that are set by the society to continue to monitor women and suppress them from fully expressing themselves. The church therefore plays a significant role in shaping and strengthening patriarchal structures, and in destroying and curtailing women's voices.

The School as strengthening Patriarchal Societies

The school shapes the life of a girl child. Depending on the family's resources, which usually favour the boy-child to have formal education, she can be deprived of education. In some families, not only does a girl fail to go to school but she also has to look after her siblings while the parents are working for the family. For those fortunate to go to school, the way the girl-child is raised at home makes her look not so intelligent. The boy is allocated more time for school work than the girl, who will get home and engage in household chores such as cooking and, cleaning the house.

This impact on the girl's performance at school, and can reduce her confidence. In most cases the girl is not very sure of what she says; her confidence is shattered, killing her voice. Kambarami (2006) observed that the Zimbabwean curriculum also perpetuates the rift in gender imbalances, "the textbooks that are used in schools depict boys as tough, rough and mentally skilled people who are adventurous whilst girls are depicted as soft, gentle people who enjoy carrying out household duties." According to UNAIDS (2004), girls accounted for only 42% of the enrolment ratio in secondary schools. Chirimuuta (2006) also noted that "by the time these children go to school, they would have already been socialized into unequal positions" (online).

It is a general observation that most girls in school trail behind boys, due to some of the limitations highlighted above. Joyce Banda, President of Malawi, tried to

correct this situation by having a school, just for girls. In an interview that I had with her in 1999 she said that, girls' only schools function much better than those which mix boys and girls; co-ed schools (co-educational schools). They bring out some strong girls who "equal to or better than men".

The debate on the advantages or disadvantages of single sex education is one which has attracted considerable research. Proponents of single sex education argue that it allows children to grow and mature at their own pace in an environment with lesser social pressures. Those who argue against it believe that coeducation break gender stereotypes.

In 2005, the US Department of Education commissioned a research on the advantages and disadvantages of single-sex education, and produced a report "Single-Sex versus Coeducational Schooling: A Systematic Review. The research indicated that Single-sex education "could be associated with a number of post–high schools, long-term positive outcomes" (US Department of Education Report, 2005:85) including better outcomes in

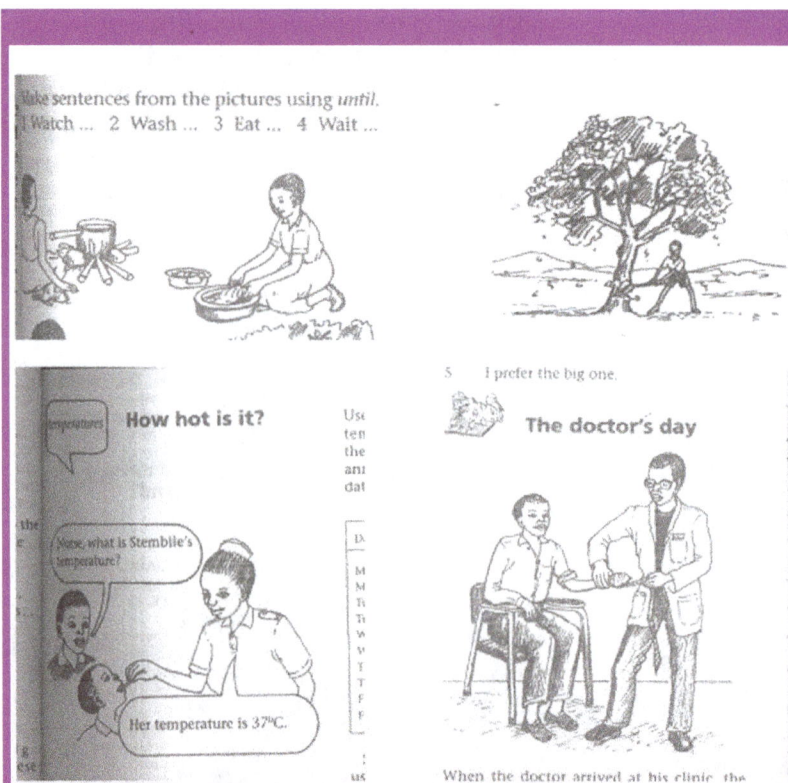

Images from a grade 5 English Text Book of how people are portrayed

post secondary school success. However, there were some downsides to single sex schools, which include eating disorders although the report highlighted the need for further research in the area.

In Zimbabwe both the Anglican and Roman Catholic Churches were instrumental in

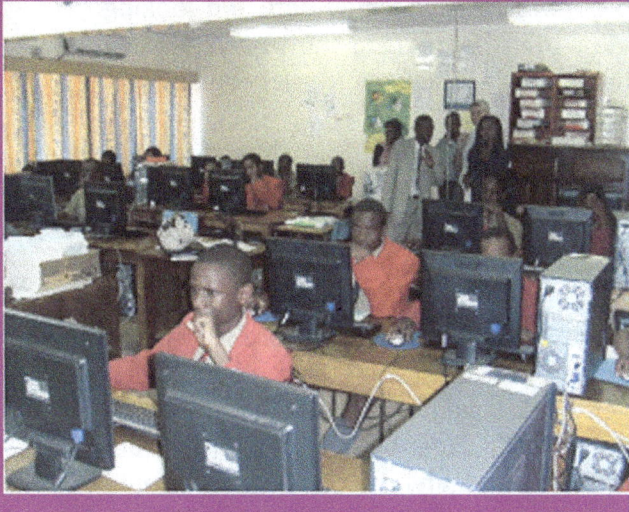

building single-sex education schools, and among them include Bonda Girls High, Bernard Mzeki College, Monte Cassino Mission, Nagle House in Marondera, Dominican Convent. The government and other institutions also contributed in having single-sex education; Hartman House, Ellis Robins, Mabelreign Girls High, Peter House Boys and Peter House Girls School. Prince Edward, Roosevelt, Evelyn Girls High, Milton High School and St George College are some of the major schools in the country that offer single sex education. Schools like St David's Bonda Girls have a high success rate in producing girls who graduate in all disciplines including medicine, agriculture (careers that would

usually be associated with men), law, and accountancy and arts subjects.

When I was in school in the 1960' s and 1970's, there were subjects designed for girls and boys respectively. Girls were supposed to do domestic science subjects, and boy's carpentry and other 'male' subjects. Domestic science subjects involved, mostly, cookery and sewing. This was designed to prepare black women to work in white people's families, and also, for them to behave as women and prepare them for their wifely duties. The school curriculum did not allow a girl child to be adventurous. One would expect that, with the domestic science knowledge that the girl child has, it would make it easy for her to get into one of the most lucrative careers like the hotel industry. No. This has been a male domain for quite a while. Although basically every work that is performed in a hotel is the same with what women do in their homes, they cannot be part of it because it is in public space and would allow women to have economic access.

The education system has continued boxing the girl-child into domestication. It has been proven that most girls do not take up science and technology subjects, but are inclined more towards social sciences, which, again prepare them to be caregivers. The issue of subject choice can also be based on or determined by how much personal time women have to invest in other subjects, which may be time consuming and may involve working during unsociable hours. Girls usually choose the subjects that can guarantee them sociable working hours, such as teaching, whereas for boys there is no limit.

When girls finish school their career choices are based on the subjects they will have done, and what is accepted by the society. Most women have resorted to teaching or nursing, secretarial or social science related courses, which are, to a large extent, associated with care-giving. However, it is through teaching in schools that some women are exposed to music as a career, that they can teach it in schools. Teaching music in schools is

Women cooking at home for family or for big function

to some extent, viewed as a respectable profession, than performing on stage. But, it is sometimes the process that one has to go through in order for them to become a qualified music teacher that ends up with a woman clashing with the society. Since most women teachers discover this career after having married and having children, it becomes a problem as they are expected to spend a lot of time on the course. The course involves the learning of music theory, instruments, and research and this takes a lot of time. Most women who I taught at the Zimbabwe College of Music

had problems balancing between looking after their homes and the two-year NCM (National Certificate in Music) course.

Some of the women were teachers and lived outside Harare where the Zimbabwe College of Music is based. They had either to leave the children at their homes and come to Harare and look for temporary lodgings that they could afford to pay for. Bringing children to Harare would mean getting a bigger place, which they could not afford since by enrolling in a full-time post-qualifying course, they would automatically loose a quarter of their salaries.

This in a way created problems for them, and some ended up dropping out of the course. In a class where there were around one-quarter women and three quarters men, this meant that less than a quarter of women would finish the programme. Together with people like Gunilla Selerud, Alpha Chapendama, I was in a group of women activists who successfully lobbied for a 50-50 enrolment at the Zimbabwe College of Music.

The Work Place

THE workplace across the board does not encourage women to be confident,

Women Music Educators at Zimbabwe College of Music

Women at work

the bedroom. They are the ones who cook the food that everyone eats but, yet they hardly enjoy it as they are either too tired to eat, or they just cooked to fulfil a duty.

From the time they are young, women are made to cook for people. Even if they are not hungry, they cannot refuse, because they have no voice. After they have cooked they do not usually get the share that a boy child gets. It is a well-known fact that some girls have to eat *sadza* with soup as relish. Traditionally, meat is mostly rationed favouring the boy-child, and the father of the house, and yet it is the girl-child who needs protein, iron and other vitamins in order to help her productive and reproductive systems to function properly, and produce healthy children.

This experience makes the girl-child feel unworthy, but there is not much that she can do. In the Zimbabwe custom, there are certain parts of meat that are supposed to be for the husband, and not the wife and kids, though it would be the woman who will have cooked the food. Women do not have the freedom to choose what they eat and when to cook.

Cooking takes most of the time from women, as people eat everyday. They also have to wash the dishes, which women always do under protest, but they have to protest quietly. Their voice is suppressed.

There are many things that a woman has to give up when she gets married; like giving up on her church and joining the husband's church, that is if they are both Christians.

adventurous, or to tap into their strengths to reach their full potential. Instead, the workplace is inconsiderate of the biology of women, when it comes to providing systems and structures for the women to function effectively in that space. The structures, also, put in different institutions seem to be in tandem with what determines how a woman will make it in the workplace. The music industry becomes one of the most affected of the work places where a woman can be vulnerable, because of its more public nature. A woman can either make it or fail in the music industry, depending on how she has been socialized to view the public.

The girl child does not usually enjoy full life when she is growing up and this follows her into her adulthood. In most cases she feels like a lesser person. When women have been groomed for marriage and they finally get married, they don't usually make major decisions in the home, from the kitchen to

Woman doing Housework

But women do it with such ease, without even questioning, as they are prepared for this, not having the freedom to choose.

The way a woman dresses has to please the man. Some women who wore trousers before they got married may also give up wearing trousers if the husbands do not approve. A woman might even be forced to change the football team she supports, and support that of the husband. She might also have to abandon her friends particularly if they are not married.

In the bedroom itself, women have suffered untold abuse. Some never experience enjoyable sexual intercourse or lovemaking. If the husband has enjoyed himself, the woman has to feel happy that she has done her job as a woman, despite not having enjoyed the sexual interaction. She is not supposed to question or show discontent.

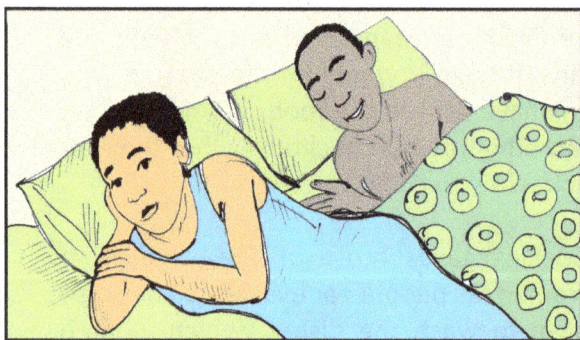

Discussing sex openly can be seen as an embarrassing subject, unlike with the women in x, who had channels to discuss sex and one of the routes was through music.

Most of today's women will suffer quietly as far as this subject is concerned. If one has no voice and cannot express themselves in their own home, how can they express themselves in public space? With this type of woman who does not have choices what kind of lyrics can we expect?

Lyrics that are supposed to be accepted by the society, that is why many women start their musical careers in churches and then graduate to sing Gospel music or for some if they start in popular music they end up in Gospel music, either to fulfill themselves spiritually or as an exit point.

Women musicians like Susan Chenjerayi-Mobape and Virginia Sillah started their musical careers as popular musicians and they made names in their respective genres, but are now considering going into recording Gospel music.

Virginia Sillah, who would like to record her music, says, "I don't think I can record my old music now because, as it is now, I've changed. As a born again Christian: if ever

Susan Chenjerayi

I want to go and record, it must be gospel. I will give my daughter all my township jazz music so that she can record it, as she is talented musically."

Susan Chenjerayi also shares the same sentiments with Virginia Sillah, as she has also become a born again Christian. She

Virginia Sillah

would like to record gospel music. For both Susan and Virginia, gospel music is an exit point in their musical career.

The musicianship of many women does not reach highest levels because of how their lives are structured. Most women do not reach the highest levels of mastery in musicianship, which comes with years of being consistent, practising and, also, creating one's confidence. The highest levels of musicianship have to do with how the voice is shaped from lyrics to how it is projected, and also, artistic expression plays an important part in bringing out a certain type of music and creating a lasting impression with one's audiences.

Because of many problems that a woman faces during the peak of her career in music, this does not allow her to compose music effectively, partly because of not having enough time to compose and arrange. Women musicians might also fail to compose music effectively because of lack of confidence with the voice inside them. The voice inside has to do with all that make up a woman, but she might find herself afraid to say it as it is. She tends to suppress the voice that wants to come out. This results in a woman fighting her inner person, editing her feelings, and

coming up with compositions that are not authentic to her - to the detriment of her career, as this affects her voice and artistic expression. For some women musicians to be accepted by society, they have written lyrics, which work against women (including themselves), as long as they are seen to be lyrics, which put a woman in her 'place'. Most women musicians are not aware that they are writing lyrics that disadvantage them as women in general.

Musicians sing about real life situations. The way women write and compose their songs comes from their life situations, and they can only go that far. They cannot reach the pinnacle because their real life situations are mostly filled with pretentious characters. Women do not live 'themselves'. Although some women musicians sing music that short changes them in a way, they will be depicting the real life situations, in most cases, not the true life they would want to live but what they are supposed to do. Because music, which has to do with woman's life situations, is supposed to help keep some order in the society, the music is aimed at a certain grouping; women who, in most cases, do not have much buying power. The media exploits this situation, and plays this type of music over and over

Botswana musician Slizer dancing at a show in Harare

again, as it is supposed to send a message and reinforce societal values. Women's music is not bought as much as the music composed by men, who are free to express themselves and know what sells better. Women musicians find themselves in a vicious cycle. They are writing songs to save the structures of the community, and yet that community is not empowering them economically by supporting their music, by way of attending shows and buying the music. Targeting female buyers (market) is not always rewarding since most of the women they target are not financially stable enough to attend shows, or they do not have the culture of going out as women to entertain themselves. This makes female musicians powerless, and they are put where the society wants them to be – powerless musicians! A woman musician ends up falling back into the structures of the society, as they are constructed to disembowel women.

The success of a woman musician also lies in the energies of the band she is involved with, and most of the band members are usually males. Women have to be comfortable with the band they sing with and get to know each other. This helps the voice of a woman to come out without fear, and she can then be able to express herself.

Because of the complications that women face in the music industry or from the structures that the society has put in place to govern them, some women musicians have entered the music industry through functions organised by the social structures – like singing for the heads of states. Although this is public space, it is a 'politcally protected public space' which might not offer much to the deveopment of their musical growth.

Recording music is an important component in the line of business of a woman musician, though this turns out to be a nightmare for many musicians because of lack of financial resources, and also not getting producers believing in their music and willing to help. Males dominate the recording industry, and they are more interested in promoting the 'boys club'. Failing to record their music at the height of their careers has seen women musicians being completely wiped out of the music industry, usually leaving no trace of the music produced during their heydays. This is also how the voice of a woman is killed, and not kept for posterity. It is important that women find ways of recording their music as a way of preserving women's voice, since in most cases women's musical careers are cut short prematurely and do not usually reach full potential.

The recording of women's music might not necessarily mean that the music will find its way to empowering women financially or their way to stardom, but it will help document their work and those who will come after them to use as reference. The music will not only help women who would want to be in the music industry, but also women in general, as this music will be a record of what was going on in the lives of women during the time the music was recorded. That is why it is important for women to record their honest feelings and what they are experiencing without being edited.

Nevertheless, if in the process of recording, a woman musician decides to edit her true feelings, the music will still serve as a record of what was taking place in that particular society. Recording of music becomes a point of reference to trace different eras lived by women, since music acts as the umbrella of the society.

While they are women who have recorded their music a number of them have complained about not achieving the quality of music that they had anticipated. Many times women musicians have complained of how the recording industry destroys their confidence resulting in destroying their voice in order to control them. Prudence is one woman musician who knows what she wants when she is in the studio, she is very clear of what she wants, she makes sure she brings out her voice and artistic expression without hinderance whatsoever. Prudence Katomeni-Mbofana is one musician who has been clear of what she wants when in the studio. Prudence has come to understand the complexity of the music industry through informal and formal education. A number of women musicians who do not have the knowledge that Katomeni-Mbofana has in the music industry, get row deals when recording as they fail to express their wishes, how they would want their music to sound. She advices women musicians to make sure that the voice and instruments blend together, failing to do so will result in the woman musician losing confidence and ending up with a mediocre product.

"My producer would say we don't just do things here we do things a certain way, and sometimes he would just do what he wants with my music without my authority and yet I would have told him that, that is not where I want to go. I would tell him with the correct terms; this is what I want for this song. One thing that I have noticed about other women musicians is that the producer decides how their music is going to be like. There is this thinking that all she has to do is to sing and therefore make decisions for her, because some of these women do not even know the key they will be singing in. This suppresses a woman's creativity because when she is singing she will be feeling that the song is supposed to go this way, she does not have the right words to speak. You see with the stronger women, the stronger characters they try to argue although sometimes from an uninformed position how they would want their music to sound, but they do not win with most producers (who are male). I overheard a male producer talking and laughing about a female musician who had just left the studio, saying 'did you hear her? What was she really trying to say?' and they laughed".

When recording it is sometimes very difficult for women to say how they would like their music to sound. The way the music is directed might not bring out voice and the artistic expression of the woman

musician. Prudence is proud that with her debut CD she was bold enough to express herself and came out with a product which she is proud of.

"This is what I want, and that's what I did. This is my journey through my album and that's why I am so proud because he (the producer) would say we should have this in your music but I would say, no, no, no, that's not what I want. What you want you can try it in your own time, and then he would understand where I want to go. Some producers are used to some women who will come to them and say all I want is to sing, and then they control everything".

The voice of women has to go through various channels for it to be heard and be

A Recording Studio

accepted. In these channels it has to be promoted and if not, then this is how it is killed. One of the channels that women musicians rely on is the media. The media is designed to inform, educate and entertain its citizens and, internationally as well. Unfortunately the media is constructed in such a way that it has to fulfil its mandate to its originators - the patriarchy. It then becomes difficult for the media to promote and encourage the voice and artistic expression of women in an honest way, without hidden agendas and stereotyping of the woman. It is through the media that most women musicians either make it or are, intentionally destroyed.

Some women musicians have pinned their

hopes onto other women in the media to publicise them in a positive manner, but in some instances, this has not worked because the woman working in the media belongs to the broad structural framework that defines society. Some women who find themselves in this establishment (the media) feel privileged and do not want to rock the boat, as they might be seen as daring by the society. This might result in them losing their jobs since the structures of the society are there to weed out exploratory characters from their institutions to keep their designed framework in place.

Women who have been able to have a voice, and also able to express themselves artistically, have been very clear with what they want in life - starting from their homes. It is these women who have overlooked the structures set by the society, to make them fail, who have managed to make it in the music industry. It is the way a woman expresses herself in her home that will filter through almost everything that they do, or have an impact on her musical career. Being able to explain to one's partner (husband) about her career is very important from the onset.

Sithembiso Gumbo of the Amakhosi Outfit feels that women should learn to explain their careers to their husbands before it is too late, they should not try to beat about the bush. They should learn to express themselves, to have a voice, because if women do not have a voice in the home, expressing themselves becomes difficult in the public sphere. If their voice and artistic expression is curtailed from their homes, then the public space becomes difficult to handle. Sithembiso has managed to stay on the music scene because she has been clear to her husband about her career, and she often wonders why women are not straight with their husbands:

"We might see as if our husbands will be hindering our progress when we are the ones who are not saying what we want. For instance if we have discussed with other women that we will meet tomorrow at such and such a place or at MaTshuma's place, for you to tell your husband you will first want to make them happy, but in fact you must first just tell him and hear what he will say. If you will make him happy for you to tell him something that will take you long, or you might fail to say anything, because- these men are different. There are some husbands who say where do you want to go, and he beats you there. It is because you are the one who lets him act like that from the beginning. You are afraid of him. You worship him. We respect our husbands, but let them give you a chance for you to do something you like as a mother/woman, so that you also appear as a noble woman. It's just that, we women, we can't talk to say our decision is this. When you marry me I will also want to do this. That's what we can't do before one is married".

Most women have had to drop out or are not consistent in the music industry, because of not being assertive in the way they explain their musical careers to their partners/husbands and the society. The problems that control their voice and artistic expression also control their existence in the music industry. Many women musicians have not been able to build trust in the music industry, which is built over the years. Building trust with one's audience plays an important role in a woman musician's life. The trust is built by knowing that if she releases music, people will be able to watch her perform, and will not cancel shows. But, if she is not consistent because of other issues that affect her life, then she will lose trust with her audience and people will stop following her music.

The trust is also built by knowing that, when her songs are played on the radio, her audience will recognize her, she becomes part of them. Her audience will recognize her by her lyrics, by her voice, or by the way she arranges her music. While some women musicians have managed to stay on the music scene, they have not been able to have full control of what they compose, and this affects them in becoming masters in the game.

When most women are coming onto the

suppress their voice, or move on with the flow.

There are few women musicians who have started with the voices they have been given by their husbands, or those who will have introduced them into music, and be able to move out of those voices and make it. The men in their lives will try and make it difficult for them because they will have become cash cows for the band. A woman who has made it by finding a new voice from the one she had been assigned by her spouse, is acclaimed diva; Tina Turner.

As discussed earlier, another entry into music is through Gospel music as it is accepted by the society. When women are in the process of finding their voices, they might touch a raw nerve of the society. Not many women musicians have been able to sing or direct their music the way they like. One woman who has been fortunate enough to be able to direct her music the way she likes is Laura Bezuidenhout: "In terms of musical direction, of course, this is different, and trust plays a huge role in developing and producing the music in the way you want it to be done. Trust is one major ingredient; the other is demonstrable mastery in the subject. Here, it is vital that a leader's credibility and musical mastery is widely accepted and trusted. And for me this has usually been the case. I have had no problem directing and arranging music in my own way, i.e., musically instructing band members".

music scene, they mainly come through music which is accepted by the community or society, or they come through the music that the male band members or the leader has written for them. And, when they finally find their voice, they either change audiences or they have to start building new audiences, which needs financial backing, which most women do not have. For women to make it in music, they either

Most of the music which is composed by men and fronted by women is mostly about selling women's sex, which appeals to the audience or patrons. Music being one of the ways to express art, sex becomes a fascinating subject. It is appealing as far as art is concerned and what becomes of concern is that, most of the time; the music that is composed by men is done in such a way that women become/are seen as mere sex objects. Women musicians are not afforded the opportunity to communicate their sexuality the way they want through music - the way that would benefit them and be treated with respect. This is because of how the music industry and

the society are structured and, by making women benefit and becoming powerful; the goal by the societal structures will not be achieved.

Laura Bezuidenhout has also observed how our paternalistic society forces women into doing what society wants and why: "It is because overall, men hold the purse: men like 'bodies', especially women's bodies, and therefore, for musicians to get some of the pie in the hands of men, they play to the likes of men, and it works! "Bodies", female "bodies", like sex, sells. It works, but it is perpetuating the trend of "objectifying" women (not just women musicians, but all women) into their bodies, their looks, their physical beauty and attractiveness.

I really don't have too much of a problem with this, as each musician must choose what works best for her. But when women allow themselves to be pictured in such a way I do feel that they are contributing to a greater problem – society's general disrespect and disregard for women as equal living beings."

Women have not been allowed to be equal human beings. One of the ways the society has achieved this is to put women into particular boxes where they expect them to perform in a manner they want.

Whether in popular or traditional music, women are supposed to observe set parameters. As stated in earlier chapters, a woman like Elizabeth Ncube refused to observe these parameters, and was nearly killed by a male imbongi. Elizabeth was not allowed to express herself freely the way she wanted. An imbongi is supposed to express itself freely.

The male imbongi felt Elizabeth was challenging him because she was not recognizing the boundary set for her as a woman. This is how she explains her ordeal:

"With this man we left together from Bulawayo, this man sings in the choir. I was judged before he was and later he came on the stage. I don't know whether he was on stage before me, so I was busy ngisenza izangelo (when I was doing praise poetry). So I did not see that there was someone coming from behind me, and he came on top of me and I thought this person wants to dance so that we could show people in Harare how we danced and yet this man wanted to challenge me. He wanted to challenge me and he wanted to hit me with a knobkerrie and I had a spear. Ngameqa (I jumped on him), ngeqa phezulu kwakhe. (I jumped over him). I don't know how I jumped and I heard everyone saying hu, hu, hu, and I saw people coming to take *me off the stage. The man disappeared and I never met him while I was in Harare until I went to Bulawayo. He would try and avoid me. I do not know why he wanted to kill me. He would say to other people he wanted to fix me. He said, 'wake wabona ngaphi umfazi otanyula inyawo pambili kwabantu', (where on earth did you ever see a woman who opens her legs in front of people).*

My ancestors really protected me. If it was not for that I would be dead by now. I just saw many people on the stage. It seems some of the people from Bulawayo knew about his mission because I just heard people shouting here is a man who wants to kill someone. People from Bulawayo must have known even if when he stood up coming to the stage. I think he must have said I am now going to beat her up. Up to now I do not know how I jumped him and found myself on the other side. I won the competition, beating the two men". (Elizabeth Ncube int. 1992)

The imbongi genre was seen as a male domain and men involved in it felt Ncube had invaded their territory and, not only did she invade it as they felt, but she proved to be better than them. As stated earlier, Ncube was the first female imbongi in Zimbabwe.

Albert Nyathi one of the famous Zimbabwe Imbongi attributes the lack of female

Elizabeth Ncube

Imbongi to some limitations that women had/have of having children and therefore could not go to war, as this was also the duty of the Imbongi to give moral support to soldiers through praise poetry. Women fought alongside men during the Zimbabwe liberation struggle. It was high time for them to be involved in the art of Imbongi. Since Elizabeth performed as an imbongi, this genre could no longer be seen as a male territory.

Although the whole music industry is male dominated, and men feel women are trampling in their territory, there is one genre which women musicians can be allowed or forgiven venturing into; this is the Gospel music genre.

As already stated, many women in Zimbabwe have found Gospel music as the easiest way of getting into music. They have used Gospel music as their entry point into music and, also, to exit from the music scene. For some women, Gospel music has been a real calling, and a way to preach and represent women and the African culture in a more positive way. Women in church have to fight different levels of oppression, as African women, and as women and the misinterpretation of African Culture through the church affects voice and artistic expression.

A woman like Shuvai Wutaunashe had to read the Bible for herself in order to interpret it in a way that did not inhibit her full self-expression in praise worship. She argues that:

"If you look in the Bible, the early church even the old church – I mean the Old Testament, this was the kind of praising; the Bible said dance, 'Come let us clap our hands to the Lord, come let us lift our hands to the Lord and people want to be free in church. The kind of God we serve wants the people who stand before Him; free to worship him, to shout praises to his name and really praise him. I really believe from the depth of my heart that music was meant for God and with all types of instruments – anything. And it's such a pity that we have left some of our

instruments to rot, like mbira. You know this is an instrument, which is specifically African, and now most of us don't know how to play it because we have let it go. It has a beautiful sound. Just because some missionaries came and said this was demonic, because it was not European. After all everything was created by God."

"These musical instruments were created to give Him praise. So I believe that any instruments that can be played should give him praise, should be played for God. I think the motive is what is important. Music progresses and you learn a lot more of music as you grow. You want to incorporate everything and I think that our African Culture is very rich especially where music is concerned, and where praising and just being joyful is concerned".

"Once you take these things and you envelope them, you put them into your singing, and then you really feel that you are actually praising and worshipping - because you are taking part of your culture, and putting it in your own context. So I found that it gets better to everybody who listens to it, it's not foreign".

"Everyone else can relate to it, and they can be lifted up and get inspiration, they can be assisted and it's no surprise that I have received letters and telephone calls people saying you know when I was listening to your song, Nditorei, I got over

Shuvai Wutaunashe

my problem. I think it's because the music is meaningful music and it's got a theme context."

"There are some people, particularly from conservative churches, who are

not comfortable seeing Shuvai dancing and clapping hands in church, but this is the way she would like to express herself: Things (in other churches) are done very differently, very quietly, and if they see me singing lifting my hands, dancing before the Lord, clapping my hands, they begin to think what is this woman doing? In earnest all I am doing is worshipping my God. It's according to the Bible and really I think where music is concerned, it wells up from within, and it is hard for me to hear a tune and just stand or even when I sing choruses I have to clap, tap or be doing something."

Mai Muchena supports Shuvai Wutaunshe that African instruments should be played in church as part of praise and worship. She says: "I don't see anything wrong with that. Why I don't like (or disagree) with people who go to church is that they see mbira as a demonic instrument. We have our God (Mwari), but we can't get straight to him, but through the mbira we get there just like Christians, but mixing it with church music is a great idea."

While Shuvai Wutaunashe finds it easy to incorporate the traditional way of worship and praise into the church, it has not been easy for some traditionalists to let the music grow. Taruwona faced resistance

Amai Muchena

when she mixed traditional music and jazz, which was a way for her to express herself. Beaulah Dyoko is one of the traditionalists who could not hide her displeasure about what Taruwona did, mixing mbira music with jazz music. Although culture is argued to be dynamic, Beaulah Dyoko did not believe when it comes to mixing mbira music with jazz.

"That was wrong of her (Taruwona) to mix the two, ignoring our culture, that's why the marimbas were created, to fuse with mbira. They are different types of mbira and neither of them needs to be mixed with a touch of English (Western). If mbira is mixed with English (Western) it will be very difficult to dance to the tune, because the tradition would have been lost."

This has not deterred Taruwona, who believes her voice is built by her upbringing and environment. The mixing of traditional music was not even accepted by her own parents, but she had made up her mind: "I never give up, and the way I feel now is that the resistance to me is healthy. Everyone is entitled to that choice and everybody has their own choice to make. I felt at that point that maybe it needs a lot of time, then I thought right, I'm my own product.

As I explained to you, I've been brought up in a very western way environment. I'm very proud of where I come from and what my family is and what my culture is and the distance between the two is quite a big distance; meaning that the upbringing that I had is not typical of the kind of person who would assimilate and perhaps would push these values (playing mbira) or feel strongly about them.

The difficulties that I have faced with pure traditionalists - I'm saying here, is even my own parents can be put in the category of traditions in terms of music. Because initially when I started with this project my mother and father were now, wait a minute, you cannot, are you sure you want to mix your songs with this instrument. To me that even made it more challenging, and I said yes I'm doing that, and I'll do it to the best of my ability and I think I'm free

to do anything I can. It was even a matter of some level of resistance that was in my own family - which said how could you take that instrument which is sacred. The fact in our culture it is sacred and it's for rituals and rituals are sacred, now you want to take that out of that era into contemporary environment. It has been done yes but it hasn't been done to the extreme as I was now putting it across e.g. English lyrics, Blues".

Taruwona feels her self-expression was nearly hampered, or confused, by her dual upbringing. When she decided to sing

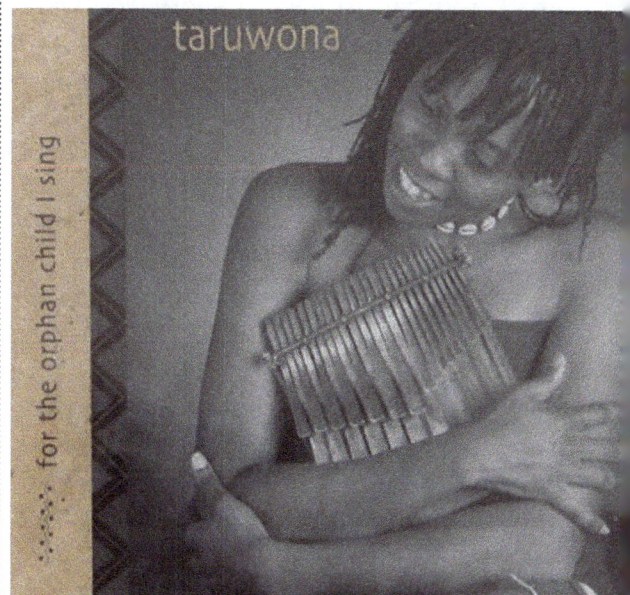

mbira songs, she had language problems as she could not speak pure Shona, which is the language mostly attached to mbira music. She had started off singing Billy Holiday's songs. Taruwona then realised that Billy Holiday is American, and she did not quite fit into that category and culture. She decided to bring the two music genres together in order to have her middle identity accepted. Although she started by singing other people's music, she later developed her own sound: "In singing other people's music, I felt there was something lacking, because the stereotypes I come across — oh she must be American. I immediately began to feel that I was at that point to be put into a category to being black American or somebody. Furthermore I actually felt that these people who wrote those songs must be proud of them, and these songs belonged to them and they are the best people who can put their songs across. If a song is written for Billy Holiday and she always did it her way and she pioneered her way and I think she'd probably be the best person to put her words across. So I began to feel that what I was doing was sort of copycat although I felt very strong about them-so it looked like aspiring to foreign music and the audience as well. It's only good when it comes from the inside, and felt that there was something wrong and missing.

Because unfortunately having gone to these schools which by law in the school you were not allowed to even braid your hair. You had to have it short. You were not allowed to be in groups as blacks on your own as you had to integrate etc. unfortunately I suffered because from the age of four to puberty age, I was at boarding school. Part of the holidays we'd go to the rural areas and stay there for like one week out of three/four. It still was not enough for me to stimulate into, actually speak the language (Shona)."

Finding her voice from her own experience and surroundings helped to bring out a unique sound in her and her first *mbira/* blues song became a hit: "Did I even know what the market wanted that time. The whole thing was a great idea I was now perhaps creating the old blues with my own feelings. That's the time I think I wrote *Dambudziko* – I was looking at our issues, the street kid who is dying in our own street here in Harare. Why can't we sing about the blues that we experience in our lives? The battered women, the drunken husband, the person dying of AIDS."

Taruwona is worried about how the mbira music/instrument is going to continue to the next generation, if it is not incorporated into our lives and fused with other music genres. The mbira instrument/music, she feels, should be allowed to grow into a dynamic instrument.

Chiwoniso Maraire also faced the same dilemma as Taruwona Mushore, as she sang mbira music in English, and also she sang church music onto mbira music.

Taruwona Mushore and Chiwoniso Maraire are some of the women musicians who have recorded their music, and the music has sold locally and internationally. However, it has not been easy for some women like Virginia Sillah to record music on her own without a group. She used to front the Harare Mambos. Although she had made a name in the music industry, which could have made it easy for her to record, it became difficult because of lack of resources. She did not want to record with the band which her husband led, because she wanted to find her voice as an individual and with a different band altogether.

Now she is no longer active on the music scene and regrets having not recorded her music then, Virginia explains why she regrets not having recorded some of her music: "It's terrible, it's terrible you know there's nothing that you leave behind. If I record I live something behind even if you died you'll still leave afterwards. It's good even to know that the people that will come after you will know, I feel terrible not to record as a musician".

By the time Virginia Sillah was a full time musician and wanted to record her music, there was a lot of monopoly in the recording industry, which has since been broken. The breaking up of recording companies' monopoly helped musicians, including women to come up with their own labels. But the stumbling block still remains that of lack of finance, as far as women musicians are concerned.

Virginia Sillah with the Harare Mambos

While Virginia Sillah managed to record some music with the Harare Mambos, she lamented how the media did not recognise her as the person who was the lead singer. Sillah was pinning her hopes on women DJs, but she felt let down, as they did not acknowledge her for the music:

"I've heard women DJs or even on the television they are the same. It's me, there, singing *Mbuya Nehanda kufa vachitaura shuwa* (Grandmother Nehanda died telling us). I'm singing taking the lead part - there is my other colleague, female DJ saying *"ndiGreen Jangano uyo neband yake Harare Mambo".* (That is Green Jangano with his group the Harare Mambos) when, in fact that wasn't Green Jangano singing. It's Virginia singing. Why not *"Ah ndimukoma Virginia avo kana kuti tete Virgie ne band re Harare Mambo."* things like that (Why not say that it is sis Virginia or aunt Virgie with the Harare Mambos band).

She feels that women in the media should support, encourage, and recognise other women musicians and give them publicity. She says that women deserve encouragement from media practitioners. She believes that her voice was suppressed by her name not being mentioned. The media took away her voice.

Busi Ncube is of the opinion that the media forces musicians to record particular types of music by not playing new types of music. She says the media can be discouraging as it sometimes has a certain type of music/ sound that it is accustomed to from certain artists, and they would like other artists to follow suit. This results in destruction of voice and expression of other musicians.

Women musicians become the most disadvantaged in this scenario, as they let men who are familiar with this territory lead them in the writing of music which can be accepted. Men write the music for obvious reasons; to control women and perpetuate male domination and superiority in the society. Virginia Sillah, with the Harare Mambos, recorded a song; *"Amainini Handeyi Kumusha",* (My sister-in-law let us go home and plough/

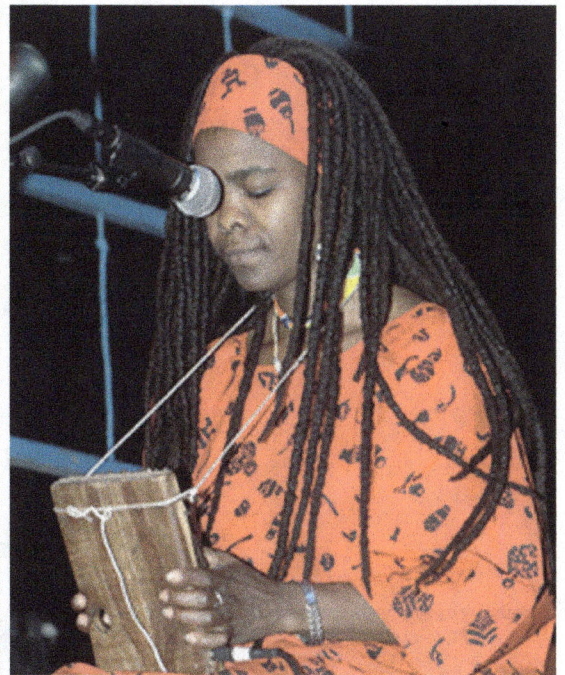

Busi Ncube

farm), a song that encourages women to go and farm in the rural areas and leave their husbands in the urban areas to enjoy themselves. This song puts a woman in a compromisingly/submissive position, although Virginia Sillah says it encourages women to support each other in times of trouble.

Some of the lyrics that women sing have contributed to the downfall of women across the board, as they feel they have to be submissive, and let men do whatever they like. Lyrics that women sing either build or destroy their confidence.

When this kind of music is played in the media, it does not only kill the voice of the musician singing the song, but sets standards out there of how women should conduct their lives, contributing to killing of women's voice in general. Popular culture plays a very important role in our lives and, the media being the strongest vehicle that drives popular culture tends to shape the way people think.

Lack of support, guidance and encouragement has failed women in the music industry. And, those who have made it are extraordinary women, who do not subscribe to the whims of the society.

Chapter 7

Encouragement

Irene Chigamba and her father Tute Chigamba

ENCOURAGEMENT plays an important role in the life of any human-being by boosting their morale, and also encouraging them in their particular fields and professions. Having moral support is important in nourishing one's success. Human-beings are social beings, hence the importance of support from both the family and society at large. Lack of encouragement, or being discouraged, can be demoralising. One can easily give up, depending on their will power. Determination can be limited to a certain extent, as the forces fighting the strength of the mind can be too powerful and overpower the spirit of determination. Without support, one can end up quitting. Encouragement comes in different forms. All the structures that control the lives of a human-being play an important role in encouraging and giving support. Encouragement and positive criticism can boost someone's confidence especially where one doubts if s/he is doing the right thing. At the same time people should be prepared to listen to others so as to understand what they are doing.

The family unit is the most important structure in a society. It is the role of the family, especially parents, to treat all children equally, and encouraging them to believe in themselves. As discussed earlier, it is at this stage that female children do not always make it due to lack of encouragement and the nature of the African patriarchy society. As outlined earlier, patriarchy families tend to mould the boy-child differently from the girl-child.

The boy is allowed to explore outside the home, whereas the girl-child is not, which contributes to the girl child not having confidence when she is finally confronted by the public space. Lack of confidence can erode one's self esteem. For women who aspire to be musicians, this can affect their talent.

While some women have found support from their families to be in music they are

those who have made it despite lack of encouragement. Women who have paved the way for musicians who came after them in some cases have encouraged the younger musicians. This has worked as a support system for the younger musician. Unfortunately some of the older female musicians who would have mentored the younger musicians leave the music

industry unceremoniously. This leaves the younger musician lost, and not knowing how to handle some pressures from her male counterparts. The support that older women musicians give to younger musicians comes in different forms including advice. The mere presence of older women on the music scene helps the younger women musicians to know that what they are doing is culturally acceptable. The absence of female mentors can make a younger woman musician to feel uncertain if she is doing the right thing.

Lack of encouragement destroys women's confidence, and they usually feel that what they are doing is not supposed to be

Dorothy Masuka

Prudence Katomeni-Mbofana

done. Some women have been confused for the rest of their lives because they have not been encouraged to take up careers that they really love to do - like music. For most women who have made it, they have been able to build support systems, or they have had a strong family background which backs them up. The support from the family can start from the time they are young; from the parents or immediate family members or from their spouses when they get married.

Women who have this kind of support feel a sense of security which enables them to handle external pressures. Encouragement can come in the form of the education system, women's support groups and social networks - Venues where women play their music and gender sensitive men, who are willing to support and give advice to women in this male dominated industry and world. Since men are usually fortunate enough to understand the music world before women, it is through men who are prepared to share their knowledge and expertise that women come to understand the music industry in a well-informed manner.

There are some men who have been supportive to women musicians in many different ways. In the 1950's, the De Black Evening Follies used to have a Christmas Show, in which they would invite the youth; both boys and girls to showcase their talent. It was through such shows that some women musicians of the 1950's were discovered. The De Black Evening Follies also recruited female musicians in their stable since their formation in 1943. Some of the musicians, in the De Black Evening Follies stable were Rennie Jones Nyamundanda, Joyce Ndoro and Mabel Bingwa.

Men like Jack Sadza used to organize Women Musicians Festivals in the 1970's. This encouraged women and helped to showcase their talent, and also to bring out new talent. In the 1990's, the patron of the Jazz Festival Gibson Mandishona also gave support to Penny Yon, who was then young and did not understand how the

festivals were run. He would introduce her to the corporate world, to get sponsorship. Gibson Mandishona also gave me a lot of support when I was writing the book on Zimbabwe Township Music which he also edited.

Chris Chabuka, who was also part of the formation of the Jazz Festivals encouraged Penny Yon to take over the running of the Jazz Festivals after the death of Simangaliso Tutani who was the Director and founder of the National Jazz Festivals. It was Simanga as we affectionately know him who encouraged and supported me, since the initial stages of my research.

Institutions in the society – like the Zimbabwe College of Music, can also play a very important role in encouraging women musicians. The college, which started with a class ratio of one female to ten male students, had increased their intake to 50:50 (female to male students) in year 2000. In discussions and debates, female students did not feel threatened by the male students, because there were equal in numbers. Amakhosi Centre in Bulawayo has helped many young women to realise their musical talents. The centre teaches and encourages women how to play instruments. Women's groups are important, as they also help women

Nomsa Ncube (Amakhosi)

musicians to come together and discuss how they can survive in the music industry, and also encourage each other.

In 1991, Mother Earth - a woman musicians' group, was formed. It was founded by some Zimbabwean women in the music industry who included Stella Chiweshe, Tsitsi Vera, Rhoda Mandaza, Virginia Sillah, Taruwona Mushore, Joyce Jenje Makwenda and Angela Impey who was from South Africa. It was a membership group for women musicians and acted as an advisory service to musicians, DJs, music promoters, music researchers and technicians. The philosophy behind the association was one of self-help and empowerment of women in the music industry. Women realised that the long awaited opportunities for greater visibility and status will develop, not through male-controlled structures within the industry, but through self-promotion and a deeper understanding of the music business and the legal aspects of the profession. Mother Earth met regularly with representatives of record companies, copyright legal advisors, band managers and other organisations to create more awareness about artists' rights in the music industry. The meetings allowed women to share their difficulties/challenges and successes. They also provided a platform for older women to advise young and aspiring musicians on how best to establish themselves in the highly competitive arena of commercial music.

Mother Earth folded in the mid 1990s, and another organisation, which represented women in the music industry, was formed, it was called Tonderai Women's Group and one of the founders was Tendai Ziyambe. Tendai had an understanding in music as she had studied music at the Zimbabwe College of Music and she was one woman in a class which the rest were male students, during the early years of the Ethnomusicology program.

The church, being one of the most powerful institutions in the society, also plays an important role in encouraging women musicians. The Two Singing Nuns - Getrude Matsika and the late Tendayi Maminimini, who were popular in the 1970s, were encouraged by the Mother Superior to perform and to record their music. If the Mother Superior had not given them her support they would have not continued, as she had some authority over them in the church.

The society as a whole can play a role in encouraging women musicians by buying their music, talking positively about them and respecting them in their various communities. Some women musicians have had positive comments from the society. The way the general public comments – upon meeting a woman

Tendai Ziyambe

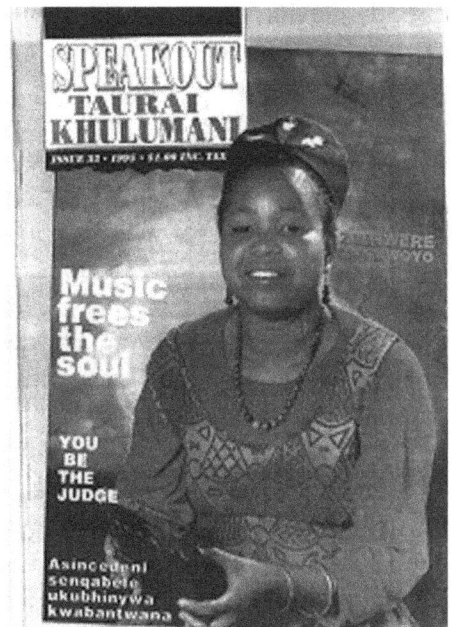

musician in the street can boost her moral, or demoralise her. The audiences also play an important role in encouraging women musicians. For instance, Penny Yon was encouraged to play her guitar by the audience. Other women, who had come to watch the band, praised her for being good at playing the guitar when they met her in the ladies room.

Cultural exchange programmes between women also help to build confidence and encourage women to share their expertise and learn from each other. But the strongest source of encouragement is the family. Musicians like Chiwoniso Maraire, Prudence Katomeni, Penny Yon had encouragement from their families.

As stated earlier, Chiwoniso Maraire's father, Dumisani Maraire, encouraged his daughter by playing mbira with her. Despite having spent the day working, when Dumisani got home he would play mbira for Chiwoniso, who would always ask her father to play mbira for her before she went to sleep. Besides mbira music being a lullaby for her, Chiwoniso learnt a lot from the way her father played *mbira*, as she was a great imitator.

This resulted in Chiwoniso playing mbira at the age of four, as and when she would pick up the instrument in the house – until her father gave her one, her first mbira instrument. At the age of nine she was already playing on stage with her parents, brothers and sisters. Chiwoniso's mother, **Linda Nemarundwe Maraire** also played an important role by encouraging her daughter and performing with her. Having her mother in the public space made Chiwoniso realise that women can after all use the public space. At school Chiwoniso was also encouraged to sing by her choir teacher, who was very much aware of her music abilities, and gave her all the support.

Chiwoniso also looked up to older women musicians, who encouraged her. Women like Beulah Dyoko, Miriam Makeba, Judy Mowart and Stella Chiweshe, were an inspiration for Chiwoniso;

Linda Nemarundwe Maraire

"I have a lot of respect for ambuya Beaulah and ambuya Stella. Why? Because those women have accepted me in a way I would have never expected. Not to sit and say I was looking for that but just because they are so much older than me and they have done these great things as far as women in Zimbabwe are concerned and they would give me the time of the day. The first experience that I had was with Stella. We were at the Stadium for musicians' day. Now my father and ambuya Stella have known each other for a long time. She used to know my mother as well. She was sitting in a Land Rover with a guy. She says to me 'Mwana'ngu, huya kuno' (My daughter, come here). She goes on, 'Ndinoda kunyatsokufundisa mupururu, ndirikuona kuti zvirikukunetsa' (I would like to teach you how to ululate). (She laughs). I look at this lady and she was completely serious and she did, and she wouldn't let me go until I could do it properly. Then ambuya Bealulah, I think it's when we were in Abidjan. She is a lot of fun. I like her she has got a youngish mood. She is one of those people who are always on the buzz and when we were in Abidjan she was really nice. Then we came back from Abidjan, I got a phone call from someone at Rooftop Promotions. They were doing a show for her in the park and they had asked if, she (Beulah Dyoko) would like to perform with

me. She said yes she would really like me to be part of her performance . There was so much fun. So just that ya.... I have got a lot of respect for those women, I really do. But you still get someone like Judy Mowatt or Miriam Makeba, you meet them all out there in some other countries. Miriam Makeba I met her in Abidjan, but after the show is over, she will come and say you have a beautiful voice, you know, and if you ever come to South Africa, if you need anything here is my address, okay. So, just like that, okay. This is a woman who has done what she has done. She doesn't have to do it anymore, but she is still concerned about the young girls who are coming after her, how these little girls are doing. 'Is there anything I can do to help you' then that is what warms my heart. That is what makes me say 'Yes, okay'.(Chiwoniso Maraire).

Irene Chigamba could have stopped playing mbira if it were not for her parents, who encouraged her while many people were discouraging her. Her peers laughed at her at school, and teachers did not encourage her as well. She nearly dropped out of school. Her teachers asked whether spirits possessed her, as they thought she was too young to play the mbira. Some relatives also discouraged her, saying that she was not going to get married if she continued to play mbira. She was reminded that she had ventured into a men's world. Irene Chigamba recounts her story:

"I'd get support from my family. My mother used to advice me to go on with mbira, so that I can pass it on to other people that it would help me some day. She also told me not to give in into people who discourage me. There was a ritual ceremony that we were invited to, and I'd be shy at first, because the men used to pass comments saying, 'A women playing mbira – it's quite boring.' Maybe that time my father would have remained behind (home) so we would be just the two of us, me and my mother. At times I'd get angry and say to myself, "Why should I play for people who do not appreciate my music". Also, my relatives used to tell my parents to stop me from playing mbira, or else I'd get bad spirits. But my mother didn't listen

to that, she answered them saying, if the bad spirits were already there, there was no way of removing them. It was too late. She would tell them".

Irene Chigamba's parents – Laiza Chigamba (mother) and Tute Chigamba (father).

Because of the encouragement that Irene got from her parents, she also encourages others not to give up on mbira, and she gives herself as an example. She tells women not to be scared to do what they love most – even if it is playing mbira. She encourages women by teaching them to play mbira. Although she says there are times when the women would want to give up, she encourages them not to give up. She also tells women to go out there in the world, and show what they can do. She is happy that the number of women playing mbira is increasing, and they are making it in the traditional/popular music.

When Ava Roger's parents realised that she had a musical talent they did all they could to nature the talent. Ava's parents noticed her talent when she was very little; they told her that she used to put ears on the radio to listen to children morning story and news, which she would do first thing in the morning, after washing and having breakfast.

At 11 years she was sent to learn and play the piano so that she could play in church because the old lady who used to play there had left. It was only when she went to Hillside College that she met the older woman there, where she was a lecturer.

Ava Rogers with her mother, her niece and Joyce Jenje Makwenda the author.

Her parents enrolled her at the Zimbabwe College of Music, then the Rhodesian College of Music which was not easy as the school did not enrol non whites. She learnt to play the piano and went on to help her father who was a sub deacon by playing the piano in church.

Her parents had foresight regarding her career, and she attributes what she has achieved in music and education to them:

"It was because I came from this gifted home where I had very intelligent parents yet had very little education and everything they achieved they made us what we are today. They had a great, great influence; they are a shining example of what you can achieve if you want to. They encouraged, they never said oh don't get involved in music, education has always been something that they drummed into, getting education and you can do as you like so I've been able to enjoy both".

She was also lucky to find a husband who supports her, "My husband loves theatre work, he enjoys music. He loves Jazz music he is very knowledgeable about Jazz and he

can tell you about different Jazz musicians. He comes from, I'd like to call it a musical family, his parents were professional Ballroom dancers. He appreciates music and he loves to see me performing, highly supportive, his only ever missed anything when he is not in the country."

Ava has done well in music and theatre productions; singing, conducting, acting and directing. She is the first black woman to conduct a combined schools choir, consisting of up to 400 students.

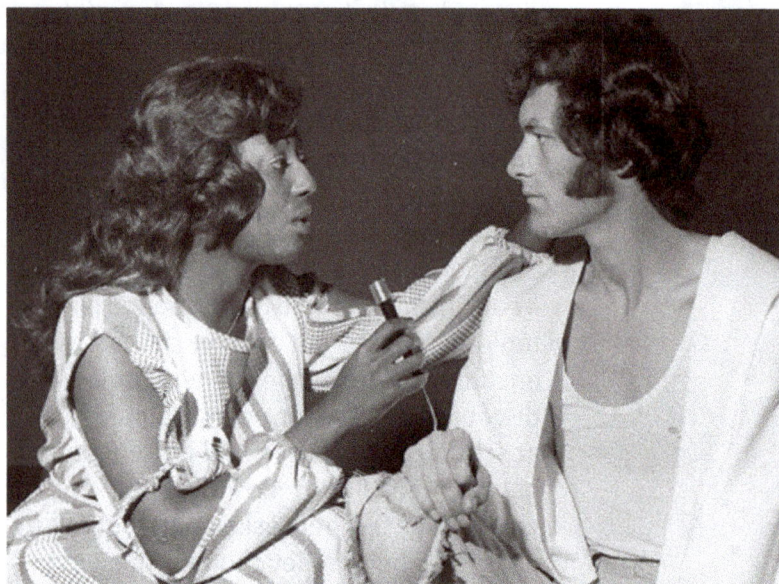

Ava Rogers doing a play in the 70's

Prudence Katomene-Mbofana has been lucky that she has had encouragement from her family; parents, husband and she has also had encouragement from institutions; at primary and secondary school. She also has had encouragement from other artists. While in primary she was encouraged by her teacher which made her realize her talent. Primary School obviously you are young and what have you, and you are trying to experiment everything but there was a brilliant music teacher, Mrs. Tessa Reynolds and she pretty much picked me and said you've got potential, she picked me in a whole group of guys and come to think of it, the group she picked I was the only girl.

Ricardo and Felix were my seniors and then Kenneth Jairos who is now Mr. Bell and Tapiwa were in my class but I must say in my case I never felt threatened singing against any of the boys, I was a tomboy. As I went to High School my mother started to discourage the tomboy character, and she said 'now you have to be a lady, you have to leave your primary school character.'

While the mother encouraged her in her music career she wanted her to be a lady, the mother would say *'uchiisa ma-brake'* (please put some breaks [in your music – the way I expressed myself and so on]). She would remind her that she was a 'woman' a 'lady', being a 'woman' or a 'lady' has its consequences, which results in a 'woman' or 'lady' not being able to fully express herself. Prudence realized that it was pressure coming from relatives who were not happy that she wanted to be in music, some of the relatives could not take it that Prudence had become *'mukadzi wemagitare'* (a woman of guitars). However; her mother continued to support her career path but with caution. Her father did not support her at first but Prudence later learned from her mother that his father was discouraged by his family from taking music seriously. Katomeni-Mbofana was told of a story of how her father's guitar was smashed in front of him by his father (her grandfather) and musical instruments were viewed as satanic. Her father continued to love music by playing it, in particular reggae music. In her debut album, Prudence dedicated a reggae track to her father.

When Prudence Katomeni-Mbofana got married she decided to end her music career, this influence may have come from her great aunt who left music when she got married and also how society views a married woman if she is involved in music. She also used to hear family members commenting negatively on her musical career. In her own words she says; "I said you know, now that I am somebody's wife and somebody's mom and somebody's *muroora* (daughter-in-law), I have to kind of conform to the tradition you know. Comfort (husband) went to where I had found a job and he said I don't think my wife should continue working here. When I confronted him he said, "Your spirit died, when I met you, you had such a beautiful spirit..." if he hadn't probably done that I wouldn't have been where I am".

Her husband encouraged her to continue with music and yet many women are discouraged by their husbands to continue in music once they get married.

Laina Gumboreshumba's family was supportive of her career from the beginning, especially her father, whom she says inspired her in many ways. Her family gave her both moral and financial support. Gumboreshumba was also encouraged by her schoolteacher to join the school choir, which helped nurture her talent.

"I remember very well the day it all began. I was in grade 6. This particular afternoon, the school choir was having one of their practice sessions. I was playing with my friend under a Musasa tree. The choirmaster, Mr Mhishi, happened to pass by. He picked me up and said to me, "Go and join the choir". I was shocked that how could he ask me to join the choir at this point in time when the choir had been practicing for over 2 months. Would I be able to catch up with the others at all! At the same time I was so excited to join the school choir".

Laina's environment encouraged her musically. Her upbringing played a major role as well in exposing her to the musical

Laina Gumboreshumba

experiences that she pursues today. Her father, according to her, was keen on preserving culture. She grew up dancing to mbira music at mapira (ancestral night vigils) and other traditional ceremonies, which her father used to hold at their home. Attending traditional ceremonies with her father made her to fall in love with mbira music at a very tender age. Her father was a gwenyambira (virtuoso mbira player) and she used to gaze, in admiration, when he played mbira.

"I also admired his philosophy about life, his wit and humour. He inspired me in so many ways, through his intriguing stories about his own experiences in life, and always emphasised that, as long as one is determined to succeed, nothing is impossible." Her father was her idol. Laina's father also taught Stella Chiweshe to play mbira.

Tambudzayi Hwaramba, who has made a name for herself in the urban grooves genre, had encouragement from her mother - who raised her and her two sisters as a single mother. She told the three girls that the sky was the limit for whatever they wanted to do, despite the fact that they were women. The three girls were raised to understand that they were not less valuable than men. They were also taught that hard, honest work always pays off. Her mother encouraged her to put her education first, so that she could be a well-informed musician and she would have the choice to do anything she wanted. Her mother helped her because Tambudzayi had a passion for music, and not because she felt she could not do anything else.

Hwaramba's mother, being a great vocalist and tumbrel leader in the Salvation Army church, greatly influenced her. In addition, if she had not instilled the belief that Tambudzayi could be what she wanted to be, she would have never seen herself become a musician. She said that she would have thought that it was only for special people on TV.

Although she got support and encouragement from her mother,

some members of society did not give Tambudzayi support because of their opinions, which were misconceptions, based on pre-conceived ideas. Women involved in music have always been perceived as 'loose' and empty-headed:

"Those perceptions are still existent. It always takes a while to change mind-sets. That is why it is more important than ever for existing female musicians to behave with consistent integrity as a way of contributing towards a change in those perceptions. Women musicians need to be positive role models so that they can empower other women in the communities they serve."
Tambudzayi Hwaramba has also had

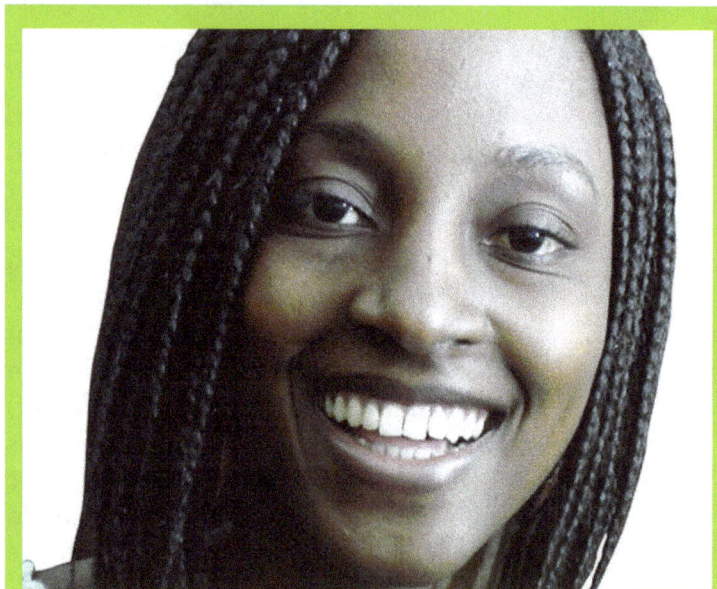
Tambudzayi Hwaramba

encouragement from her husband who is a musician, Roy Gomo of Roy and Royce Fame. Having a husband who sings, she says, has grown her to be more humane and to be humble, because when she is home, she does not demand to be recognised as someone special because her husband has the same talent. They do not fight for recognition or fame at all because they realise that, although they have the same talents, they are gifted differently. Complimenting each other is encouraging for Tambudzayi:

"We have different voices, different strengths, different styles and even a different audience. When we do sing

together, however, the fusion of the two different styles is phenomenal!"

Tambudzayi found it to be an advantage – marrying someone who is also a musician, someone with the same passion for music as herself. Because of this, she is free to rehearse outside the home with bands, or alone at home:

> *"That husband might not have understood the fact that music needs to be high on my priority list – way below cleaning the windows or the carpets of the house. Likewise, it's an advantage for him to have married someone who understands when he wants to lock himself in the study while he writes music. I think that the support I get from my family strengthens me, giving me an advantage over other female musicians. It keeps me grounded on knowing who I am and what my worth is. It also protects me from being discouraged by those that look down on female musicians."*

Tambudzayi Hwaramba feels the society does not adequately encourage women to be musicians. While there is stigma attached to the idea of a woman becoming a musician, she believes this can be changed. She also laments that there are few women musicians who are exposed to the opportunity to play instruments and, even fewer, actively seek to play instruments.

"There almost seems to be an unspoken belief that instruments are better played by men and that women are not really that good at playing them. I find that really sad and I would like to see that change."

Some of the women who have been in music before her that have inspired Tambudzayi include Cesária Évora and Miriam Makeba. They have played big roles in her life. She has always looked up to them. Tambudzayi taps into their wisdom, and admires how they have gained respect from people. She admires them due to the fact that both of them managed to succeed in their careers

without selling themselves short.

I also encouraged my daughter Naome and my granddaughter Mya to take up music and they did well on the music scene.

My family loves music and my daughter Naome Makwenda was born into a family, which is, literally, immersed in music. From a tender age she sang with me and singing became part of her life. During her pre-school days, she and some of her friends had a singing group. While others were playing with different toys, my daughter and her friends would be singing. A teacher at the pre-school once said, "Naome and her friends have their own special corner where they go to sing. She likes music and singing very much. It would be sad if you just let that talent go to waste". This really encouraged me, as the mother, to carry on with what I had already been doing – encouraging my daughter to pick up the music mantle, and run with it.

Not only did I mentor her in voice perfection, but after noticing her keen interest in music, I also went on to recruit a personal mbira tutor for the family. Naome grabbed this opportunity with both hands and capitalized on it. She then burst into the limelight when she featured in *"Senzeni*

Naome Makwenda

Na" - a musical video that became the talk of her home city, Harare, and well beyond. Those who had witnessed her early leanings towards music were not surprised, save to be proud of and be associated with her. The song was composed by Albert Nyathi, and was initially sung by Prudence Katomeni-Mbofana.

At time of making the video, Prudence was busy, and Albert asked for Naome – who was 11 years old then to stand in for Prudence. He gave me the words of the song so that I could help Naome with the rehearsals, as she only had a day to practice. I went through the song with her, explaining what the Ndebele song meant. Her knowledge of the Ndebele language was very limited then.

After she got the meaning of the song, the rest was history. When she went to the studio to have the video recorded, it was amazing how she expressed the song – through both voice and body language.

Senzeni Na? video was in the top 3 in the Top 100 Chart of the Zimbabwe Broadcasting Corporation (ZBC-TV) in 1995. The video elevated Naomi to great heights in music, and the arts in general. She became a professional musician at the age of 11. She had shows with Albert Nyathi and his group, Imbongi. She also went on to do tours and other performances with the group and others.

Her performances with Albert Nyathi included Ihawu LeSizwe and Albert Nyathi at the UNESCO HIV/Aids Workshop for Southern Africa; Soul Brothers and Albert Nyathi at the City Stadium (Bulawayo); Soul Brothers and Albert Nyathi (Hwange); Albert Nyathi at the Alliance Francaise de HARARE; show held at the Harare Polytechnic College (Harare); Child Survival and Development Foundation's Children's Festival.

Naome also went into acting, and some of the productions that she was involved in for television were TAKA (1996), and Mo Money Mo Problems (1998).

Before coming into music professionally, she did a modelling course in 1993 - and actually graduated with an A+ and honours. She continued with modelling and advertising, whilst doing music and acting.

Naome is currently living in the UK and, although not into music full time, she sometimes does sessions with some bands (including a rock group) in Coventry, where she stays. She still plays the *mbira* and is also learning how to play other instruments. I also went on to encourage my granddaughter Mya Madzudzo.

Mya Madzudzo's musical talent manifested itself whilst she was staying with me, her maternal grandmother. She accompanied me when I was doing piano lessons at the Zimbabwe College of Music during Saturday

Naome Makwenda being encouraged to learn how to play drums (Coventry UK - 2006)

Pop Workshops in 2004, and it became more evident that she was a musician. Mya was then enrolled in a class which started as a play-centre/pre-school, which had been established to look after the children of parents and guardians who were involved in Saturday Pop Workshops.

Mya joined the pre-school later than the rest of her class. Although she was behind by three weeks in her mbira lessons class, she managed to catch up with the rest and went on to become one of the best mbira pupils in her group. At an early age of four she surprised many by the seriousness that

Mya Nontando Madzudzo

her mother who is my daughter Tandiwe). Mya was elated.

At the age of four, Mya wrote her first book, *"Mya's Story"*. This was a story she used to tell me, and I decided to record her and transcribed it into a book. This made Mya the youngest writer in Zimbabwe then. Her book was the pride of her school, and she was also featured in the *Coventry Telegraph* for her achievement.

Though now based in the UK, Mya still rehearses the mbira almost every Saturday. Her love for music and the arts in general,

she displayed, her concentration, and her understanding of the fact that she was doing something important. When the pre-school held its graduation, Mya was one of the top students. At the same event, her class did a presentation of their work, and Mya proved her outstanding artistry. She was a star as she danced in a manner that dazzled the audience and made them laugh at the same time – a soft, jazzy style.

Mya somehow adapted the way she played the mbira tunes on to the piano. She has a certain way of playing the piano that was influenced by the mbira. She can play the mbira without looking at the instrument, and can even put it behind her back, and play.

When I was invited by the British-Zimbabwe Society (Oxford University, UK) to talk about my works were I also included a book she wrote – *Mya's Story* which is a story she kept telling me until I decided to translate it into a book. Mya opened the talk at Oxford University with a mbira song. She also played the next day at the workshop.

In 2008 Mya was involved in a contest in the Coventry Shopping Mall (UK), which was organized by the City Council, and she won the contest. She sang a song by Beyonce – *Irreplaceable* – *To the left to the left*. She won a cash price and the organisers brought her a big bouquet of flowers at their home (were she stays with

Joyce Jenje Makwenda with granddaughter Mya Nonthando Madzudzo (2004)

lives on. She is also involved in dancing. Beaulah Dyoko is a woman who got support from her male counterparts and those who were in influential positions, to have her music recorded. The Rhodesia Broadcasting Corporation male broadcasters, some of them, Dominic Mandizha, Webster Shamu and Benedict Mazonde, spotted Beaulah's talent. Because of the encouragement she got from the F.B.C. Producers, she also encouraged the man who she was playing with to come along, and add his mbira on the recording. The man that she played with had given her support and told her that she was actually a better mbira player than some men, which was a big encouragement to her. Beaulah Dyoko became the first woman to record mbira music in the 1960's.

She recorded the songs, Nhema Musasa and Bhuka Tiende. She was paid twenty pounds, which was a lot of money those days. She gave half to the man who had played the other mbira for her, and his family appreciated very much. The man had two wives, who showed their appreciation of what Beaulah had done for them by taking warm water to Beaulah's house every morning - as a sign of appreciation, and thanking her. This was very encouraging to Beaulah as the society (the family of the man she played with and his two wives) demonstrated appreciation. It gave her the urge to go on. This is another form of encouragement, which is also very important.

Beaulah Dyoko has also encouraged other women to play mbira. In the 1990's, she assembled a band, which consisted of women only. Unfortunately, the two women she played with in her band died. (Beaulah Dyoko died this year 2013 in June). She has also encouraged women in mbira, and music in general, through women's groups that she has been a member of, like Mother Earth and Tonderai. With Tonderai she helped organize shows for women to show case their talent.

Unlike Chiwoniso, Irene Chigamba and others, Laura Bezuidenhout did not have support from her parents, as far as music is concerned. Her family frowned upon her passion and dream. They never talked about it, and she did not get any encouragement from them. Her family background was extremely conservative, and she thought one of the reasons they did not want to take her music very seriously was that they felt it was an insecure industry. They were also discouraged by the social environment

Beaular Dyoko with band

and conditions in which music takes place. This is also something, she thinks, they may be afraid of or be uncomfortable with:

"Actually, it is a miracle that I ever discovered the musician in me. Even now, I struggle against that ingrained upbringing every day, to free my artistic self. We were four girls and one boy. My eldest sister became a nurse, and my brother, a teacher. The rest of us were all destined for secretarial college. I wanted to be a vet, but my father said that wasn't a job for a woman".

Laura Bezuidenhout

She also believes that society has let down women musicians, and feels other women musicians can open doors for other younger musicians:

"I don't think society encourages women into music. Generally, society, culture and tradition play an enormous part in predefining a woman's role as that of eventual mother and wife. Period! Women are generally raised for very little else, in my opinion. I think other musicians encourage women into music. Visible, successful female musicians raise awareness and point to music as a potential career path for many youngsters who have become aware of their own talent. Professional or experienced musicians do a great job of recruiting, teaching and grooming new musicians, both male and female. Still, as a woman musician you really have to know your stuff and hold your own if you do not want to be used, abused or relegated to backing singer".

The late Elizabeth Ncube is one musician who did not have encouragement from her family, but was encouraged by members of the society, though there were some who felt that what she was doing as a woman was going to bring bad luck. Influential people like Joshua Nkomo (Father Zimbabwe), and also international people who admired her talent, supported her. In an interview that I did with her in 1993, she said, *"I was called by Joshua Nkomo, and he said. 'My daughter, the thing you are doing is very good, but it is not supposed to be done by a woman. But then it was given to you as a woman. Continue doing it'. I have done praise poet for Joshua Nkomo and for Lookout Masuku. People now know me because of the ZAPU meetings which used to take place."*

An old man who was a family friend also confirmed what Joshua Nkomo had said, that the talent was given to her, and it was hers. The man also explained the importance of this talent to Elizabeth Ncube's parents, who were not supportive of their daughter's talent. At one of her performances in Bulawayo, she met a woman from America, Mary Permmington, who was working with Amakhosi and other groups in Bulawayo. When she went back to America, she invited Elizabeth Ncube to perform in New York in 1991.

Elizabeth Ncube also felt that it was important for husbands to encourage their wives: She felt in many instances that if a

husband marries a musician, he would not want his wife to continue with her career. She cited travelling as one of the causes of problems, which has caused most women to abandon the music industry because their husbands are not supportive:

"Sometimes he (husband) feels that there are some men who are after you. They always think that if they are not around

Elizabeth Ncube

you, you are with other men, sometimes he becomes jealous because of the praise that you get from people then he says 'Why can't you involve me? Why can't you involve me, maybe as a secretary or something?' That is where the problem is. He always wants to go with you wherever. He would even want to be the master of ceremony, 'since I am your husband'. Or be the stage manager, 'I must control you or direct you.'

Stella Chiweshe who, when she was growing up, did not understand why women were criticised for playing mbira, asked her grandfather and was told that women were supposed to stay at home. She now understands, as she is always on the road. Women who played mbira when Stella was growing up were supposed to play at biras (ancestral night vigils), and this did not please men. Some of these biras were held far from their homes. This was not good for the women, as they would travel far – and yet they were supposed to be looking after the home. Women were also discouraged from playing mbira when they got married, as they were seen as outsiders who were not related to the family they had married into, so they could not evoke the spirits of that particular family. This meant that women could not play mbira freely before and after marriage.

Dorothy Masuka had to leave Zimbabwe. She felt that she was not as recognised and encouraged here in Zimbabwe as she was/is in South Africa; although she is still not very much recognised in South Africa, for instance, in the "Hall of Fame" street at Newtown, in Johannesburg. Dorothy Masuka does not appear. There is Miriam Makeba and others. Hers is a catch 22 situation, of expectations against reality between home and South Africa.

She was recognized for the work she has done by the Women's University of Africa, in Zimbabwe, in 2007 she was honoured with a degree in Sociology. In 2011 in March she was honoured at the inaugural Harare Jazz Festival Lifetime Achievement Award for her contribution to township jazz music. But, in South Africa, she has not been given the recognition that she deserves. A sense of belonging gives one confidence and encouragement. In an interview that I had with her in 1994 she said:

"I am finding very little to say about my career anymore, except that I have been very busy in the last decade. So, seriously, there is nothing much to talk about anymore, as far as my career in Zimbabwe is concerned. I have had to come back to South Africa where my career is respected and I, also, am respected and recognized. Although, of course, I was born in Zimbabwe but I have a feeling there is nothing for me in Zimbabwe, music–wise. So, this is why I am really pleased that I have come back to South Africa where my colleagues and everybody is, where I am really working. I am really doing my thing. People in Zimbabwe – the people who are responsible for music, when they know that you are very good they want to sit on your head (hinder your progress), and they continue to do so. They still sit on musicians' heads because they want to promote so and so, who they think they can manipulate or take advantage of their selfish gains or, maybe, due to tribalism or nepotism. The Lord knows. Really this is the reason why I am more recognized in South Africa than in Zimbabwe."

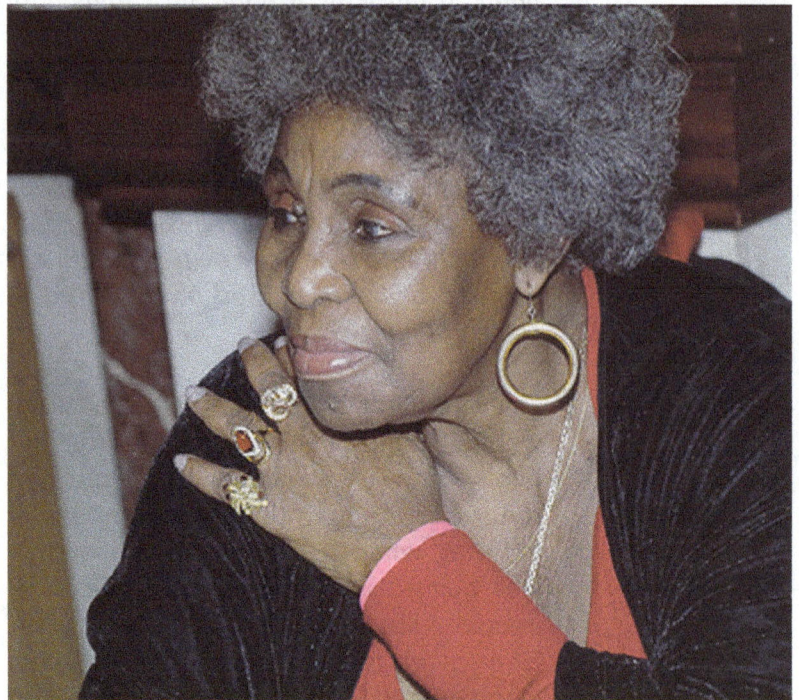

Dorothy Masuka

It is important for women to also perform on their own as it gives them the sense and feeling of not being overshadowed or threatened by men. In the 1970's, the late Jack Sadza used to organize festivals for women musicians only. Sadza is considered to be one of the best music promoters in the history of Zimbabwe. He was gender sensitive and considerate to the plight of women musicians. He saw the need for encouraging them through such initiatives.

Jane Chenjerayi, reminiscing on the shows, said that Jack Sadza was a good man who gave moral support to women by encouraging them. In the 1990's, Mother Earth and Tonderayi (women musicians groups) continued with the trend that Sadza had set. They organized a women's only festival, which was funded by the government through the Ministry of Education Arts and Culture. It is important for women, across the board, to get encouragement from the family, institutions and structures that run the society.

Chapter 8

Access to Financial Resources

LIMITED access to financial resources makes it difficult for women to function in the music sphere as bandleaders, managers, promoters and producers. As a result, women end up as backing vocalists and dancers, at the mercy of their male bosses.

To be a bandleader, manager, promoter or producer needs financial back up, which women do not usually have access to. As a result, men end up dominating the positions of power in the music industry, making important decisions on what happens in the music industry because they have the financial resources. Some men enjoy connections with influential people, and they can also access bank loans. This economic disadvantage that women endure has roots in the patriarchy society; which in many ways disempowers women. Property inheritance also discriminates on women; both as a daughter or a wife. Thus as discussed earlier, lack of access to economic power sees women taking up any job that will be available in the music industry, usually starting as backing vocalists or dancers and may not progress beyond that.

While women contribute to the family in so many ways in their families as daughters and as wives, they are usually at the receiving end. This is because they are "owned" as daughters, and as wives, whatever they bring to the family becomes family property, just like they themselves may be seen as family investments. For centuries economic power has been associated with authority. The way money has been presented to women is as if it is associated with some 'evil' but with men it is associated with glory and status. Although it is said that "money is the root of all-evil", the opposite is very true: More money appropriately used is the root of happiness, stability, status and power. Women should understand that and not be ashamed of having money – even in abundance.

Lack of resources also hampers women not to make it in the music industry. The understanding of how music is run is very important and, also to know how to choose people to work with as a woman musician. Choosing the wrong manager or promoter, including band members, can lead to exploitation. Some women may choose to manage themselves, which is not advisable as it affects the artistic creativity and expression. What makes women choose the wrong people to work with is that they are not quite conversant with the business world or the public space, and how it functions.

Not many women musicians have been able to find economic viability from music, whether as backing vocalists or as bandleaders. Some have been able to generate income for themselves through musical performances, although it is usually barely enough and more of "hand-to –mouth" situation. Music has to some extent, given women another potential avenue for income-generation. Music has not yet developed into a fully-fledged industry in Zimbabwe, for both men and women musicians; it is still in the stages of "cottage industry", very much seen and being treated as a cash-generating project.

However, despite the economic obstacles, few women have done relatively well in their musical careers. They have been able to generate sizeable incomes for themselves, thereby benefiting economically from music. These are the women who have had to work very hard doing more than one thing in the music and the arts industry. But, as an artist, taking up a lot of work and not specialising may hamper one's focus and creativity. However, this represents only a very small proportion of women in music today. They have read into the whole spectrum of the music terrain in order to understand its other components, which are not just music performance.

Women bandleaders benefit more, as they are in control of their finances. Women who team up with their husbands, may, or may not, benefit that much – depending on their marital relationships. Every active and performing musician is probably earning an income, but very few women have made significant financial gains in the music industry. Right now, women benefit much less economically, from music, than most men do. This is due to the mere fact that the local music industry is primarily in male hands.

The historical background of black women in Zimbabwe has also affected them in understanding how the public space works in regards to relating to music. They have to deal with a number of layers in the society in order for them to understand the outside world. However, for white women musicians the situation may be different due to historical imbalances between blacks and whites, which have negatively affected black women in the music industry, just like in any other professions and fields. Research, over the years, has proven that white women are more likely to have a sound financial backing. However I am not suggesting that white women venture into the music industry only because they have the financial resources to do so, but do it is because they love the music industry. Just like black women,(a proven fact) they are sometimes not understood by their families and communities. Some had to fight and convince their families and societies to understand the career that they had taken up; that of being music promoters and managers. This was especially the case in the 1950s, when race relations where divided by colour.

The 1950s saw white women promoters such as Eileen Haddon, Monica Marsden and Barbara Tredgold, who were interested in the black music and theatre. They worked hard to promote township music and theatre. The 1990's saw another woman from the white community, Debbie Metcalf, who was Oliver Mtukudzi's manager.

"Until January 2007, I maintained my position as Manager of both artists (Steve Dyer and Oliver Mtukudzi)."

Monica Marsden

During the time Debbie was his manager/promoter, Oliver's musical career reached higher levels.

Laura Bezuidenhout, a white female musician, made a name for herself in the music industry in the 1970s. She came in as an instrumentalist, playing piano for the group, Movement. Playing an instrument put her in a better position on the music landscape as she was paid better as compared to other musicians in the music industry, who were backing vocalists. Management usually pays backing vocalists less than those who play instruments, while the bandleader or the lead vocalists get more.

Laura had enough resources because of her background. Resources for African musicians in general have always been scarce, except for a few who come from privileged backgrounds or families who understand music. Female musicians are the most disadvantaged in the music arena. They have to be able to deal with performance outlets and venues, support, respect, money, opportunities, trust, appreciation, equipment, transportation, safety and the list goes on. It is extremely difficult for a female musician to develop and obtain the necessary resources to launch and maintain her chosen career because of the obstacles mentioned. Women do not usually last in the music industry. Laura attributes her ability to find respect on the music scene to the resources she has had since childhood. She explains her advantageous position in the society as compared to black women:

"Unlike myself, no early exposure to musical instruments and/or education in music from a young age, background of poverty and different culture – how many African parents have a piano, cello or guitar lying about for children to experiment with? Different priorities (culturally), for how many African parents is it a MUST (as did "older-fashioned-Europeans") to send their children for musical instruction? You know for Europeans and their descendants in Africa, musical education has always been part of a "fully-rounded" grooming, especially for girls. Many women come to music as a career out of luck or desperation – she can't find "normal" work, and her ability to sing can bring her an income (provided she meets the right opportunity at the right time) – ie., no formal training, just inherent talent and musicality that does not require any additional resources (such as equipment/instruments) – i.e., it is cheaper, quicker and easier to sing than to obtain, learn and play an instrument".

For some musicians to survive the industry, they need side-jobs to finance their musical projects since it is not always guaranteed that one can make a living through music alone. Laura is one musician who has subsidized her musical career with a side job.

"It takes a very "big" heart to keep going. I, on the other hand, do not have such a big heart, but am rather a coward, choosing to fall back on other skills from time to time to recuperate financially and obtain the necessary resources. I'm lucky in that I have other skills and capabilities that allow me to earn an income outside of the music industry. I have used this over the years to procure the necessary resources to be able to remain independent. It has meant "dropping out of musical circulation" for years at a time, working and saving for whatever the necessities are: keyboards, amplifiers & peripherals, a car, etc. I doubt that I would have managed in any other way, given the poverty, abuse and disrespect encountered in the local music industry. That is why I have determined to remain independent, even at the risk of being musically dormant for long periods of time".

It is therefore important to have other sources of income to sustain the musical career, because in most cases music alone does not pay that much in Zimbabwe. Because a lot of women are just backing vocalists or dancing girls, there are not many women who become financially viable in music, as there are not many female instrumentalists, even bandleaders.

Taruwona Mushore has managed to own musical instruments by subsidising her music project with her other job. I interviewed her in 1995, and she had this to say:

"I am fortunate enough to have another occupation because I would be disillusioned, if solely relied on music. It's something that I'm very interested in doing. I could work more towards it to try and make a living.

But what does that involve? You can't sell cassettes in this country and make a living out of it. **(This interview was done when cassettes were used to sell music)** *It would involve a lot of external travelling. It would consider me maybe basing myself even out of the country and, at this point in time I don't want. I want to spend my life here in Zimbabwe. I don't want to be based out of the country, for the interest of family and myself."*

A woman who relies on other jobs to support her musical career usually disappears from the music industry for long periods to earn money, before she returns again. Jane Chenjerayi's first love is music. She started music at an early age and, had she had it her way, she would just be in music and not any other place. But unfortunately like some of her colleagues, she disappears from the music scene in order to work so that she can be able to survive. In the 1970s, she used to combine music and her other job, until she became a full time musician. When she realized that the music business was going down, she went back to work outside music.

Rhoda Mandaza, who has also been in the music industry for a long time, has had to disappear and take up other jobs in order to stay afloat.

Although there are few women musicians who are doing well, or did well in the music industry, and across the board, not many women own musical instruments, or the venues were music is played. There are also not many women in the recording industry, or as bandleaders.

Generally, in the workplace women are not well paid, (historically). This makes it difficult for them to support other women in the entertainment industry by attending their shows, as they would want to spread the little they have on 'important family activities'. There is a mentality that women should earn less. This is a mentality that the society uses even when paying women musicians.

Women in Zimbabwe had to fight with their male counterparts for equal pay across the board and, women in the music business are no exception.

Some musicians are forced to end up running their own music businesses because some managers and promoters either do not understand how the music business is supposed to be run, or they just want to use musicians for their own benefit. Some managers and promoters may be very genuine in the way that they would like to promote musicians, but may not understand how the music or the arts industry operates. They would then want to run it like any other business. The complexities that go with the music business should be understood before a manager/promoter embarks on wanting to promote a musician.

Musicians end up in a catch twenty-two situation; managing themselves or deciding to engage a manager or promoter who in most cases does not fully understand the music industry. Women musicians who have made it on the music scene are either coming from backgrounds where their families were in music for a long time, or from a business background, where they combine art and business and find a middle ground. They may also have been educated on how the music industry is run, or they have taken time to study and understand the music industry in its entirety. It then becomes easy for them to know what they are supposed to get in their music deals, and what a manager or promoter is also supposed to get. Debbie Metcalf became a manager after being in the music business for a long time.

Debbie Metcalf has been in the music industry for decades. In 1985, Debbie in partnership with two sound engineers, established, co-owned and managed a 16/24 track recording studio in Harare called Frontliine Studio where all major Zimbabwean groups on the charts came to record some of them were the Bhundu Boys, Thomas Mapfumo, Oliver Mtukudzi and regional artists.

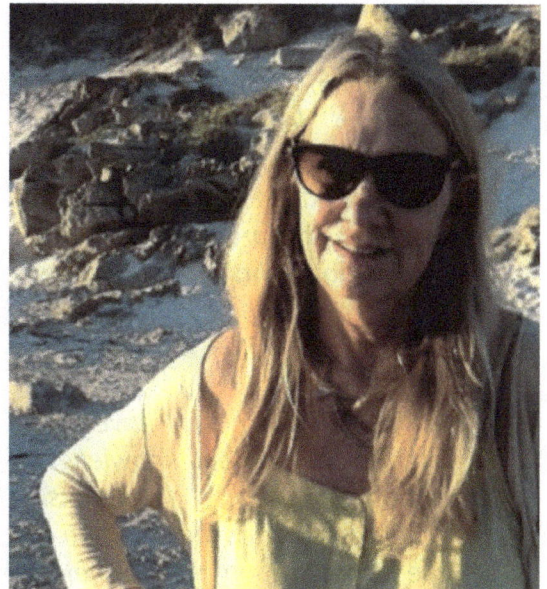

Debbie Metcalf

The acquisition of a stadium-capacity professional sound system saw the company serve well over a hundred major 'live' music events all over Zimbabwe and many more smaller events (corporates / club and conference centres).

By 1994, she assumed full-time management of Oliver Mtukudzi who she began working closely with after the recording of his album 'Strange Isn't It" at Frontline Studio in 1985.

> "I never considered becoming an artist manager and only learnt what it entailed from my early dealings with Oliver (and the Black Spirits) and Steve Dyer (with Southern Freeway) with whom I seemed to find a natural affinity from the day I met them and we effectively built our careers together. I have always enjoyed the contact with the musicians the most, bottom-up approach one could call it, but it was those relationships that kept me buoyant when the going got tough which was regularly!"

Tsungi Zvobgo explains how her work as manager entails.

> "In the Zimbabwean music industry I find that there is generally a lack of understanding on the part of both the manager and the artist as to the role a manager is supposed to play.

Furthermore, not enough musicians take the time to learn what is required to properly manage their own careers which can leave them open to profiteers. The assumption is that all a manager has to do is book gigs and maybe do a little promoting and that's it. That's not right. A good manager will be someone that IS RESPECTED in the industry.

This individual should have good references, and a good knowledge of the music industry, and contacts. A manager represents the musician and is the "front person" in the majority of areas regarding the musician's career. Therefore, the musician must depend on their manager to portray them in the way they want to be projected and above all, to protect their interests, and relay information to the artist completely and accurately. The musician will be judged by many venues and markets by the way their manager represents them and their act. So musicians have to be very careful when they choose a manager. Managers can make or break a musician's career. Choosing the wrong manager can lead to the artist being financially ripped off and their professional image/reputation being compromised."

It also goes back to understanding the music business, in order to be financially or economically empowered through music. How does one chose the right people to work with? Who will control the finances? Will the manager/promoter make it possible for the female musicians to be able to continue with the music business uninterrupted? How does one do this if they are not exposed to the real world of money; or if money has not been presented as an important asset in one's life? While it is important to monitor and control one's finances, it could also have a detrimental effect on their performance, or one's artistic creativity, as management alone is a full–time job. Looking after finances can affect a musician's artistic expression. Balancing the two becomes a challenge to most artists and, more so to women musicians.

Chiwoniso Maraire was in music for a long time. She managed to have managers who were helpful in her musical career. She also understood the music business, which was part of most of her life. She explained:

"...there was a lot of luck (favour in my life) that was happening at that time; I never had to deal with money situations personally because it was always either our bandleader, or the manager (to deal with that). The only time that I would have to deal with money situation was when I was dealing with something personally that was my own show, and usually they paid me upfront before I did the show. But, as far as the club scene is concerned for big bands, there are a lot of sharks out there. I wish the promoters will be a lot straighter with the musicians. It's already unfair the way most of these promoters in this country (Zimbabwe) treat musicians. It's terrible. What happens is that if you are a musician who has a lot of respect for what happens, you tend to become very, almost very staunch about the way you deal with your business. There are a lot of musicians who would be paid their money and they don't show up for their gigs. I think there needs to be more respect

Tsungirirai Zvobgo and Chiwoniso Maraire

Chiwoniso Maraire Advert 2011

benefit from it - just like their male counterparts. In the first chapter, I mentioned how Miriam Makeba re-arranged traditional lullabies into popular music, and got some financial rewards from it.

between musicians and promoters and club owners and staff like that, to realize that we are helping each other make money instead of sitting there and saying, mine, mine. You know I am helping you in order to make better sales; you are helping me pay the rest of my band, so let's work in harmony here. Yah? The money situation, as far as paying musicians is concerned, can be very difficult so that is something that I wish could change in this country."

It is important for women to see opportunities in the music industry and to be innovative, for instance, how women can benefit from traditional music. Some women traditional popular musicians have had problems taking the music to greater heights because of the rituals that the traditional music is associated with. Lack of confidence can make them to feel that they are not doing the right thing, and yet male musicians have found an opportunity in popularizing the traditional songs and making money out of the music. Male musicians have popularized the music to the extent that they have even taken over some of the music, which was sung by women traditionally; This maybe because some women do not have the knowledge that they can also change/adapt the traditional music into popular music, and

Many male musicians have rearranged traditional music into popular music, amongst them musicians like Thomas Mapfumo and Salif Keita, just to name a few. These men have done it with a clear conscience but some female musicians would want to be apologetic about it. Elizabeth Ncube did well as the first female Imbongi (praise poet), which was mostly a male domain. Despite having done well in this field she still had mixed feelings on the way traditional music was being presented; and felt that it was no longer the same with how it was presented in the olden days. She said,

"We held a traditional dance between rural and urban women; I realized that there was a big difference between the dances. Women in the city are no longer dancing as we did in the rural areas. It's diluted. Even if they are dancing isitshikitsha, it's not like traditional (isitshikitsha esasibekelwa) (isitshikitsha; a traditional Ndebele dance) (esasibekelwa – the kind of isitshikitsha which was soft, isitshikitsha came from praise poetry and esasibekelwa means soft, this is according to Pathisa Nyathi who has done extensive research on the Ndebele culture, [Pathisa Nyathi 2011]). People are now dancing fast, even the clapping of hands, it's now too fast, even the Hosana.

If, for instance, I play drums with a person from the rural areas, it is no longer the same, because things have changed. I see that I am also changing some of the traditional music, like Hosana, and putting it into records. It's now mixed with guitars. Not that I am saying it's wrong because, even long ago, we had some guitars in our tradition. It depends ngokuntshintsha kwezinto, kodwa amadhlozi kajabuli nxa kungabikwanga, ngokuhamba kumele kubikwe. (It depends on how things are changing, but ancestral spirits are not happy. But, anyway, ancestral spirits should be informed about whatever we will be doing and the reasons why we will be doing it). Because if we were to follow the old traditions – then we were not supposed to let out our culture be known to other people and other nations. Because of the situation that we are in today, we are left with no choice but to go outside the country to sing because we want money. We want to eat. It has become some sort of employment. But I think it is also good for people outside the country to know what we are doing as women musicians".

Elizabeth Ncube managed to be financially stable from singing traditional music, and travelled to many countries outside Zimbabwe, where she showcased this music. She also recorded the traditional music.

A woman like Stella Chiweshe has recorded almost all the music that she played at all the night vigils where she was invited to play, so that people can listen to the music whenever they would want —cassettes, CDs, DVDs and so on.

While recording is important for women's music in order for it to be archived or kept for posterity, and also give them financial rewards, many musicians have felt let down by recording companies. They feel they are not paid what they are supposed to be paid. For women it becomes even more complicated. But for those who have been able to get something from the recording companies, music becomes a worthwhile venture.

When veteran mbira musician Stella Chiweshe recorded her first song she was paid $49.00 (forty nine dollars), but what she did not understand was that these were the royalties, which were a two and half pence (a tickey) for every record. This made her question how royalties were paid. With time she understood the music business, and has made it in the tradition/popular genre. Fortunately, for Stella, she has managed to make it as a musician by recording her music internationally, mainly in Germany.

It is important for women musicians to have knowledge of how recording companies work, which ones to use, and

also to know how to monitor the sales of one's recordings. According to Jane Chenjerayi, the radio hit parade helped her to know how her music was doing. Jane's song, which she recorded in 1977, went on to number 3 on the hit parade and she was paid $1,000- (one thousand dollars) and was paid royalties up to 1981. Her sister, **Daisy Chenjerayi's** song, *Zai Regondo*, recorded in 1989 went up to number one on hit parade, but the royalties that she got were nowhere near that of her sister, Jane.

Daisy Chenjerai

Shuvai Wutawunashe

Jane finds this strange as she thinks her sister's song *Zai Regondo* should have gotten more royalties, since it went on to be number one on the hit parade. She encourages women musicians to shop around for recording companies which add value to their work. They should have knowledge of how the recording companies work. It is also important for women musicians to understand the contracts that they sign with recording companies.

The media plays an important part in giving airplay to the songs that women sing. This also helps to create interest for people to buy the music. Shuvai Wutaunashe's song, *Ngayipenye Zimbabwe*, got a boost in its sales because of the airplay it got in the media after it had been used at the inauguration of President Banana in 1980. This also helped some of her songs, which, also managed to get airplay because of the song *Ngayipenye Zimbabwe*. Shuvai Wutaunashe is also one of the very few female producers who own a recording studio (jointly with her husband).

Mai Muchena made money at biras by charging a fee. This show that even at traditional events, a musician can charge money, since musicians have to make a living through their music. The modern situation requires a payment in cash, unlike long ago when one could be paid in kind. Music has to be taken just like any other business in terms of profits, although it has to be handled differently from other kinds of business.

A musician should not feel that they are not supposed to charge at traditional gatherings, as going to those gatherings accrues costs in transport and the time the musician has to spend at the vigil, whereas she could be entertaining people elsewhere. Beaulah Dyoko would even charge those who came to attend the night vigil, just like she would do at any concert. She would also have separate charges for the rattle player and the drummer, but the mbira player would be paid more than all the instrumentalists. She played for rituals held in the rural areas or in the city.

Access to resources is very important for women in order for them not to be taken advantage of by males who own most resources, like instruments. Susan Mapfumo was lucky to have instruments bought for her by West Nkosi in 1979. But, because she had a band full of men, she felt they confused her when she was buying the instruments. This is how Susan

narrates her ordeal.

"I asked West Nkosi to buy me some instruments. Then West said, 'go and look for the instruments'. So I went to a second hand shop at Rezende Street bus terminus. I chose what I wanted. He gave me the amount which was $5, 500; in 1979, in a cheque form, from Bulawayo. Then the guys (in the band) came and said; 'no sisi, we can't waste money buying such expensive instruments. There is another guy who sells instruments.' And then I said to them, 'What are you trying to do?' I asked where the guy was. He was outside with the instruments, and they were for $2, 500. I sent the $5, 500 cheque back and I got a $2, 500 cheque. I took the kit to my flat because that was the safest place, corner 7th and Central. But the kit was not enough. There were two missing speakers. The guy came sweating, begging for mercy from me when I told him that he could never cheat me, and I wouldn't forgive him. Then I phoned Bulawayo to tell them to release the cheque, even though he didn't bring the speakers, and the microphones were crooked. But we decided to just use them like that."

The problems between Susan and the band escalated to a point where according to her, the male band members would help themselves to instruments without her consent. West had to come from South Africa to solve the problem.

"I then telephoned West to come and solve the problem. He then came and asked for the instruments, I told him they were in Mufakose. But the guys were not there. And then somebody told us they were playing at St. Peters. We went there, West asked Zexie Manatsa for his combi, it was raining. We got there. They were playing. He told them to stop and pack the kit in the car. People had paid. The kit was taken and locked in at Gallo. West then told them that we were going to go to the lawyers to see who the owner of the kit was. He didn't take their money away. It was theirs, but the instruments were for us. This happened on a Friday."

Susan finally got her instruments back because of the intervention by West Nkosi, this was an important resource for Susan Mapfumo and not having her instruments meant that she was crippled, she could not do her work.

Women musicians should have equipment in order for them to be able to be independent. It is high time that all stakeholders, including the government,

Susan Mapfumo
Musician 1970s to 1990s

take the music industry seriously. Recently in 2000, the government introduced a law which allowed musical instruments to be imported into the country duty-free, as a way of facilitating easy access to instruments to musicians.

Having no instruments has hampered women musicians' success. It even becomes difficult for them to play instruments, which require regular practising. Nomsa Ncube, who played drums for Amakhosi Women's group, stressed the importance for women to have instruments of their own.

It is usually difficult for female musicians

to make full use of this resource without risking their reputation for integrity. Tambudzayi Hwaramba says, "In a male dominated industry, it means that they would have to spend quality time with male musicians. Unfortunately, they are often frowned upon when they do this. What's more? It is difficult to trust that every male musician is only interested in your professional worth, and nothing else."

Having composed and recorded her music, Susan Mapfumo had the knowledge of how royalties were administered and she got her royalties through ZIMRA (Zimbabwe Music Rights Association). She got paid royalties whenever her music was played on radio. (NB: Every song that plays on the radio generates royalties, which the producer of the particular programme has to compile and send to ZIMRA (Zimbabwe Music Rights Association), which then pays the royalties to the artist. The recording company, Gallo, recorded almost 25 songs for Susan.

Beulah Dyoko is also one female musician who got royalties from her music. From the late 1960's, she would get her royalties after (which) improved her economic status. It is important for musicians to know about their royalties, especially women musicians.

Zimbabwe's attainment of independence in 1980 brought opportunities for musicians to go and perform in other countries. Beaulah Dyoko was one of the musicians to go international in the early 1980's. This helped boost her financial base. She explains how she got the opportunity to go international.

"One night we were playing at the Front Page Restaurant. Then a white man from Finland approached us and asked us how we would like to hold workshops in Finland. We said it was fine. He asked us for some of our music so that he could play for the Finish Government. Then he wrote me a letter and said I should come to Finland in May 1992. This was before the two women that I was singing with died. We

were provided with transport. But the two women had no passports. So I went with Everisto, Lavett and Pancho Nzirawa, who was the sound engineer. We stayed there for two lovely exciting weeks. We also went to Malaysia with Amai Nyakudya. It was also very exciting. From Malaysia we went to Germany and Holland."

While it is important to play to international audiences, Beulah continued to play in her home country, Zimbabwe. This is how a musician can make their name in their home country but remuneration wise, most musicians say they make

Beaular Dyoko

better fortunes outside their country. It is imperative though to balance the two: the local and the international audiences.

For one to enjoy fame it also has to go with economic benefits. In most cases some women just want to be seen as stars but not making much money. This is something they should come out of. Sometimes women destroy their chances of making it in the music business by looking for validation from men. When they come with a brilliant idea, they want to involve men, so that it can look authentic. Rhoda

Mandaza has had problems in some of her projects by involving men as a way of seeking validation. The men have ended up taking over the projects. She says this has blocked access for women from sustaining themselves economically. The men end up being the owners of the project, involving even more men along the way, in the end as a woman, ends up invisible.

Rhoda says that in one of her projects, she had planned that women would supply food at the venue as a way of empowering women who are in the food industry. The men that she had involved ended up bringing their own food, purchased from the established food industry. She narrates: *"All the plans that I had made that of involving grassroots women to be the ones who would cook sadza were not to be realized. The men hijacked the whole thing; instead they took over the catering and made money out of it. They made money out of the whole venture. If this had gone according to plan, then it could have empowered other women financially, who were going to be in charge of catering."*

Rhoda advises women in the music industry to understand contracts, and know how to draft contracts, so that they can be covered in situations of misunderstanding with business partners. The understanding of how the music business is run is also very critical, Rhoda continues to explain:" When going into partnerships, women should set out parameters and understand what it is the other partner is bringing. One must know how much percentage they are bringing and how everything is going to be divided, in percentages, with what you will also be bringing. Women should not be afraid to ask from the beginning how they are going to share – who owns what at the end of the day. And have a contract, even if it is sometimes embarrassing to ask a friend as this was the case with me, since I looked up to the person I had involved in my music venture as a friend."

Some married women musicians have found it difficult to explain or educate their husbands about their careers, especially when they become famous. The fame and money that women musicians get as they rise in their professions can bring unhappiness in their marriages, or see the marriage breaking up altogether. There are few husbands who will understand and support their wives in the music industry, especially when the financial gains, which go along with fame, become visible. Prudence Katomeni Mbofana's husband, Comfort Mbofana, does not see it as a problem that his wife is in the limelight and sometimes earns more than him.

Prudence confirmed this on a phone – in a radio programme in which, Comfort participated. The talk show was on what men or husbands feel when their wives are more popular than them, or if they are making more money than their husbands, Prudence recounts what happened that day during the phone in programme:

"One of the men to comment was like; God made men to be the head of the family and to be bread winners. And the DJ was saying, 'Yah that is the wife that God gave you and it's the one that's successful.' My husband was listening

Rhodha Mandaza (right) with the author Joyce Jenje Makwenda

to this and he called in, and he said, my name is Comfort Mbofana and I'm married to Prudence Mbofana. She makes more money than I do. She is more successful than I am. Do you see me mourning. I'm a very happy man. The money comes to the family, kumba (home), you know. I am a very happy man. I'm very happy you know my wife is not poor. She is making a decent living. If she's gonna earn more money than I am, hey, I'm the one who's going to be eating good at the end of the day. Am I complaining? No. I'm happy. Hey, what's your problem man?" (2003)

It is men or husbands like Comfort Mbofana who make it easy for their wives to continue to bloom in the music industry, enjoy the fame, and the financial gains that come with it.

Busi Ncube feels she has not made enough financial gains in the music industry as compared to what she has put in. She says access to economic power through music, especially live shows is still a pipe dream, but she has been able to sustain herself though. She attributes this to the good and transparent management skills that she has, and the openness that she had with her band. She made sure that all the band members had access to the ledger books, and everyone was satisfied:

"This way everyone in the group is kept in the picture, and whatever money we will have made at any show is shared accordingly." Not being transparent amongst band members has seen musical groups disbanding

Busi Ncube also planned on her retirement and to be able to survive on the music products she has composed/recorded. She encouraged musicians to compose music rather and not just depend on performances, as the stage has its limit. (She said this during the time when musicians could make money through royalties, but now because of piracy, it is difficult for musicians to make music through selling their music). Busi is a member of ZIMURA (Zimbabwe Music

Busi Ncube

Rights Association.) ZIMURA established a pension fund for musicians. Busi now lives in Norway, she has recorded 13 albums to date.

Through my interviews with various female musicians, I have managed to demonstrate how lack of financial resources, compounded with the shaky music industry in Zimbabwe, can hinder female musicians to follow their dreams. It is therefore advised that artists plan for a rainy day. Many artists, especially women end up living in poverty when they are no longer performing. It is also other opportunities that music presents, which, women musicians should take advantage of to prepare for their retirement.

Women should strive to create enough resources to cushion them when they are no longer active on stage. They should also take time to understand how the music industry is run in order to maximize their financial rewards, and also, not to be ashamed about taking music as a business venture. This will help them have a comfortable life, be respected by the community, and also inspire other young women who want to venture into the field.

Chapter 9

Women and Music Education

Rumbidzai Chipendo (Standing)– Zimbabwe Music Educators conducting a workshop with members of ZAME and also with Music Educators from the SADC Region.

I N earlier chapters I discussed how patriarchy societies can control women by limiting their aspirations and ability to dream. In this chapter I will explore the role played by education in reinforcing this negative perception, and also how the society can benefit from music in terms of educational development.

In some families, formal education is

often made available to the boy child more than the girl child. Furthermore, boys are allowed to experiment, and if they fail, they are still encouraged and given support. On the other hand girls are generally not expected to fail. Consequently, fear of failure hinders women from trying out new things. This includes getting access to knowledge and skills.

Educational institutions, among other institutions, shape the life of a girl–child. She might not go to school depending on the family's resources. In some families, not only does a girl fail to go to school, but she also has to look after her siblings while the parents are working for the family. In cases where she goes to school, the

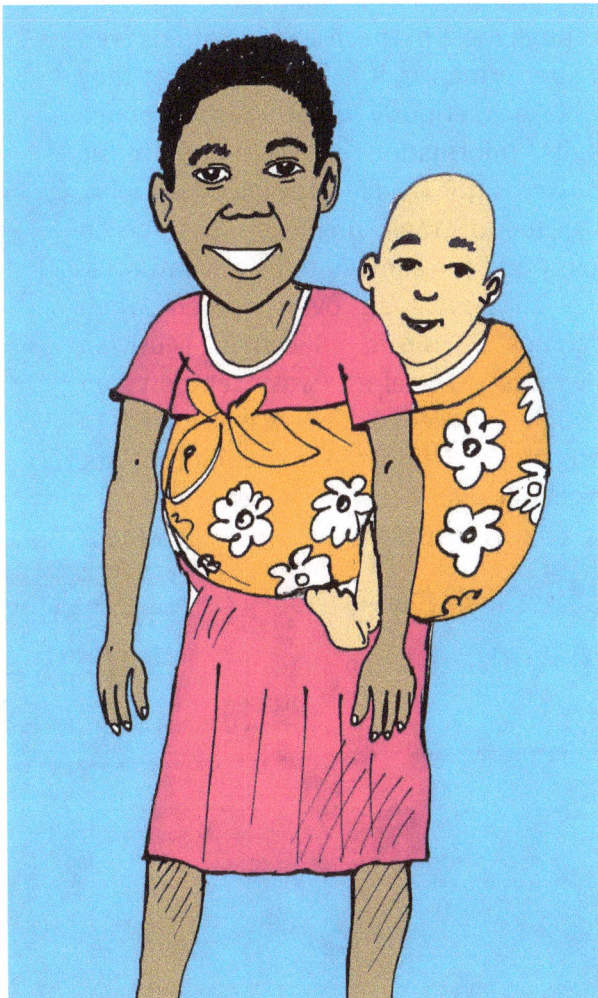

way the girl-child is raised at home makes her look not so intelligent. The boy can have more time allocated for homework than the girl, who often has to perform the household chores when the boy is socialising or reading. This, as stated earlier, can impact on the girl's confidence

and most girls trail behind boys in school. The education system contributes to

the domestication of the girl child. It has been proven that most girls do not take up science and technology subjects but are inclined more to social sciences, which again, prepares them to be more of caregivers.

The issue of subject choice can also be based on or determined by how much personal time women have to invest in 'demanding' subjects, which will lead to similar working environment in future.

The Contribution of One's Background Towards Career in Music

Most women who have come to understand the broad spectrum of music have been able to do so mostly because of either the families they come from or their environment. Music is mostly known from the performance point of view. Little knowledge has been passed to the society about how broad the music profession and industry is. Just like any other profession, music has to create a feeder system. This means that it has to start from the first grade in primary school, to secondary level, and then to university. In music education one can go as far as Masters Degree, and even PhD, specializing in a particular field. For instance, there is musicology, ethnomusicology, and performance and so on. Unfortunately, music education has

not been taken seriously. It is taken more as an extramural activity.

Although it is taught at some schools, there are no exams as with other subjects. Music is the umbrella of the society. Music can also make it possible for one to understand the history of the country or the continent. Through music one can trace the original inhabitants of a particular country.

For instance, an instrument, which is found in Mali, may also have been found in Egypt, this helps one to study how it is associated with that particular place. The power of music is underestimated and yet, if it is taken seriously, people may have more knowledge than through some of the channels used to get education. During pasichigare music was used to teach. Music made it easy for one to understand issues because it was not heavy. It made life's issues lighter and more understandable. With the complexities surrounding it, music understanding has been accessible to only a few, and mostly men.

I personally came to understand the importance of music education through my parents, who recognized my music talent at an early age. They encouraged me to perform and to take a music course at the Rhodesia College of Music, way back in the 1970's, although I did not do it at the time. Instead I decided to go into research and then became a lecturer at the Zimbabwe College of Music.

The music industry has different career specialisations. It needs performers, promoters, managers, sound engineers, venue owners, etc. Most of the people who end up working in the music industry do not fully understand how the music business is run. It takes some time to see results of success as far as music is concerned.

Although most of these specialisations feed into performance, it is important that they are taken seriously in order to produce results. Information on the entire music industry is not readily available. Men who, by virtue of their privileged position in society and are allowed to be adventurous, have an advantage over women when it comes to music education. Musician Chiwoniso Maraire was empowered through knowledge. She was allowed to learn, and had time to practice until she got it right. She was allowed to dream:

"I was just born into an environment

Simamngaliso Tutani, Joyce Jenje Makwenda and Louis Mhlanga (1991) – Ethnomusicology in Luck Street

where there was teaching in the house. So there was music playing like 24 hours and 7 days a week, all of the time. If you wanted to walk into the rehearsal room you could. They (her parents) never fussed about us being in their space where they were teaching and playing. They loved us being there. So it was just a natural thing. It came out naturally."

Laura Bezuidenhout was the only woman

Dumisani Maraire – Chiwoniso's father

in the group, Movement. She played the piano when she joined the group. She performed with the group for seven years. The group helped her understand a number of things regarding performance and working with men:

"Movement was my very own personalised seven-year "apprenticeship" in music, and my first introduction to contemporary African music, which has remained my specialty ever since. I'm a pianist and electronic keyboardist. I grew up with an acoustic piano at home. I would listen to tunes on the radio, and then go and fiddle on the piano, until I could play these tunes. I had a good ear right from the start. My parents made me take classical piano lessons when I started primary school. It gave me a good theoretical grounding, even though I hated every minute of it. European classical music has always had a depressing effect on me – I have several negative associations with it. After leaving school, I found my ability to learn and

play new styles of music, and this has continuously developed as I grew in years and experience."

Having resources was a big advantage to

Laura, as she spent more time with the instrument. Women who have access to resources such as musical instruments have more time to spend with the instrument, perfecting their skills. Laura was also fortunate to get proper skills through an institution. This helped to ground her into the instrument, and also help her to understand the theatrical aspects of the instrument.

It is mostly women who come from privileged backgrounds who are able to access musical instruments, as music is generally not taken seriously in terms of human development. Many countries in Southern Africa have other priorities as far as education is concerned. There is a tremendous backlog in educational standards and achievements across the various population groups in the region. Generally, national priorities would be towards raising the level and standard of general education for all, which then makes music to remain inaccessible. For a long time, European classical music education has dominated the form of musical education that was available in musical institutions, from the lower to the highest level. Recent scholars have made all efforts to introduce other forms of music, such as ethnomusicology.

Education that comes from old people is often not taken seriously, and it disappears with them when they die. Music does not only come from formal education, but also from those around us. Older people's knowledge should be taken seriously as this is the link to the source of our music. Understanding music that is passed on through generations helps to understand the history of women and why certain songs were sung – such songs as work songs, lullabies, protest songs and wedding songs. Elizabeth Ncube, who benefited from traditional music and took the music to another level, said:

"It is important to teach young women, especially the traditional songs, as they will disappear. I still remember there was an old woman who had called us to learn the traditional wedding songs but we were taking our time, until she died. The songs were not recorded as she had always wished, because some men were refusing their wives to go and get these songs from gogo (the old woman). But there are still some people, especially in places like Nkayi, where I went to conduct research. There are isitshikitsha songs, they have wedding songs, and they can explain to you isitshikitsha songs – Leyingeyomendiso, leyi ngeyokuquba intombi, leyi ngeyokucola. (This one is for weddings, this one is for welcoming the bribe into the new home and this one is for sending her away to her husband.) They explain all these songs to you in detail.

Some people are good at learning through observation, as Stella Chiweshe did. She spent most of her time at ritual ceremonies with her mother. It was easy for her to play instruments like rattles and drums. She also learnt the rhythm for dance, but she needed someone to teach her the skills of playing mbira. Trying to get someone to teach her how to play mbira

was a problem because of the myths that surrounds mbira, and the knowledge being held mostly by men. However after a long search for a mentor, her uncle Gwanzura Gumboreshumba helped her (the father of Laina Gumboreshumba, Laina is also featured in this book).

Besides learning how to play instruments and performing, women have also tried to understand and learn more about the recording industry. Education on how the recording industry works comes with the amount of time that one spends in the industry, which is why it is important for women to be consistent in the music industry. Busi Ncube is one-woman musician who has been in the music industry for a long time, and has come to understand how the industry operates in broader terms, including contracts, running a musical group professionally.

Music education has also come through family connections. This has been very helpful to some upcoming women musicians. Jane Chanjerayi benefited from her mother's colleagues as they came home to do rehearsals. Her mother's home provided a good environment for music education. It then becomes easier for a woman to learn, when the right environment is provided for her. Jane Chenjerayi reminisces:

"I was taught music by Jack Maravanyika, while he was coming to practice with my mother. He started teaching me copyrights. They used to come with records or just singing by head. They taught me how to play the guitar. I used to sing with them and my mother. So that's where the Pied Pipers saw me – at my mother's house. They used to come with those guys – Jack Maravanyika and Neganje. And then I started singing copyrights. It was a success."

Irene Chigamba's home environment provided a good opportunity which enabled her to do well in the music industry. She performed with her family, and the public space became familiar. This also created confidence in her. She got educated in music through her parents: "The first two songs that I mastered very well were 'Karigamombe' and 'Kuzanga' – some call it 'Mukaranga' and 'Shanje'. From then on I have never looked back, until we were being invited to ritual ceremonies as a family."

Irene's father Tute Chigamba who had learnt how to play the mbira from his wife (Irene's mother) taught his daughter (Irene) to play mbira. Although he did not encourage his wife to continue playing the mbira, Irene's father ended up travelling and performing with her daughters; Irene and Julia. Some men do not appreciate to learn from their wives, like what Irene's father did, because in most cases the man expects to teach the wife. Knowledge is associated with power; and in a patriarchy society the man yields the power. According to Irene, her father later claimed that he was the one who taught his wife how to play the mbira. Men usually feel threatened by getting information from women. They would want to be the ones who teach women, especially an instrument. Education or knowledge, particularly the teachings of instruments, has to come from men and not from women, as far as men and the society are concerned.

Irene was taught by her father not only to play the mbira, but also to repair the instrument: *"He took me as his daughter, not as someone who did not matter,*

Madzimai Mbira, from right: Julia Chigamba Erica Azim and Kelly Orphan

Julia Chigamba and Chinyakare Ensemble

because he saw my love for the mbira, and since I was the only girl in the family who was interested (then). He also enjoyed and loved teaching me the mbira. He also taught me to make the instrument; he can also repair the mbira."

When someone is given knowledge they also want to pass it to others, and on to the younger generation, as Irene did that. She and other performers formed the National Dance Company. She played mbira and rattles, and also danced, amongst other things. She got invited by the Ministry of Education to go for training with other instructors. The other instructors were for choral music, Jerusarema dance, Shangara

Irene Chigamba and her father Tute Chigamba

dance, Chinyambera dance, Muchongoyo dance, Dinhe dance, Korekore dance (from Gweshe), and also a mbira instructor. When they started the National Dance Company, there were 37 of them, including Stella Chiweshe.

Irene Chigamba went on to research on the meaning of the dances that she was teaching. The dances became a source of history, as a certain dance would bring out a whole lot of knowledge. Irene started teaching youngsters in 1984. She taught dancing at Frank Johnson School (Waterfalls, Harare). She was training children from 7-11 years, and they mastered very well. The group was called The Young Zimbabweans. Through Irene's experiences, we learn the importance of passing on knowledge/education to the younger generation through both the formal and informal education systems, so that the legacy can live on.

Irene was teaching the dances just out of love. The dancing company sometimes paid her, but there were instances where she had to use her own money.

She empowered the kids she was teaching dances by also paying them financially.

"When there was a show, and my kids performed and got paid – that's where we got money. Myself, as a person who was working in the dancing company, I wasn't expecting to get paid. I was just doing it for the kids, so that they can grow up knowing these dances. If I didn't teach them, who was going to do so? I taught those kids until 1987. And then I started with the older ones, those who had finished high school and had nothing to do – school leavers. Some of them are now in the police band. Up until now I have taught them the mbira, dancing, singing, marimba. I'm training at Zororo Center in Highfields. I'm not getting paid by anyone. I was hoping I would get funding from the donors. Sometimes I end up using my own money so that I can pay them a little, because they work very

hard." (Irene said this in an interview I had with her in 1995)
Irene Chigamba started learning drums

Chidren Playing Instruments

in 1981. She went to different places researching why certain drums were being played. Because of her love for music she kept on learning and, in no time, she mastered the drums.

However, she admits that playing drums needs passion and dedication as the first few days can be painful and stressful, even the breasts can be affected; the palms turn red – hot – but she kept on playing the drums, she overcame this by exercising regularly, for example jogging. Pain and physical strain may be the reason why other women do not like playing instruments, but Irene says;

"Some of them are shy, and some say drums are for men. That's what they were taught as they were growing up. Even the mbira, they say it's for men. They are also scared that if they play the mbira they might get evil spirits. Even the students that I teach, some of them they don't like the drums and mbira lessons but they just attend for the sake of attending. But when it's time for the guitar, they run like nobody's business. I asked the other student why it's like that and she said she grew up in a Christian family. So the mbira

and the ngoma were something that was frightening her. I then explained to her that it wasn't like that – in church the ngoma is played e.g. in the Roman Catholic. Where do you think they got the skin to make the drums? It could be from an animal, which was killed on somebody's grave. She understood what I was trying to say. I told her that it was important that she knows her culture – traditional instruments, so that in case she goes out of the country and she is asked to show other people what their traditional music is like, she will be well informed. She can't stand up and sing Ragga with the guitars. She has to play the mbira, drums, e.t.c."

Irene wishes women could take time to learn instruments. She has realized that women are scared and have a certain inner pride, but she sits them down, individually, and talks to them. Generally, women's confidence has been shattered, and they need to be encouraged.

Shuvai Wutaunashe's musical talent could not have reached high levels, had it not been for her formal education. Formal education was an added advantage to her music career. It gave her confidence. Formal education can help one to understand certain issues, which someone without formal education might not be able to understand.

Susan Mapfumo used her musical talent to train young musicians how to sing. She passed on the knowledge about the importance of training on the voice:

"I met the Fantasy. The name came from Tobias Arekete and his brothers. They were called Fantasy, playing in the Queens Hotel. Then this man, the owner of these instruments, was called Max. He had two sets of instruments, for Pied Pipers and the others were for Fantasy. So he saw me. He said, 'Suzy come and teach these guys (Fantasy),' I said, 'Alright.' They were playing these songs with the high note. So I went outside the Queens Hotel, because you could hear the vibration outside. Then I came back and I said, 'Right the guitars are fine, but don't sing the Jacksons here, don't. I want you to use your own voice.' I then told them to sing somebody else's song but using their own voices."

Some women musicians have not made much progress as the learning of instruments is concerned but, for Nomsa Ncube playing drums is something that she is proud of. She has done well with time and practice, because she was willing to learn:

"At first it looked very complicated. You know when the teacher was showing me how fast you play the drums, like rounding them all, it was very complicated. It was so difficult. When it was time to go and play drums, I would want to run away. If you have an interest in something, you can do it."

Women should learn to persevere, and

Nomsa Ncube

create time, if they are to learn how to play any instrument. It helps to play instruments because it puts them in charge of their music. It also seems that women who play instruments are more respected than backing vocalists.

Netsai Chingwendere is one woman who has invested her time in learning how to play musical instruments, she can play the guitar and mbira.
Tambudzayi Hwaramba encourages young

Netsai Chigwendere

women musicians to explore their creativity through using real instruments, as this will allow them more radical creativity and freedom. Tambudzayi would like to see a proliferation of music schools in Zimbabwe, where female musicians will be able to attend music lessons with no hindrances and no fear of being taken advantage of by male counterparts. She feels the education system is not doing enough:

"The education system is not doing enough to educate anyone in music — male or female. I feel that we don't have enough music schools in Zimbabwe for the amount of talent that you will find in our country. Men tend to educate each other in music, but women do not get the same opportunities. The creation of music schools would build a neutral and fair environment in which female musicians could learn and thrive. It is important for institutions to support women."

A centre like Amakhosi Theatre has made it possible for women to gain access to knowledge, like the playing of instruments, and also helps women in the arts.

The Zimbabwe College of music is another institution, which has been a training ground for women in music education. Nyasha Bare, who is now a teacher at Avondale Primary School, did her training in Ethnomusicology at the Zimbabwe College of Music.

"People didn't understand what I would do in life with such a course. Some thought a person who did such a course would join a band, not knowing that it's just like any other course, whereby you have practical and oral lessons and also sit for exams. Music is just like any other subject. So people used to look down upon what I was doing (the course). They didn't see it as a decent profession, especially for women." She said in an interview.

Nyasha's family did not understand about music education, and they had to see her conduct lessons, in order to believe and understand what she was doing. It is important for families to be given understanding on music education. It was a big surprise for Nyasha's family when she started working. They did not really understand how she did it. Society has to be educated on formal music education, and also be shown that it can be part of mainstream education.

It is also important to have music teachers at primary and secondary school level, so that a feeder system can be created for secondary schools and tertiary colleges

Amakhosi Women's Group

Nyasha Bare
Ndirori Shoko

"This course was very enriching musically, and it reinforced my orientation towards ethnomusicology. I lectured music at Nyadire Teachers College (2003-2005). In 2006 I did a Bachelor of Arts with Honours at University of the Witwatersrand, S.A, where I also taught mbira and marimba."

She then did a Masters of Arts degree in Ethnomusicology at Rhodes University (South Africa), where she also taught mbira to second and third year ethnomusicology students. She worked at the International Library of African Music in Grahams Town in South Africa, and is currently a PhD student at Rhodes University in Grahams Town. She intends to explore the performance side of music and record:

"Not to say I will abandon the music education side. I love and enjoy teaching music very much. I am also more inclined to ethnomusicology. I very much treasure our own indigenous traditional 'musics' of Africa and vie for their perpetuated existence. They should not die but continue to thrive alongside (without being overshadowed by) the 'modern' music, lest we lose sight of our precious heritage."

Women musicians get their music education in different ways, and for different reasons. Taruwona Mushore had

The Zimbabwe College of music is another institution, which has been a training ground for women in music education. Nyasha Bare, who is now a teacher at Avondale Primary School, did her training in Ethnomusicology at the Zimbabwe College of Music.

done very well in her formal education, as it was a requirement by her family that she had to fulfill. Her education helped her to get a well paying job, and also to have confidence. But the germ for music had

and then back to the schools again.

As I stated earlier, Laina Gumboreshumba, who was exposed to music at a tender age by her father, has reached higher levels of music education – acquiring a Master's Degree and working on her PhD program: "Of late things have changed for the better. With the prevailing gospel on gender equality, men and women are given equal opportunities in the education system, including music education, and the society is gradually changing its attitude towards women musicians."

Primarily, Laina is a music educator. She teaches and conducts workshops on mbira, marimba, drumming, traditional dances, choral music and percussion.

After she graduated from Nyadire Teacher's College in 1997, she taught in primary schools (in Mutoko, Murehwa and Harare) until 2003. During this period she conducted school choirs, percussion bands and taught traditional dances. She was also an adjudicator in the above – mentioned disciplines. She obtained a National Certificate in Music at the Zimbabwe College of Music in 2002:

been biting, and she wanted to play mbira, and fuse it with Blues. She had to learn how to play the instrument, and also to understand it from a cultural perspective. She feels that attending former Group A schools which were reserved for whites only, impacted on her ability to master her Shona culture and customs. Her parents worked from 6am till 11 pm in their grocery shop to give their children the best.

As a result, she and her siblings had to go to boarding schools. At the boarding schools they were not allowed to speak in Shona, and even to plait their hair. During the holidays she would go to the rural area for a short while, which enabled her to understand a bit of the Shona culture and customs, including the mbira instrument. Hers had to be a different kind of education, since it was not provided for in the formal education system. She had to find people to teach her how to play the mbira, people who understood what she wanted to do – to fuse the mbira and blues! This was a real challenge for her.

She had started with Blues, and played with a band at Manhattan Bar, with Simangaliso Tutani, "Jonny Papas" whose real name was John Homo and Chris Chabuka. Besides singing/performing, she decided to learn how to play the piano. She would get score sheets, so that she understood the music she was playing on the piano.

The time she spent working with the group of top jazz musicians helped her to understand how music was run, which made it easier for her when she was on her own as she had decided to fuse Blues and Mbira music:

"To be able to sing with a disciplined group, and to do the moves and sync with that group, and catch up onto the new answers that are being put across. I remember from the beginning, Simanga saying to me, 'Massie (my other name is Massie), what level are you doing? G or F, or whatever, and I would say, ' I do not have a clue.' 'But

Massie you are singing this song – so do you want it in this level?' And then I would start again, and he would say, 'Is this all right for you?' And I would say 'ah-ah-ah a bit higher.' But, then, I learnt a lot. I learnt to perform. I learnt about to be flexible. I learnt about to be versatile. I learnt about what it is as a woman performer in a male – dominated environment. Then, at one point, I was with Chris Chabuka. He was doing piano at that time. So I then said could I come at lunchtime because I had a full time job. I asked him if I could go with him at Stoddard Hall where they were practicing – just practicing – and I think Chris started thinking that I was crazy. I think he realized how serious I was, because I had written the music scores for these old blues numbers because Chris didn't have them. So I brought them along all the time. If I knew somebody who was going out (out of the country) I'd say, 'Please look up for these kinds of scores for me,' and they did that for me. I'd photocopy and bring them back, and I'd say to Chris, 'Chris, I'm bringing this to you.' During lunchtime we'd go through all renditions of this and that. He'd practice and we'd do the numbers and, occasionally I'd now go to Manhattan bar and I'd sing some of the songs with the group. It was a very good experience for me."

However, she agrees that getting someone to teach her mbira was not easy. At first some did not take her seriously. Some were even making sexual advances, and she had to be very clear with them that she just wanted to be taught the mbira, and that was all. She went to the rural area were her uncle was willing to teach her, but did not understand why and how she was going to fuse the mbira with blues. She also had to educate her parents, who also did not understand how she could fuse the mbira music with blues. She finally found a group to work with, the Mujuru Brothers, but fusing the mbira and blues was also new to them. They taught her the mbira but, because she is left handed, and it was complicated for her, she decided not to pursue the instrument. Because of her visionary qualities she became the leader and the artistic director of the group instead. Her music, Mbira Blues was born. Her formal education had made it possible for her to be confident and to articulate what she wanted to learn and achieve in music:

"I was introduced to Simon Mujuru. For the first three or four sessions I felt there is something there. I thought: let me bring my tape recorder, let me record, and do some research. I played for people at home, and they loved it. And it was just jamming. This was in the 80's."

The understanding of music education

Taruwona Mushore

leads to the understanding of music in its broader sense: the different levels that it operates in; how to use performance to get to one's audience; how institutions of learning can add value in the understanding of music; and the feeder system of music. Organizations which help lobby for the promotion of music and institutions and how those who are part of the music industry can also, benefit mutually.

Cultural Exchange Programs have been very important in the diversification of music and the musicians themselves. These are provided by organizations, which are helping facilitate the advancement of music and musicians. One such organization is Zimbabwe Music Educators ZAME, (Zimbabwe Association of Music Educators), which is led by Rumbidzai Chipendo.

Rumbidzai is one person who has been educated to understand the different levels that music operates in. She taught music at the Seke Teacher's Training College and also taught at the Zimbabwe College of Music. She started off by training as a general teacher. She then took music as the main subject. She chose music as a major because she loved it. She used to sing in church but for her to understand music she had to be educated formally:

"So I took up music and then I did my 3 years training. And, when I went up to teach in the schools, I was one of the music people who would help with music curricular activities. But that didn't change me much and, also, I think I wasn't that confident to take it up and say this is what I could do in music. I had just done it in 3 years. Everybody was looking at me to say: 'What should we do.' And people said you said: 'You have trained in music.' I was a very good singer, and I did know how to play piano very well. I wasn't very active in extra mural activities, because I wasn't very confident with people."

Even though she had trained in music for three years, she had to train again as a music teacher in order to have confidence in how music is taught. Music is an important subject, just like any other, and should be taken seriously. One should go through all its various levels:

"I went to Hillside Teachers College for one year to learn music, so that I could teach it. And there, I think, I became more

confident. I went to teach at Seke Teachers College. There were already two people that were already teaching in that college. We didn't have any specialization for the students. I think it was for 8 hours a week that we would share the 3 of us in the music department. So what happened is I was asked to teach something else, and then have half of my time doing music."

To enrich her music education Rumbidzai studied psychology, and was teaching theory of psychology in education. A new department was created which had some music component. She was in charge of the music programme, where she trained the Infant Teachers – preparing them to teach Grade One children. This helped to create a feeder system, which raised teachers to teach music from Grade One in schools.

A two-year National Certificate in Music

Rumbidzai Chipendo

(NCM) programme at Zimbabwe College of Music where she got a certificate also added to her wealth of music education. The two-year program focused on African culture and the playing of the marimba, the mbira – different types of the mbira (nyunga-nyunga), njari and dzevadzimu amongst others). The course also included traditional dance, history of western music, theory of western music, the theory of African music and culture, and ethnic history. All this helped the understanding of culture in music.

The late Dr Dumisani Maraire started

the Zimbabwe Association of Music Educators (ZAME). In 1994, Rumbidzai was chosen as secretary, and started learning about Zimbabwean cultural music. She was the only woman in ZAME, but her spirit of wanting to learn saw her rise to Chairperson, and took the organization to a higher level. The association promoted the learning of African music among other subjects, although the main emphasis was to develop African music. The association is meant for teacher's colleges, but anybody that is in music education can be an affiliate member of the association.

ZAME, among other things, organizes exchange programs. Attending exchange programs made Rumbidzai more confident in what she was doing and especially in African music exchanges. She had to work with people from other cultures, from as far as Norway. The organization (ZAME) sends two students from the Zimbabwe College of Music every year and also gets students from Norway.

While working with Maraire in ZAME, she was encouraged to perform in the mbira group, which, he led:

"I became involved in performance, I was co-opted into the group. And there was another lady –she is late now – Thandi. She was playing the mbira. I was playing the mbira and also singing. Doctor Maraire wanted, especially, women singers to do exactly what other members of the group where doing.

And that's when I became very confident in mbira playing. We would go out and perform, not for a lot of money, but for the love of it. And people who we performed for really loved our music. They wished we had made recordings. When Dumisani Maraire passed away we still maintained the group.

Education, in all forms, is vital for the development of women in music.

Chapter 10

Limited Personal Time

IN this chapter I will explore the importance for a woman to explore personal time. Women's personal time is determined by their family and by society. Patriarchy aims to confine women to the home where they do un-acknowledged or unpaid work. They usually combine the responsibilities of working to earn a wage and doing the domestic work. Unfair division of labour may mean that girls have less time to nurture their talents. As stated earlier patriarchy societies confine women to the domestic sphere with limited public space. They are not supposed to develop a public persona.

There are some women who try to fight all

odds when they are still young, and attain their goals, but when they get to a certain age, for instance if they get married, the structures set by the society remind them that they are 'women' and they give up on their dreams. This has contributed to a large extent to women lacking personal time to continue with their aspirations.

It becomes even more difficult when a woman wants to be in a field or profession that will take her away during odd hours, or for a long time, away from home. Women who have chosen music as a career have had to find ways of dealing with their families, or society, in order for them to make it. It is relatively easier when they are still single but, once they decide to marry and have a family, it becomes a challenge. With marriage comes the responsibility of re-arranging priorities. As a wife, she is called to put her husband's needs before her own. This often means compromising on the amount of time she spends on music, if her husband is at all interested in her continuing with music. In this day and age, whereby women usually

need to work to supplement the family income, it becomes almost impossible to be an effective wife, a good mother, a reliable employee and a great musician, all at the same time. When the demanding lifestyle becomes stressful, music is often the first thing to be taken off the list.

Laura Bezuidenhout, who has been in music since the 1970's, both in Zimbabwe and South Africa, has made the following observations as regards women musicians and personal time:

"I think some women are themselves to blame for this – in a lot of cases, her passion and drive to perform and earn an income from music disappears once she's married and has a husband to 'look after her'. Also, once married, she now has to keep a home, bear and raise children, and play the expected role of wife and mother, which leaves her little or no time and energy to pursue her talent. Remember, it is an extremely hard life to be a musician under the current industry conditions. It is hard, harsh, unsafe, uncomfortable, many times unrewarding and vicious.

As a woman, the alternative of being a homemaker is often a much less taxing option. But not all women are to blame for this. The reverse is also true – a lot of men who marry female musicians tend to become possessive and jealous after the marriage, and they often force their new wives to choose between their careers and their marriage. Society also plays a role here – music is seen as an activity for youngsters, carefree, without responsibilities and, more often than not, a little on the frivolous side. Society expects a married woman to conduct herself as such, and the negative associations with music is often too overbearing for general societal acceptance. In the paternalistic society we live in, women are tossed from side to side when trying to chart their lives, and they are often not allowed to make the necessary decisions that will accommodate both her 'talents and her in-laws', so to speak..."

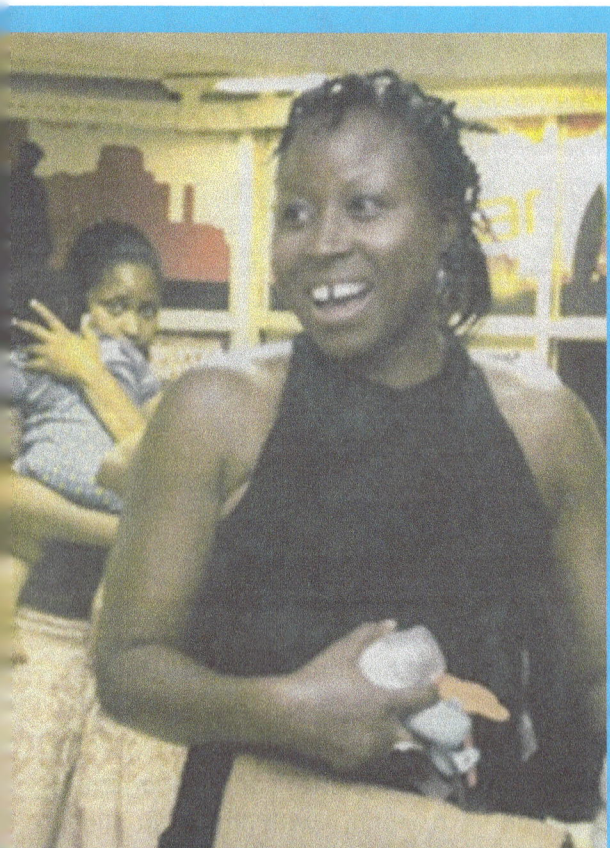

Prudence Katomeni with baby and baby sitter preparing for a performance.

Lina Mattaka and Evelyn Juba who were some of the first women to make a name for themselves in popular music in the 1930's, and became popular in the 1950's but had to leave the music industry because their families were growing, and they had to look after the children. The African Daily Newspaper reported on the two women when they left the music scene:

"As the old MaShona proverb aptly puts it, 'It was the sound of a drum about to crack. And indeed it was, for that was the last Northern Rhodesia saw of Lina and what a fitting finale to life so full of gaiety and splendour. On returning to Salisbury Lina quit the stage for her family of four." (4, February 1958 –Socialite).

The African Daily News paper also reported on Evelyn Juba:

"Concert goers of the early 1936 would focus on the name; Evelyn Juba. Eve, as fans in showbiz knew her, held sway in musical showbiz until 1952, long after the advent of the old jazz era. She soon retired from active stage work to give more attention to her growing family, having been active for more than 16 years; such an achievement is her singular honour and memorable contribution. Evelyn Juba made her debut in Bulawayo during 1936, at the newly built Stanley Hall with the Merry Makers." (8 March 1958- Socialite)

Ava Rodgers became the first black woman musical director. She got involved with the Reps Theatre soon after college, and produced a musical –Motown, which was quite unique, and another hit, Soul Train. During 1978-79 she featured in a high-flying production; *"Svikiro"* which was written by Arthur Chipunza. During the same period, she starred in a musical drama: Rock and Revolution, by Margarita Bouzanis, which aroused a stir in parliament.

In 1989 Ava became the first black conductor of the junior combined schools

choirs.

Ava recorded the good-time tunes of the old Township Music era.

At some point in her life, she had to give up music to look after her children, and only went back when her third child was about two. *"I got married in 1978. When I started my family it is when I also stopped going to do any more (music), and bring up my children, and when the 3rd born was about two, I then went back to it (music)."* Said Ava Rogers in an interview I had with her in 2003.

The responsibility of raising a family

Ava Rodgers

becomes overwhelming to women and, in most cases; they leave music and become fulltime housewives in order to look after the family.

The structures of the society are designed in such a way that women find it difficult to work outside the home. This puts pressure on the women, as they often have to choose between continuing to work outside the home or to work within the home. Usually it is the home that they have to choose, as they are brought up to feel that they are obliged to run the home smoothly and, if it does not, they feel they have failed the family and society.

Laina Gumboreshumba started her musical career at a young age, and she had time to pursue her musical dream. She came from a musical family, and would accompany her father to play at bira's (ancestral night vigils). Laina has taken her music career to another level and she now has a Master of Arts in Music, she is working on her PhD at Rhodes University. While she has been one of the lucky few women musicians who have fulfilled their aspirations she feels that the demands of music and marriage often clash.

"I think the demands of a musical career and the demands of marriage for a woman as expected by the husband and the society at large, clash. Being a musician demands many hours of practising, and some performances are done outside the 'normal' day hours. As a result many men are not comfortable with their wives tackling the heavy schedule and working odd hours. The demands of the family weigh down on the woman and in the end she has to make a choice and drop the other. So married women musicians really need their husbands' and families' support for their careers to succeed," says Laina Gumboreshumba.

Virginia Sillah, a jazz musician of the 1960's –1990's, also feels that marriage is viewed as the ultimate goal for women and, when they achieve it, everything else has to come after marriage.

"Yes, when we grew up we always looked forward to being married as African women. .... it was something special. But I wouldn't advise the young women of today to look to marriage as the only solution to life. Marriage is not a solution to life. When we grew up it was like 'ah akatatwanga he-e', (she is not married), but now women are making it on their own. You don't need a man to succeed in life. At times a man can be an obstruction coming your way. Marriage...... can also.... I don't know whether it's an object or it's a ......, what should I call it? What would you call it?... can also be a hindrance, getting in your way, and then you don't do things like you'd love

to do. Each time you have to consult so-and-so, instead of doing exactly what's in your head, what you want to do at the moment. Every time you think of doing something, you have to ask and, if that someone says 'No', that's it."

One of the few women instrumentalists, Penny Yon, attributes the lack of women playing instruments to not having enough personal time, among other things. Penny managed to learn how to play piano and the guitar because of the time that she was allowed to freely learn and experiment when she was growing up. She was not forced to cook like what was expected of other girls. Her parents encouraged her to take up music, and did what they could to see to it that she realised her dream. She is always grateful to her parents, who nurtured her musical talent, particularly playing instruments. Most women have not been able to do so because they do not have sufficient personal time. Penny narrates how her parents supported her musical career:

"My father thought that was something (the music talent) that just being out from having handed down his father also that it's important to learn musical instruments and to work hard and learning to become proficient and enjoy and give pleasure to other people. When I was a very small girl in Grade Two my father sacrificed for piano lessons at the school. I was at Convent at the time. I was one of the first non-white children to be allowed into that school. This was in the 60's. He encouraged me and paid for piano lessons. So I started when I was six years old, on the piano. When I was ten years my mother bought me a guitar, acoustic - which I still have - from a second hand shop, $17, 00! It was a lot of money then." Since the parents had invested in the instruments they acquired for their daughter, they made sure she found time to play and practice on the instruments: "Because my father used to listen to my piano when I was learning, I used to spend at least one hour when I was a small child, when other kids were doing their cooking with their mums in the kitchen, preparing supper, I was on my piano."

But like many women musicians, Penny had to leave music for a while to look after her growing family. However, she came back to it and is contributing to music in many ways.

Penny Yon

She has been at the helm of a project, which encourages upcoming women musicians, called FLAME (Female Literary Arts & Music Enterprise), with Pamberi Trust.

Despite the structures of society, which have made it impossible for women to fulfil their aspirations, some women musicians have learnt how to create time in order to have their place on the music scene. Prudence Katomeni-Mbofana, one of the best Jazz musicians and a renowned actor, was once asked to be part of a musical play at a time when she was breastfeeding her second child. She says the show was such a success that even the producer did not know how she was able to pull it off, as she would breastfeed her child in between performing. She created time for the musical play to be successful.

A mother of four, Prudence has managed to stay in the arts industry by creating time, she encourages women to create and manage time in order to achieve their goals as artists, such as playing instruments which needs a lot of dedicated time. She does not only sing but she also plays instruments, which takes a lot of dedicated time for a musician to master an instrument, especially women musicians, taking into consideration the house chores they have to deal with. Women are left with not enough personal time but Prudence advices that it is how one manages their time that they will be able to create personal time, for instance learning how to play instruments. Prudence explains how one does not need a lot of time to learn an instrument; she says it is about prioritizing what is important and having interest.

Once you are in it and you are focused you will find time. One thing I have learnt as well is that it's not about 2 hours, it's about 10 to 15 minutes, you say to yourself after 10 minutes I want to have achieved a,b,c. Let's say a piano, even if you haven't mastered it, to play it smoothly it's locked up there and it will come back and the regularly you do it for 10 minutes you will get somewhere. I know women watch a soap opera for 30 minutes; you can take 10 minutes from there, because the soap is not going to teach you anything that is going to help you in your music industry. Its time management and knowing that this is important and this is unnecessary, you structure your things in such a way that; this is low in my priorities or is this high, you do that and it works.

I believe if you can't, you will remain a slave to somebody, some other musician arrangement. You will always remain a slave. You will be having an idea of how you want the instrument to sound like but because you don't know how to play an instrument you cannot explain how to hit a certain note, because you don't know whether it is pitch or what.

Prudence Katomeni-Mbofana's career started while she was in high school, and

Venue : Alliance Francaise
Date : 28 March 2013
Time : 8pm
Price : $10

Mabangu NaPru
Night Of The Guitar

Sponsored By:

she seems to be going stronger, despite being a mother of four and a wife. She also gets support from her husband, Comfort Mbofana as stated earlier.

Tambudzayi Hwaramba, who made her name in the urban grooves genre in the 90's, was involved in music from a tender age. She managed to do this by creating personal time to accommodate her music in whatever she did:

"I've always had a passion for song and dance. When I was in primary school I used to invite my friends over to my house for singing and dancing competitions. We would compete to see who could sing popular songs by musicians, like Yvonne Chaka Chaka, best. Of course, I would practice all week so that I could know every song by heart. I would watch all the music

programmes on TV and imitate the dances and performances. At this stage, I just thought I enjoyed music but didn't realize that God had given me a particular gift. I didn't even realize that there was potential for creativity in me."

Tambudzayi continued with her music when she went to secondary school:

"I went to High School (Arundel Girls High School). However, this was when I became aware of the fact that I had a God-given talent. I met a girl called Dumisani Nkala, who was a brilliant piano-player. We became friends, and we would sit together in one of the school piano rooms while

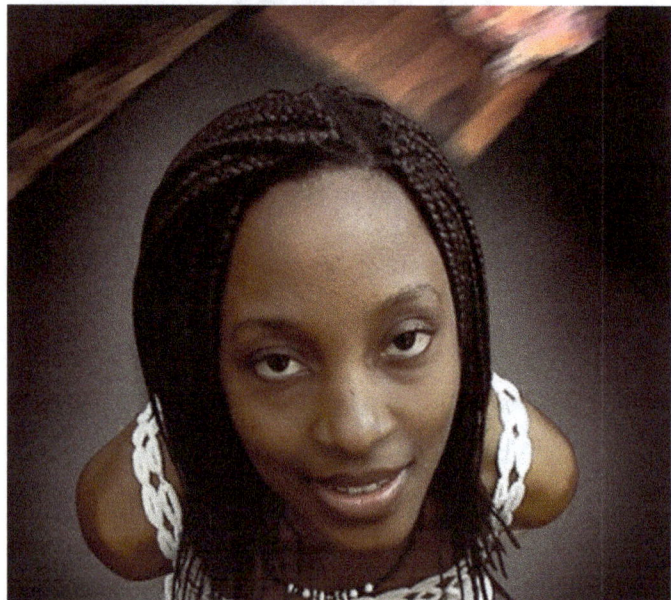

Tambudzayi Hwaramba

she practiced. As time went on, and as we got comfortable around each other, we began singing together and writing songs together. By the time we were in our second last year of High School, Dumi and I were part of an all-girls gospel band, called Milele. Other members of the band included Farirai Mukonoweshuro, Ratidzai Magura and Nyaradzo Ngwerume. Milele performed at a few concerts in their time."

Tambudzayi feels she still needs to create time to go back to learning how to play instruments, as this would make her to be an all-rounded musician.

The Two Singing Nuns, who became very popular guitarists in the 1970's, learnt how to play the instruments when they were at university, and by that time they were novices. A friend, who was also a nun, taught the two how to play the guitar. They created time in between studying for their degrees. Not many women can play instruments because they do not assign enough time to learning and practising the instruments. What also made it easy for the two nuns is that they did not have husbands, who would likely have discouraged them, and also they did not have children to look after; although Sister Gertrude Matsika

The Two Singing Nuns

later decided to get married. She however continued to sing and play the guitar, and taught music at the school where she was also the Head. Both nuns, at some point, had to stop actively playing the guitar and being involved in music in the public space. Sister Helen Maminimini, before her tragic death, was the Order Superior-General of The Little Children of the Blessed Lady (LCBL) General and, because of the duties that she had to perform, she could not be involved in music as before.

The late Elizabeth Ncube, was not all that lucky when she started her musical career. She was always reminded of housework and that, as a woman, she should stay

at home. Elizabeth resisted this kind of treatment, and followed her heart, became the first female Imbongi, and her parents were impressed. In an interview that I had with her in the early 90's, she said:

"I knew I was going to perform, but I did not know what to say to my parents. It was difficult for me to tell them, as they used to say that a woman must not be exposed too much to the outside world (umuntu wesifazana kumele ahlale pansi). A woman was not supposed to go to beer halls. A woman was just supposed to look after children at home, sweep the house, etc. But, then, what I had was too powerful for me. My parents were now the ones asking

Shuvai Wutawunashe

me when next I was going to perform."

Shuvai Wutaunashe, a celebrated Gospel musician since the late 70's, encourages women to create time in order for them to be able to succeed in the music industry. *"It takes effort, and a woman has to be able to divide her time. Because I am a married woman, I am a wife, and I have two children. There are the things I take seriously and am fortunate that my family supports me. But a woman in my position needs to have time (for family) and, at the same time, working."*

Women musicians should learn to create personal time in order to fulfil their musical dreams and aspirations. ▪

Conclusion

I have taken you through almost the 75-year journey that it took women musicians to get to where they are today. The journey has not been an easy one, which has been filled with joy and pain, but it is the product that came out of this sweet and bitter journey that we celebrate; We celebrate - **WOMEN'S STRUGGLE FOR VOICE AND ARTISTIC EXPRESSION – IN VERY CHALLENGING CIRCUMSTANCES WHICH IS A TALE OF RESILIENCE, DETERMINATION AND TRIUMPH!** I hope that by outlining the obstacles that many women face, not only in the music industry, but in other fields as well, that the society can open up and encourage women to explore their talents.

Some of the musicians that I interviewed have since passed on, but through their musical recordings and recorded performances, their spirits still live on.

It is important to document the history of women musicians for posterity, to avoid the distortion of the history of women. It was difficult to find the songs that were written for Lozikeyi because it was not recorded, it is only now that some composers have composed songs to honour Lozikeyi. It is not that this music was never there but maybe those who had the power to document history decided to allocate the music to a certain section of people knowingly or unknowingly. In her research Walker explains why women's histories disappear undocumented;

"In the case of great mass of women, documentary silence may be erroneously equated with historical passivity or, even worse, with historical insignificance, so that women simply disappear from our view of the past. Where women's presence is acknowledged, it is often to subsume them within family or hide then behind abstractions such as 'reproduction' and 'oppression' – even 'gender'- so that the full complexity of their lives, as well as their historical agency, becomes obscured". (Walker 1990,3).

That is why it is important to document women's stories using all forms of documentation in dynamic and accessible ways of telling their stories. The Women Musicians project has documented and told their story in many ways – Women Musicians Book, Diary Notebook, Children's Book, Thesis, Women's Voices of Zimbabwe CD and Film Documentary, (Film documentary is on its way). This will cater for specific groups of people across the board. Thus the story of women is documented and disseminated so that their historical significance is acknowledged.

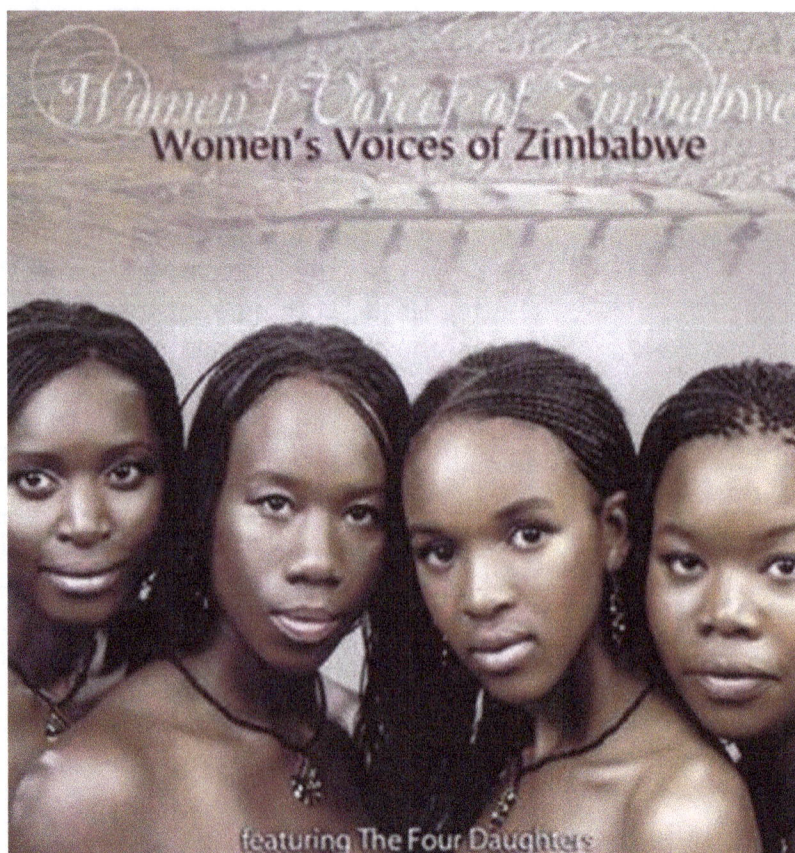

Women's Voices of Zimbabwe

featuring The Four Daughters

Discography

Lina Mattaka (Mattaka Family) (1930s)
Juju Maqeko   Idiko zito Ratenzi   Oh wait

Evelyn Juba (Merry Makers) (1930s)
Go tell your mother   Elokitishini

Faith Dauti
Rosvika Zuva   Hama Neva Bereki   Ngatipemberei,   Shoko Rasvika

Susan Chenjerayi
Isaac hauchandida here   Mwedzi Muchena   Dali iwe
KwaHunyani   Ndatemwa negogo   Ndoita sei
Amai mwana ndanyara *(collaboration withSafiriyo Madzikatire)* Hondo Yechindunduma

Jane Chenjerayi
Usandimirire Pagedhi   Kuwomesa Mutambo

The Two Singing Nuns
Tatetereka   Kundenderedzana   Baba vemwana
Nditakanurei Mambo   Baba ndipfavireiwo

Susan Mapfumo (1970s

Hama Dzangu	ABC 3 4310/FYF127	Nguva Yandai Kuda	ABC34311/ "
Muchanyara	ABC34396/ FYF 132	Chitema	ABC 34397/ "
Ndisiye Yiso	ABC34596/ JR502	Vakomana Vemazuva Ano	ABC 3472/ "
Godo Iro	ABC34722/JR511	Baba VaMunyaradzi	ABC34597/"
Kwamurewa	ABC35094/JR 518	Makeyi	ABC 35095/ "
Hwiza	ABC 35096/JR 519	Ngarava Ya Nowa	ABC35097/ "
Mukoma Teacher	ABC 35098/JR 520	Muchengeri	ABC35099/"
Mhesva Mukono	ABC 35230/JR 523	Ndofireiko	ABC 35231/ "
Vanopururudza	ABC 35434/ JR 531	Ndinokuda	ABC 35618/ JR 537
Hwiza	ABC 35619/ "	Kura Uzvionere	ABC 34922/ JR 514
Pasi Pano	ABC 34923/ "	Tamba Wakachenjera	ABC 35276/ FYF 404
Chawira Mugomba	ABC 35277/ "	Mandisinyongoro	ABC 35435/JR 531
Totopira Mudzimu	ABC 35436/ JR 532	Varume Vema Birifikesi	ABC 35437 "
Pachavo	ABC 35510/ JR 534	Muroora	ABC 35511/"
Handeyi Tese	ABC 35512/ JR 535	Baba Vamuki	ABC 35513/ "

Bybit Mtukudzi
Tanga wanamata 1989

1981 10 tracks

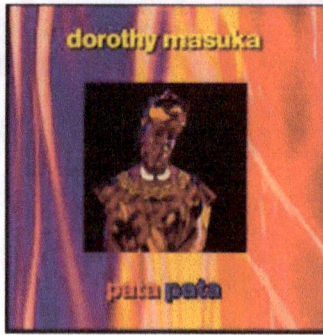
1991 15 tracks

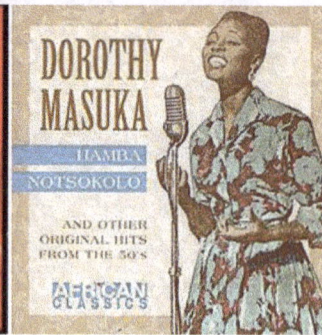
Dec 2, 1997 22 tracks

May 14, 2002 10 tracks

2002 20 tracks

1994 6 tracks

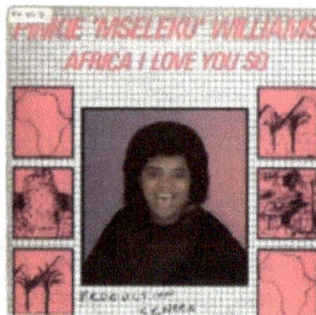
1984 10 tracks

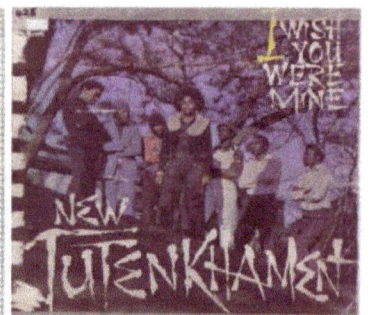

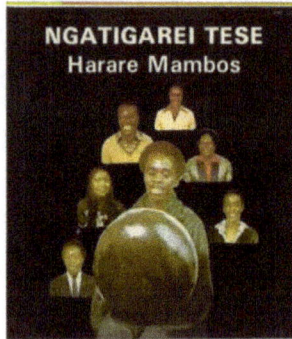
1985 10 tracks

1989 10 tracks

2001 12 tracks

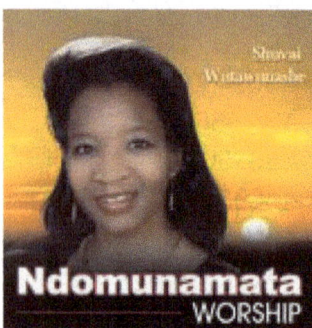
1 Jan 2007 5 tracks

Sep 01, 2002 8 tracks

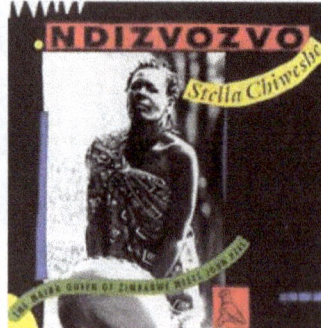
1988 4 tracks

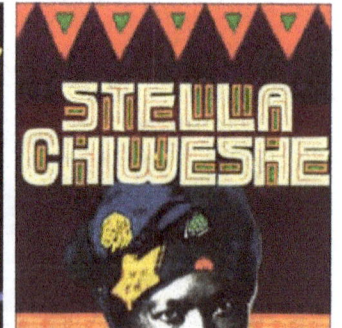
Sep 17, 1990 9 tracks

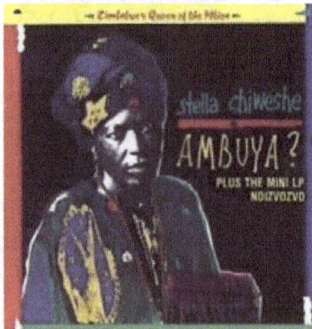
Sep 21, 1994 13 tracks

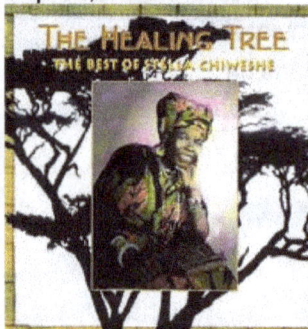
Jan 20, 1998 12 tracks

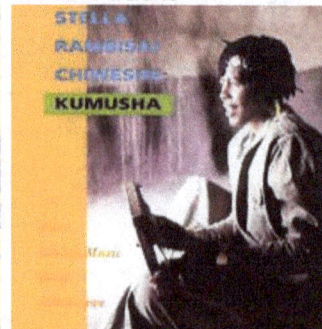
Mar 30, 1999 8 tracks

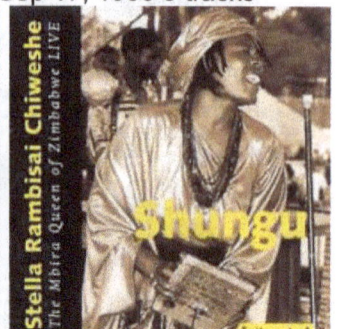
Mar 30, 1999 9 tracks

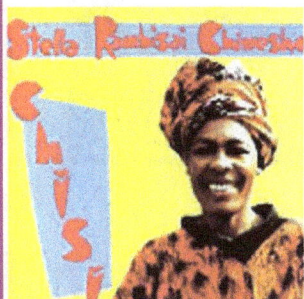
Mar 30, 1999 15 tracks

Jun 11, 2002 10 tracks

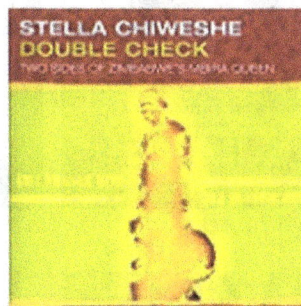
Mar 07, 2006 22 tracks

1993 6 tracks

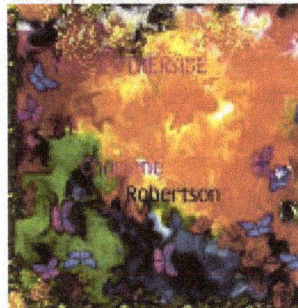
Feb 05, 2008 10 tracks

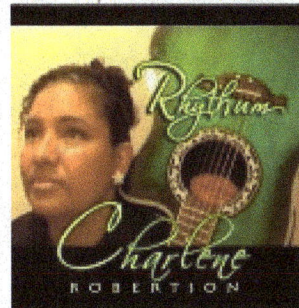
Apr 01, 2008 9 tracks

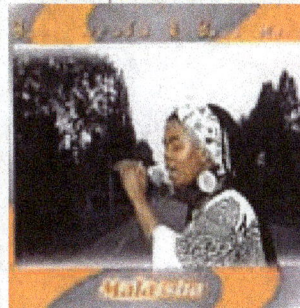
Jan 31, 2011 – 10 Tracks

2011-01-12 - 12 tracks

1989 10 tracks

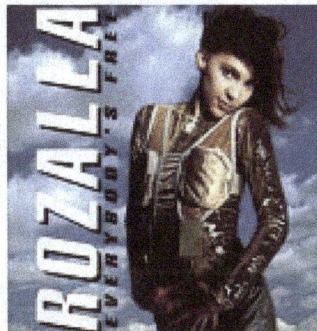
1992 12 tracks

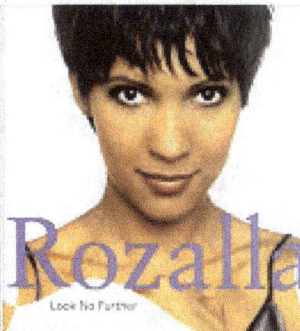
1995 12 tracks

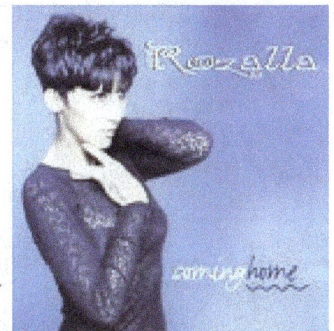
1998 12 tracks

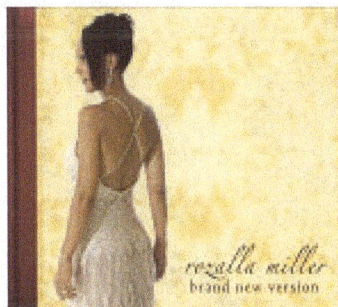
Feb 2, 2009 11 tracks

Sep 02 2008 – 12 Tracks

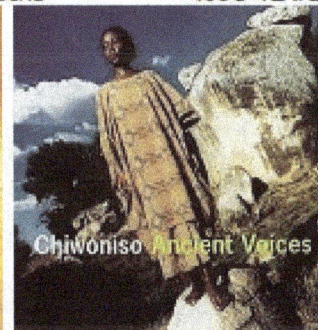
Mar 09, 2001 – 10 Tracks

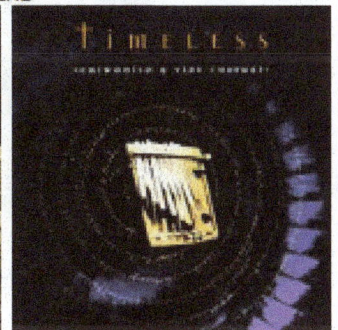
2004 - 12 tracks

1994 8 tracks

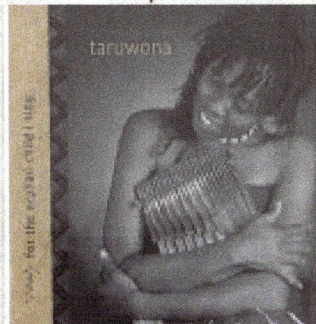
2003 9 tracks

2000 6 tracks

20 tracks

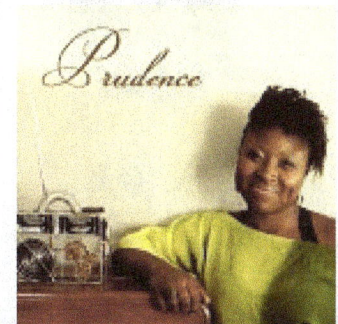
Feb 08, 2011- 16 tracks

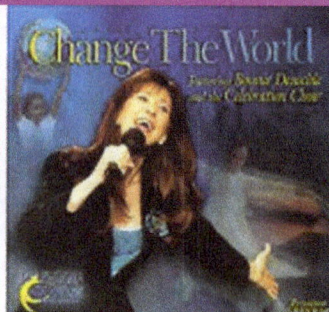
Feb 08, 2011- 16 tracks

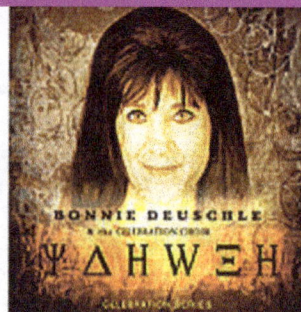
2012 – 13 tracks

11 tracks   Mar 21, 2007

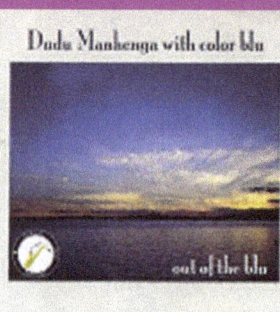
04 Aug 2008 9 Tracks

2008   2 tracks

Jul 08, 2011 10 tracks

Apr 17, 2013 11 tracks

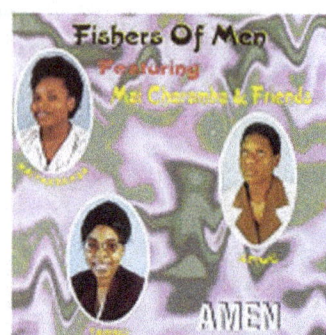
20 Feb 2004 10 tracks

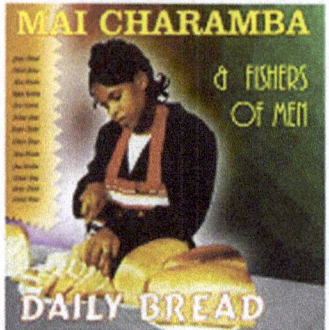
15 Mar 2004 9 tracks

2007 8 tracks,

Zvanaka 1995 10 tracks ,Huyai 1998 10 tracks,

2000 10 tracks

10 tracks – 2002

8 tracks 2003

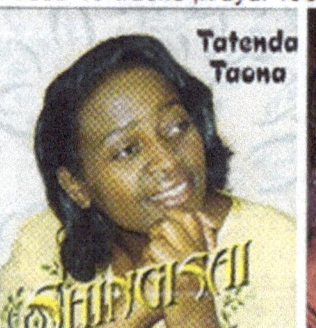
11 tracks – 2004

9 Sep 2006 17 tracks

2009 10 tracks

14 tracks

2002 12 tracks

2012 14 songs

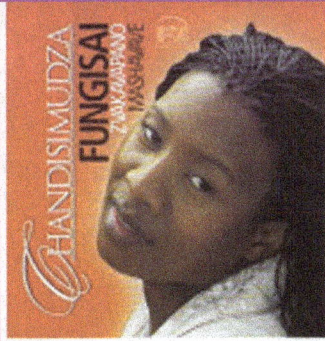  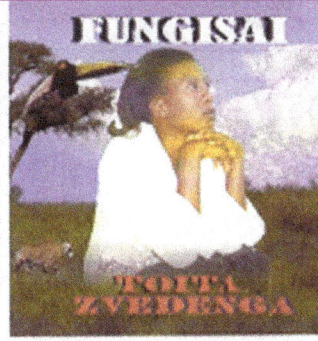 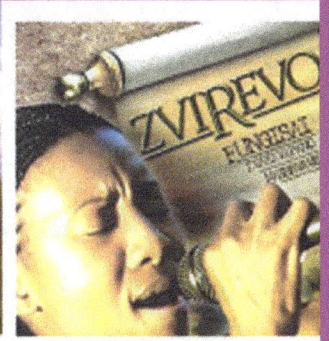

2009 8tracks   2010 8 tracks   2002 7 tracks   2006 8 tracks

 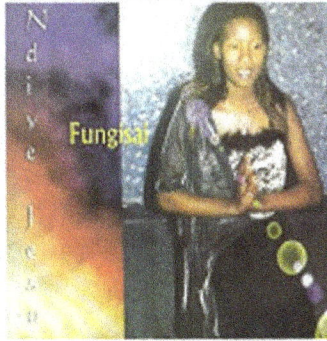  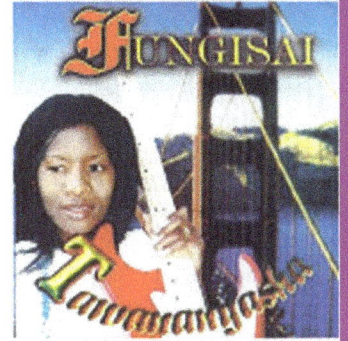

Nov 11, 2011   8 tracks   2001   8 Tracks   2005 8 tracks

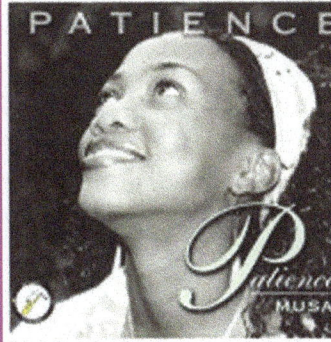 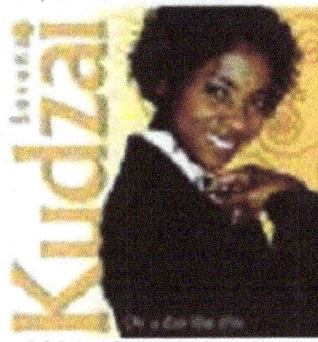 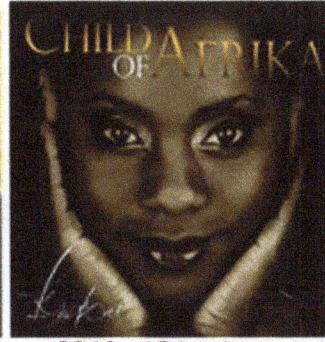 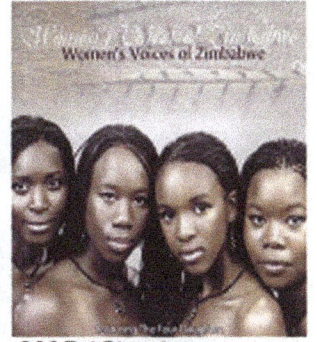

2005   8 tracks   2004 10 tracks   2010   12 tracks   2007 12tracks

   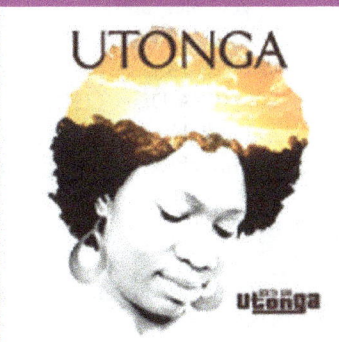

2004   Jul 11 2006   2009   12 tracks   2009 10   tracks

 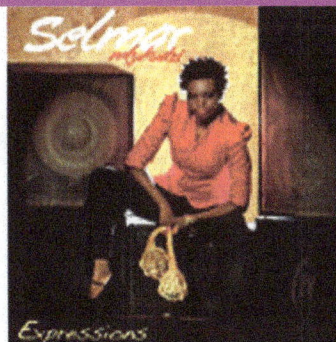  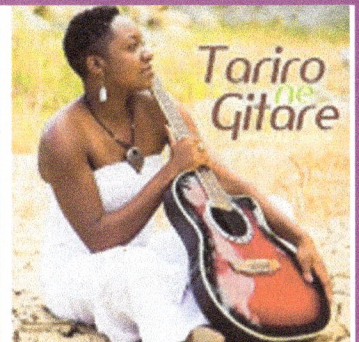

2009, 9 tracks   2013, 12 tracks   2011, 10 tracks   2013, 10 tracks

Index

Bibliography and References

- African Broadcasting Corporation
- African Daily Newspaper
- African Press
- Allen 2000
- Amadiuni (1995)
- British Broadcasting Corperation (BBC)
- Blake (1977)
- Central Daily News
- Chifamba Barnes (2008)
- Chirimuuta (2006)
- Clarke (2000)
- Daily News
- The Herald
- Kambarami (2006)
- Krige et al 1943
- Mudenge 1988
- Mya's Story
- Oliver 2004
- Pongweni
- African Daily News – Socialite
- Speak Out Magazine
- The African Weekly
- The African Parade
- The Radio Post
- The Rhodesia Broadcasting Corporation (FBC)
- The Sunday Mail
- Venables, 2003
- Walker 1990,
- Weiss 1983
- WICSA Diary (1992)
- Zimbabwe Broadcasting Corporation (ZBC)
- Zimbabwe Township Music Book(2005)

JOURNALS

- (IAWM) International Alliance for Women in Music
- Southern Rhodesia Report of the Director of Census, May 1926
- UNESCO, 2009: Representative List of the Intangible Cultural Heritage of Humanity
- US Department of Education Report, 2005

VIDEOS/CDS

- A Christmas to remember – With Early Township Dwellers Documentary (1994)
- Epworth Theatrical Strutters Film Documentary (1994)
- Omasiganda-African Trobadours-One Man Band Guitarists Documentary (1995)
- The Bantu Actors/Mattaka Family Documentary (1998)
- Women's Voices CD (2007)
- Rebel Woman (2008)
- Zimbabwe Township Music documentary Documentary (1992)

Glossary

African Service -	Rhodesian Broadcast for non-English service
Afro pop music 7 -	African pop music played on electric instruments and inspired by Western pop or soul music.
Akatatwanga -	Term given to mature women who are not married.
Austin Cambridge -	A motor car range sold by the Austin Motor Company in several generations from September 1954 through to 1969.
Ballroom dancers -	Any of various social dances, such as the fox trot, tango, or waltz, in which couples follow a conventional pattern of steps.
Bira -	(Night vigils) Ritual feast of (eg. mhondoro or vadzimu).
BSAC -	The British South Africa Company founded by Cecil Rhodes colonized Southern Africa in 1889 and in 1923 it became the self-governing British colony of Southern Rhodesia.
Chihwani -	A traditional brew which takes one day to make.
Chinyambera dance -	A hunting and gathering dance, originated within the Karanga people of Masvingo province in Zimbabwe. Females show their fruit gathering skills, and males their hunting skills.
Dinhe dance -	A dance, singing and drum style also known as makwingwindo. It is mostly found in the Dande area. It is a fast paced drum and dance style performed mostly at harvest celebrations.
Dombo -	Representative in marriage negotiations. In Ndebele pronounced as (dhombo) it is also known as (Munyayi) in Shona. The word dombo in Shona can also mean a stone.
Dzepfunde -	Encouraging teller of folk tale or acknowledging to the folk tale teller that you are listening
Esasibekelwa -	Soft (Isitshikitsha).
Ethnomusicologist -	Is a person who does a comparative study of music of different cultures.
Ethnomusicology program -	The study of folk or native music, especially of non-Western cultures, and its relationship to the society to which it belongs.
Federation of Rhodesia Nyasaland -	Also known as the Central African Federation (CAF), was a semi-independent state in southern Africa that existed from 1953 to the end of 1963, comprising the former self-governing colony of Southern Rhodesia and the British protectorates of Northern Rhodesia and Nyasaland.
General Service -	Rhodesian Broadcast for English service and it catered for people of European decent (Rhodesians).
Gospel Music -	A kind of Christian music based on American folk music, marked by strong rhythms and elaborated refrains, and incorporating elements of spirituals, blues, and jazz.
Gramophones -	The first device for recording and replaying sound.
Hall of Fame -	A building housing memorial items honoring illustrious persons.
Imbongi -	A composer and orator of poems praising a King/Chief or other figurehead.
Internal Settlement -	It was the agreement between Rhodesian Prime Minister Ian Smith and Abel Muzorewa in 1978. After almost 15 years of civil war, and under pressure from the sanctions placed on Rhodesia by the international community, and political pressure from South Africa, Great Britain and the United States, the Rhodesian government met with some moderate black nationalist leaders to reach an agreement.
Isitshikitsha -	A tribal dance brought to Zimbabwe by the Ndebele people who migrated from South Africa under King UMzilikazi kaMatshobana and settled in Southern Zimbabwe. Isitshikitsha is performed at social gatherings—weddings or first fruits ceremonies.
Isitshwala/sadza -	A thick porridge which is prepared using mealie meal.
Jazz music -	A style of music, native to America, characterized by a strong but flexible rhythmic understructure with solo and ensemble improvisations on basic tunes and chord patterns and, more recently, a highly sophisticated harmonic idiom.
Jenaguru -	Full moon.
Jerusarema/ Mbende dance –	A popular dance style practiced by the Zezuru /Shona people living in the Murehwa and Uzumba-Maramba Pfungwe districts, it is characterized by sensual and acrobatic movements by women in

	unison with men, also known as the fertility dance.
Jiti -	Shona secular songs and dance formerly known as Jikinya, performed in the manner of a jive.
Kanindo music -	East African rumba, jit (jiti) type of music.
Korekore dance –	A dance by the Kore-Kore people in the North-Eastern Zimbabwe and Mozambique to summon the Mhondoro spirit.
Kushonongora mwenga -	To show acceptance of the bride by giving her money, and also to honour her.
Land Apportionment Act in 1930 -	The Division of the Colony of Southern Rhodesia into six specified areas as follows, The Native Reserves, The Native Areas, The European Areas, The Undetermined Area, The Forest Area and the Unassigned Area.
Madanha omugudza -	Using the totem to express gratitude in the form of praise poetry after sexual intercourse.
Marabi -	Urban black music developed in the 1920's in South Africa, Blending Western chord polyphonic systems and harmonization with African rhythms.
Marimba -	A percussion instrument with wooden bars tuned to produce a chromatic scale and with resonators; played with small mallets.
Mbaqanga music -	Originally the 1950s popular commercial African jazz in South Africa using African melody, marabi and American Jazz. Later it combined new urban traditional sounds and marabi using modern Western musical instruments.
Mbira -	Also commonly referred to as the (hand piano),it is the main instrument in the performance of the Shona Spirit and secular music and dance of the same name. It can be played alone or accompanied by drums and rattles.
Mbira Dzevadzimu –	A set of carefully shaped and sized metal keys that produce different tones. The keys are mounted on a rectangular wooden sound board that acts as a first level amplifier.
Mother Superior -	A nun in charge of a Christian religious order or congregation, a convent or house of women under vows.
Muchongoyo dance -	Secular Tshangani traditional song and dance popular in the Eastern Districts of Zimbabwe and closely resembling the Zulu war dance.
Munhumutapa -	Ruler of the Mutapa Empire which stretched between the Zambezi and Limpopo rivers ofsouthern Africa in the modern states of Zimbabwe and Mozambique.
Negro Spirituals Jazz -	Religious music of American origin, particularly associated with African-American Protestants of the Southern United States, characterized by syncopation, polyrhythmic structure, and the pentatonic scale of five whole tones and above all is deeply emotional with words most often related to biblical passages.
Ngoma -	African type of drum.
Njari –	A less common type of Shona mbira originally introduced from Mozambique.
Nyamaropa tune -	Nyamaropa, which literally means "meat and blood," has been described ... as referring to the period after a hunt when meat is all around, as "a war song to arouse feelings before the battle, as the scene of a battlefield after fighting when blood and flesh is everywhere," and as having "to do with the blood of a beast when it is sacrificed for the [ancestral spirits].
Nyunganyunga mbira -	Similar in construction to the Mbira Dzavadzimu, the Nyunga Nyunga has fewer keys, in two rows, and no hole in the soundboard. Key pitches radiate out from the center, rather than left to right. It is typically played by holding both sides of the instrument in one's hands.
Pennywhistle (Kwela) music -	street music from southern Africa with jazzy underpinnings and a distinctive, skiffle-like beat. It evolved from the marabi sound and brought South African music to international prominence in the 1950s, the pennywhistle is a simple, six holed woodwind instrument.
Pioneer column -	A force raised by Cecil Rhodes and his British South Africa Company in 1890 and used in his efforts to annexe the territory of Mashonaland, later part of Southern Rhodesia (now Zimbabwe).
Pop -	Music of general appeal to teenagers; a bland watered-down version of rock'n'roll with more rhythm and harmony and an emphasis on romantic love.
R 'n B -	A style of music developed by African Americans that combines blues and jazz, characterized by a strong backbeat and repeated variations on syncopated instrumental phrases.

Ragga -	A style of reggae music that incorporates hip-hop and rhythm and blues elements. Also called dancehall.
Rattles -	Percussion instrument consisting of resonant objects strung together and set in a sliding frame or enclosed in a container such that when it is shaken the parts strike against each other, producing sounds.
Rave -	Name given to various types of dance music, such as techno, house that feature fast electronically synthesized rhythm
Rhumba Music -	Music combining complex footwork with a pronounced movement of the hips.
	Rock music - A genre of popular music originating in the 1950s; a blend of black rhythm-and-blues with white country-and-western; "rock is a generic term for the range of styles that evolved out of rock'n'roll.
Rungano -	Folk tale.
Second Chimurenga -	Chimurenga is a word in the Shona language, roughly meaning "revolutionary struggle. It is the war fought between black nationalist guerrillas and the predominantly white Rhodesian government during the 1960s and 1970s.
Seven Days -	A Traditional brew which takes seven days to make.
Shabeen -	An unlicensed drinking establishment.
Shabeen Queen 34,	The lady patron of the shabeen.
Shangara dance -	Term covering several types of traditional Shona circular song and dance performed with two or more drums, or with singing and clapping only.
Simanje-Manje -	A form of South African music that became popular in the 1960s. The Zulu term means "things of now-now".
Soul -	A popular music genre that originated in the United States in the 1950s and early 1960s. It combined elements of African American gospel music, rhythm and blues, and often jazz.
Squatter camps -	Slum settlements of plywood, corrugated metal, sheets of plastic, and cardboard boxes. They are usually found on the periphery of cities, public parks, or near railroad tracks, rivers, lagoons or city trash dump sites.
Sungura (growth point) music -	This is the local genre of the Zimbabwe music industry. Sungura music became popular in the early 1980s
Tribal Trust Lands -	The term communal land in Zimbabwe refers to certain rural areas within Zimbabwe. Communal lands were formerly called Tribal Trust Lands in the Rhodesia Government.
Tsaba, tsaba -	1940s music which combined African melody with American swing and jazz. Tsaba-tsaba was essentially a working class form of dance music and eventually evolved into "kwela".
UDI -	The Unilateral Declaration of Independence was a statement adopted by the Cabinet of Rhodesia on 11 November 1965, announcing that Rhodesia a British territory in southern Africa that had governed itself since 1923, now regarded itself as an independent sovereign state.
Ukuhaya -	A celebration which is done so as to welcome the new bride into the family.
Uphini -	A utensil made out of wood used to make traditional meals such as isitshwala/sadza.
Urban Grooves -	Coming on the Zimbabwe music scene in the late 1990s and early 2000s, Urban Grooves takes in American Rap, Hip Hop, R&B, Soul and other international music genres, often melded with traditional Zimbabwean music.
Usaziwatshela –	Wash clothes for us.
Vimbuza Healing Dance -	A healing dance among the Tumbuka people living in Northen Malawi, it is an important manifestation of ng'oma, a healing complex found throughout Bantu-speaking Africa.
Vinyl -	Commonly known as "a record' is analog sound storage medium in the form of a flat polyvinyl chloride disc with an inscribed, modulated spiral groove. The groove usually starts near the periphery, and ends near the center of the disc, and are generally described by their diameter.

ETHNIC GROUPS

Balobedi people -	An African tribe of the Northern Sotho group under the Balobedu Kingdom, within the Limpopo

Province of South Africa with a female ruler, the Rain Queen Modjadji. Their language is known as Khelobedu, which is a "non-Pedi" dialect of Northern Sotho.

Europeans - The various ethnic groups that reside in the nations of Europe, in Africa white people are mostly referred to as Europeans.

Ndebele People - An African ethnic group located in South Africa and Zimbabwe and their language is Ndebele.

Nguni - A cluster of related Bantu-speaking ethnic groups living in South Africa, Swaziland, and Zimbabwe, whose ancestors inhabited a broad band of upland territory extending from the Great Fish River, in what is now Eastern Cape province, northward to Kosi Bay, near the border of KwaZulu/Natal province and Mozambique, that paralleled the Indian Ocean. They speak the Bantu languages such as Xhosa, Zulu which are unique in that they have imploded "clicking" phonemes.

Nnobi - a small rural town in the hinterland of Igboland of Eastern Nigeria

Portuguese - A Western nation and ethnic group native to the country of Portugal, in the west of the Iberian Peninsula of Southwestern Europe. Their language is Portuguese, and Roman Catholicism is their predominant religion.

Shona People - The Shona tribe is Zimbabwe's largest indigenous group, their tribal language is also called Shona (Bantu) They are found in Zimbabwe, Botswana and southern Mozambique in Southern Africa and bordering South Africa. There are five main Shona language groups: Korekore, Zezuru Manyika, Ndau, and Karanga.

Sotho - Sotho, also called Suthu or Suto, linguistic and cultural group of peoples occupying the high grasslands of southern Africa. The main groups are customarily classified as the Transvaal, or northern, Sotho (Pedi, Lovedu, and others); the western Sotho, or Tswana; and the southern Sotho (often called Basuto) of Lesotho and adjoining areas.

Swahili people - (Waswahili) are a Bantu ethnic group and culture found in the eastern African Great Lakes region. Members mainly reside on the Swahili Coast, in an area encompassing the Zanzibar archipelago, coastal Kenya, the Tanzania seaboard, and northern Mozambique. The name Swahili is derived from the Arabic word Sawahil, meaning "coastal dwellers". The Swahili speak the Swahili language, which belongs to the Niger-Congo family.

Tonga people - Also called 'Batonga' are a Bantu ethnic group of southern Zambia and northern Zimbabwe, and to a lesser extent, in Mozambique.

Tumbuka people - Also called Kamanga, or Henga, are a people who live on the lightly wooded plateau between the northwestern shore of Lake Nyasa (Lake Malaŵi) and the Luangwa River valley of eastern Zambia. They speak a Bantu language closely related to those of their immediate neighbours, the lakeside Tonga, the Chewa, and the Senga.

Venda People - The Venda (Vhavhenda or Vhangona) are a Southern African people living mostly near the South African-Zimbabwean border.

Zezuru people - People of the Shona dialect Zezuru spoken in Mashonaland and central Zimbabwe, near Harare.

NAMES

VENUES

PUBLICATIONS

SONGS

PICTURE CREDITS

Sam Mhirizhonga
(p2 and 3) Ava Rodgers, (p31) Agnes Jenje with granddaughter Mya, (p63) Victoria Zimuwandeyi and Dadirai Manatse, (p96)Rhodha Mandaza, (p128)Ava Rodgers with her mother, her niece and Joyce Jenje Makwenda the author, (148) Rhoda Mandaza with Joyce Jenje Makwenda, (p162)Rumbidzai Chipendo (p165) Ava Rodgers

Tandiwe Jenje
(p4) Mya Madzudzo,
(p133) Mya Madzudzo
Penny Yon and Book Café
(p5) Women Musicians-Flame Celebrations, (p89) FLAME Advert, (p143) Chiwoniso Maraire Advert 2011, (p190) Women Musicians, (p196) Chiwoniso Maraire

David Kofi
(p7)Tabeth Kapuya, Joyce Jenje Makwenda and Victoria Chingate, (p44)Beular Dyoko with band, (p60) Tabeth Kapuya and Victoria Chingate, (p99)Victoria Chingate -90s, (p134)Beaular Dyoko with band, (p152)Simangaliso Tutani, Joyce Jenje Makwenda and Louis Mhlanga (1991) – Ethnomusicology in Luck Street

National Archives
(p9) Shona women pounding corn, (p12) Ndebele Girls, (p15) Shona Girls, (p22) Mbuya Nehanda (p23)Lozikeyi Dlodlo c.1860, (p24)Queen Lozikeyi (Later years), (p27)A Childminder (nanny) (p29) Amai Musodzi, (p36)Lina Mattaka-50s, (p37)Evelyn Juba -50s, (p39) Dorothy Masuka, (p46) Susan Chenjerayi, Dorothy Masuka, (p47) Dorothy Masuka, (p55) The Mattaka Family, (p56) The Merry

Makers, Flora Dick, Faith Dauti, Mary Mabhena, (p57) Dorothy Masuka, Dorothy Masuka, singer Tandi and Rose, (p60) Joyce Ndoro, (p61)Mabel Bingwa, (p65) Virginia Sillah and the OK Success Band, (p66) Izintombi, ZakaMtwkazi, Sakaza Sisters –Bulawayo, (p67) Susan Chenjerayi with her 2 children -70s, (p99) Victoria Chingate -50s, (p100) Sylvia Sondo, (p139)Monica Marsden

Miriam Mlambo
(p11) Ambuya Miriam Mlambo

ZWICCT/WICSA
Margaret Waller- (p13)Woman beating water with a stick, (p37) Evelyn Juba -1990s, (p40) Eileen Haddon, (p45) Stella Chiweshe, Taruwona Mushore, (p54) Traditional Dancers, (p73) Irene Chigamba, (p74) Chiwoniso Mararire, (p77) Elizabeth Taderera (Katarina), (p82) University of Zimbabwe Students, (p87) Taruwona Mushore 1993, (p95) Bertha (Mattaka) Msora, (p117 Elizabeth Ncube, (p118) Amai Muchena, (p145)Beular Dyoko and Amai Muchena, (p158) Amakhosi Women's Group,
Tessa Colvin - (p41) Virginia Sillah

Canaan Jenje
(p16) Malandu Mateza Dube (Mangena), (28) Canaan Jenje (Mateza)

Simon Kofi
(p17) Women singing for a bride at a wedding

Susan Chenjerayi
(p25) Susan Chenjerayi, Safiriyo Madzikatire and an unidentified actress

The Herald
(p28)Angeline Makwavarara (Mrs Mhlanga), (p30 and 31) Early women and urbanization article (p43) Women Soldiers, (pg 44) Chiwoniso Maraire (p46) Susan Mapfumo, (p54) Jerusarema Dancers,(p78) Betty Makaya, (p81)Edna Makanda and Sons, Mambokadzi, (p110) Woman Sleeping with man, (p111) Botswana musician Slizer dancing at a show in Harare,

(p116) Woman Dancing with man,

Hope Bakasa Sadza
(p28)Sarah Bakasa

Mavis Moyo
(p28) Mavis Moyo

Katie Chitumba
(p30) Katie Chitumba

Gladys Hanyani
(p33)Gladys Hanyani, Martha Kuvheya

Joyce Jenje Makwenda Collections
(p36) Lina Mattaka -2000s, (p49) Rozalla Millar LP, Charlene Robertson LP, (p61) Pinkie Mseleku, (p71) Beulah Dyoko LP Cover, (p75) Lina Gumboreshumba, (p90) Kenneth and Lina Mattaka, Evelyn and Simon Juba, (p97) Nomsa Mhlanga and her father Louis Mhlanga 8 August 2008, (p109) Women Music Educators at Zimbabwe College of Music, (p110) Virginia Sillah, (p125) Tendai Ziyambe, (p129) Laina Gumboreshumba, (p144) Stella Chiweshe album Cover – Chisi, (p150) Rumbidzai Chipendo conducting a workshop with members of ZAME (p195) Zimbabwe Township Music Dvd Cover, Gupuro Book Cover, Zimbabwe Township Music Book Cover, Usenzeni Book Cover, Divorce Toke Book Cover, Mya's Story Book Cover, Women Musicians of Zimbabwe 1930s – 2013 Book Cover, Women Musicians of Zimbabwe Thesis Cover, Women Musicians of Zimbabwe Diary Notebook Cover, Please Gogo can I have the mic featuring Women Musicians Children's Book Cover

Gibson Mandishona
(p38 and p98) The Gay Gaeties posing

Rob Allingam
(p39) Dorothy Masuka (2000s), (pg123) Dorothy Masuka

David Tredgold, Carine
(p40) Barbara Tredgold

Josephine Jenje Mudimbu

(p41) Ava Rodgers, (p84) Irene Gwaze, (p133) Joyce Jenje Makwenda with granddaughter Mya Nonthando Madzudzo (2004)

Shingi Keith Phiri
(p41) Prudence Katomene Mbofana

Ava Rodges
(p41) Biddy Patridge, Kundisai Mtero, Penny Yon and Ava Rodgers (Big Sister), (p128) Ava Rodgers doing a play in the 70's

SPEAK OUT Magazine
(p42) Susan Mapfumo, (p69) Susan Mapfumo, (p72) Beaulah Dyoko and her son, (p125) Tendai Ziyambe, (p146) Susan Mapfumo, (p147) Beaular Dyoko

Elizabeth Ncube
(p44) Elizabeth Ncube, (p73) Elizabeth Ncube, (p135) Elizabeth Ncube

Irene Chigamba
(p44) Irene Chigamba

Sister Helen Mamimini
(p46) Two Singing Nuns, (p47) The Two singing Nuns, (p69)The Two Singing Nuns, (p169) The Two Singing Nuns

Mike Mwale
(p48)Jordan Chataika with sisters Addena, Joyce and Molly Chataika LP Cover

Jane Chenjerayi
(p48) Jane Chenjerayi

Shuvai Wutawunashe
(p48) Shuvai Wutaunashe, (p76) Shuvai Wutaunashe, (p118) Shuvai Wutaunashe, (p145) Shuvai Wutawunashe, (p169) Shuvai Wutawunashe,

Zimbojam
(p49) Busi Ncube, (p102) Dudu Manhenga, (p149) Busi Ncube,

Benita Tarupiwa
(p50)Benita Tarupiwa album Cover

Patricia Matongo

Google

(p35) White woman at shabeen - www.urbanadventures.com
(p41) Dudu Manhenga -www.zimbablog.com, (p53) Miriam Makeba pg - www.okayafrica.com, (p76) Rozalla Miller- www.flickr.comp, (p77) Sandra Ndebele -zimbabwenewsonline.com, (p78) Plaxedes Wenyika-www.plaxedeswenyika.com, (p79)Shingisai Suluma-sphotos-b.xx.fbcdn.net, Fungisai Zvakavapano-Mashavave- www.thestandard.co.zw, Ivy Kombo www.newzimbabwe.com, (p83) Debbie Metcalfe -www.newzimbabwe.com (p84) Tsungirirai Zvobgo -www.zimbabweonlinepress.com, Jackie Cahi - kufunda.org, Nomsa Mwamuka – flickriver.com (85) Portia Gwanzura,- scoopweb.com, Hope Masike- quinaineafriquaine.unblog.fr,

(p87) Kudzai Sevenzo-flowerstapiwa.wordpress.com,
Dudu Manhenga -www.newzimbabwe.com, (p95) Chiwoniso Maraire- www.misszimdiamond.com, (p101) Edith Weutonga – HIFA, (p107) Arundel Students- brickproject2016.com, St Georges College Students - www.amazingvictoriafalls.com, (p108) Women cooking at home gmrpr.files.wordpress.com and funeral or wedding - www.paleostyle.co.il, (p109) Women at work - madamenoire.com, (p109) Women doing Housework - 5to9branding.com, (p110) Susan Chenjerayi - relzim.org, (p121) Busi Ncube- flickriver.com, (p 123)Photo of a family- thegrio.files.wordpress.com, (p136) Dorothy Masuka -farm4.static.flickr.com, Women selling vegetables - www.mamagenas.

com, (p151) Young girl carrying a baby on her back -www-i5.informatik.rwth-aachen.de, Young girls carrying firewood - photos.travelblog.org, (p152) Children dancing-img.thezimbabwean.co.uk/chipawo, (p153) Chiwoniso Maraire-zimbeatnews.blogspot.com, (p154) Julia Chigamba, Erica Azim and Kelly Orphan -worldartwest.org, Julia Chigamba and Chinyakare Ensemble-www.livesv.com (p156) Chidren Playing Instruments, (p158) Netsayi Chigwendere - bbc.preview.somethinelse.com, (p208) Women at work with baby - nationalurbanmedia.com

Thanda Richardson, Prudence Katomene-Mbofana, Hope Masike, Rumbidzai Tapfuma, Adiona Maboreke-Chidzonga, Kundisai Mutero, Cecilia Geskemo and Dudu Manhenga.

Acknowledgements and Dedication

MY gratitude goes to all those who made this book possible, mainly The Ford Foundation for funding the research, writing and also my Masters program at the University of Witwatersrand. In addition I would like to thank the following people at The Ford Foundation– Nume (Farai) Mashinini and John Butler Adams, for believing in this project, Betty Amunga for assisting wherever possible. I would like to thank Alice Brown The Ford Foundation Country Representative (during the time I got funding), for seeing the importance of the project and funding it and also the encouragement. The project took more time than I had anticipated. Thank you so much FORD FOUNDATION for giving me time and space to dream in order to bring out – THE VOICE AND ARTISTIC EXPRESSION OF WOMEN MUSICIANS IN THIS BOOK.

Initially the project included the book and the thesis but because of the time and space I had, a diary notebook and a Children's Book on Women Musicians of Zimbabwe were added. A film documentary is on the way.

In 1994/1995 I received a grant from NOVIB for research and writing the first draft, but unfortunately NOVIB could not fund the project beyond the first draft. At NOVIB I would like to thank in particular Judith Uyerterland who made it possible for me to get funding for the early research and writing. I would also like to thank Megan Alladice, a colleague, who encouraged me to apply for funding from NOVIB. I had to shelve the project until 2006 when I got funding from The Ford Foundation.

However, from 1995 to 2006, a lot had changed on the music scene and I had to carry out new research to incorporate the new changes in a fast changing industry. The book took a new angle which was no longer narrative, but is written thematically.

I would like to thank all those who supported the project in various ways;

My appreciation to Prof. Lara Allen who was my first supervisor on my Master's Thesis entitled "Women Musicians in Zimbabwe 1930-2005: A Struggle for Voice and Artistic Expression", which is also the title of the book. Lara Allen introduced me to the academic world and academic thinking. Thank you so much Lara for nurturing the project. *Ndinotenda zvikuru!* (Thank you so much!)

Thank you so much Prof. Tawana Khupe, for introducing me to Lara Allen, and encouraging me to apply to study at the University of Witwatersrand, it has been a great experience.

Let me take this opportunity to thank my current supervisor Dr. Marie Jorritsma for the support and encouragement.

I would also like to thank Sarudzayi Chifamba-Barnes for editing the book. Working with an artist can be a challenge, but you took time to understand what I wanted without changing the content and context of the book. It was a blessing to have someone like you edit the book because you understand where I am coming from; my feminist beliefs, my African way of thinking, my journalistic, artistic views and my new found academic views. *Ndinotenda zvikuru 'Jerry' wangu.*

Many thanks goes to Louis Mhlanga for the encouragement and advice on music matters, on this project and a lot of my other music projects. Nolitha Sondo Patterson (Aunt Nollie) for being my cheerleader, (men siger tusind tak) thousand thanks. Rob Allingham, as always your library was accessible to me and your door was open whenever I wanted advice on a number of issues concerning the music industry. Mike Mwale for access to your rich music library, and the informative discussions. Alexander Kanengoni thank you for your invaluable comments, and always ready to listen to my new ideas and seeing them unfolding. Margaret Dongo (muroora), for the 'compulsory' retreats at your rural villa, you helped me to take the necessary breaks when my mind was getting tired. Sis Babs (Barbra Nkala) for the encouragement and support I know I can always count on you. Hope Chigudu – sister dear – thanks for always assuring me that I can do it and for being a great listener. Mary Ann Mandishona (VaNdai), for the encouragement and for advice on a number of issues and for holding forte at Chipo Changu project in order for (Mama J) to find time to work on this project. Rumbidzai Chipendo my friend, thanks for being a great listener and guide. Rhoda Mandaza my Ekse, what more can I say. Masepeke Sekhukhuni (Mae) thanks for being there for me in many ways that I cannot list. Beauty Ncube (Musikana) - for the encouragement on my Master's Degree, you were so happy when I went back to 'school' – thank you. Charity Hodzi Sibanda for the encouragement and support you gave to (Mama Jenje) in many ways. Florence Matsikiwa and Barbara Mutambu, (vaning'ina), thanks a lot for being there during my three years in Joburg, I knew I could count on you. Patricia Phaka, thanks for everything for all the support you gave me while working on this project. MacArfthur Park, Joburg could not have been the same without you (baby sister). I would also like to thank my sister Ngonidzaishe Moyo, who encouraged me to write about my two daughters who are into music; Sasani Naome (my daughter) and Nontando Mya Cecilia (my granddaughter), and to treat them like all other musicians as sometimes writing about your family members can be seen as bias, but Ngoni wanted the two to be awarded the merits they deserve in music by appearing in the book. Priscilla Sithole (mnawami), thank you for facilitating interviews in Bulawayo and for the hospitality. Tambudzai Madzimure (MaNgwenya), thank you for facilitating (Gogo Jenje) during the early stages of writing this book by offering me space at SACOD (Johannesburg) while I was waiting for my grant, thanks to SACOD for understanding.

To Yolanda Birivadi thank you for everything and for laying out the pages of the book and for the index. Mention also goes to Jeffrey Milanzi for the wonderful designs and Josh Sithole for the fantastic cover.

My gratitude also goes to colleagues, friends and members of the family who helped with the editorial when the project was in its initial stages, and as it progressed, they gave their comments and

Acknowledgements and Dedication

suggestions. Some of them are my sister Glandina Nhamo who also guided me to understand some ethnomusicology issues, and my friends Mike Mwale, Thedias "T.C." Chikukura.

I will always be grateful to a colleague – Dr. Gibson Mandishona –for editing the *Zimbabwe Township Music Book*, it is through that experience that it has been easier for me to work on the *Women Musicians Book*.

I would like to thank members of my family who have assisted me in many ways I cannot recount; from giving moral support, advice, financial support, and helping in the production of this book. My projects could not have reached fruition without your unwavering support. My heartfelt gratitude. Countless thanks to my children who have accommodated my work, and grown up with it, the research which goes back 27 years. You are wonderful; Tandiwe, Simbarashe, Naome and Edward; My grandchildren, Mya Nontando Cecilia, Thami (Thamsanqa) Emmanuel Farai, Joshua Jabulani and Thando. I will spend time with you and see animals and sing for you, my bundles of joy.

To the father of my children, (Ada Makwenda) Edward Makwenda snr, for all the support (*Ndawonga Ada, muje kutali ndimotu*). I wish to extend my gratitude to my sisters; Juliet, Joseline and Josephine, and my brother Emmanuel. You have always wished me the best, thank you so much. Mama Sheilah Matindike thanks for everything MaDube. To my late uncle (*umalume*) Caleb Dube I wish you were here, thank you for opening the door into this big house.

I wish to pay homage to my six parents (my two grandmothers, my two grandfathers and my mother and father) I wish there were here to see how the seeds they planted have germinated. They created a storyteller in me, a musician, a music critic, analyst, a journalist, a researcher, archivist, historian, ethnomusicologist, artist, I can go on and on. To my four grandparents: Marko Jenje Mhembere, Agnes Chihute Jenje Mhembere, *Ndinotenda zvikuru*, Malandu (Mangena) Mateza Dube and Mateza (Tarara) Dube, Ngiyabonga Kakhulu.

I will always be indebted to my parents; my father David (Murehwa) Jenje and my mother Canaan (MaDube) Mateza Jenje for the support and the encouragement you gave me and guiding me in my career path since I was young. *Ndinotenda zvikuru, Ngiyabonga kakhulu* (Thank you).

Time and space do not permit the mention of several contributors, for their liberal assistance in the fulfilment of my aspired project book.

NDINOTENDA! NGIYABONGA! THANK YOU ALL!

Joyce Jenje Makwenda
2013, August HARARE

Julia Chigamba

About the Author

AN Archivist-Historian, Researcher, Author, Producer, Lecturer and Ethnomusicologist – Joyce Jenje-Makwenda was born in Mbare Township, Salisbury (Harare) in 1958. For the past 27 years, she carried out research and interviews on early urban culture, music, politics, education, religion, media, fashion, taboo, sexual and cultural issues and women's histories in Zimbabwe.

Joyce has written a book on *Zimbabwe Township Music Book* which was published in 2005, which has been widely read locally and internationally. She has also written two novels in Shona and Ndebele; *Gupuro* and *USenzeni* on women's issues and the girlchild. Gupuro was translated into English and the title is *Divorce Token*. She also co-authored a children's book with her grandchild Mya – *Mya's Story*.

Being a dynamic storyteller who uses different forms to tell a story and make it accessible she produced and directed an award winning documentary in 1992 – *Zimbabwe Township Music 1930-1960s*. She produced several other documentaries including – *"A Christmas to Remember – With Early Township Dwellers"* December (1994); Omasiganda – *African Troubadours - One man band guitarists* (1995); The Epworth Theatrical Strutters – Musical Group from the 1940s. 1997; The Bantu Actors/Mattaka Family (A Family Musical Group which goes back to the 30s) – 1998

Radio being one of the most powerful ways of disseminating information, Joyce has used it to tell the story of Zimbabwe music, she worked with the BBC to compile a radio program on Township Jazz of the 50s -1992; she produced a 13 week Radio Program for ZBC on Early Musicians (Shona & Ndebele) 1992. Researched, Compiled and presented radio programmes on Township Music 1930s – 1960s: A Social History, for the Audio Visual Services, (Ministry of Education and Culture) 1994.

With all the information that she had gathered

Joyce Jenje-Makwenda

on musicians in Zimbabwe she decided to impart the knowledge and she was a lecturer for 15 years (1991-2005), at the Zimbabwe College of Music (Ethnomusicology Dept) and she introduced Gender Studies in music and also compiled a Gender in Music Handbook which is yet to published.

She has also given talks and presented papers on music on a number of forums - locally and internationally.

As a way of documenting women's histories in 2007, she was Executive Producer of the CD – *Women's Voices of Zimbabwe* were she took four young women and they sang 12 songs of women musicians from the 50s.

Joyce Jenje Makwenda owns a private music collection/archive at her house, which consists of interviews on music, on audio, video, and some of it transcribed and also press cuttings, LP's and music artefacts, such as gramophones.

She has been honoured with the following awards:

Zimbabwe Township Music Documentary got a special mention; Southern African Film Festival - (1993).

About the Author

Best T.V. Producer of the Year (Entertainment, music, drama) – The National Journalist and Media Awards for 1993 – Zimbabwe, Sponsored by REUTERS.

Second best T.V. Producer of the Year 1994 National Journalistic Awards, Zimbabwe Sponsored by REUTERS.

Freelance Woman Journalist of the Year 1999 funded by UNIFEM hosted by The Federation of Media Women of Zimbabwe.

Population Development and Gender Writer of The Year (Overall Winner) funded by UNFPA hosted by Zimbabwe Union of Journalists (ZUJ) 2002.

Special award The Triple T award – "tackling taboo topics" (New Category) – Gender Links/ GEMSA Awards – Gender Mainstreaming – Johannesburg 2010

Jenje Makwenda is a lucky female artist who got support from her parents Canaan and David Jenje who encouraged her when she was young to take up music and also when she embarked on the research on early musicians and early urban culture there were there to give her support and guide her.

She is a mother of four; Tandiwe and Naome, Simbarashe and Edward. She is a grandmother of four; Mya Nontando Cecilia, Thamsanqa Emmanuel Farai, Joshua Jabulani and Thando.

Joyce Jenje-Makwenda in her Archive/Library (7/10/2013)

Publications and Productions by the Author

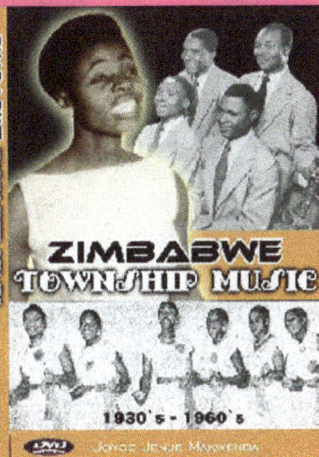

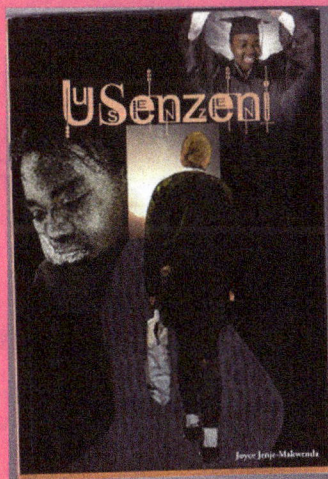

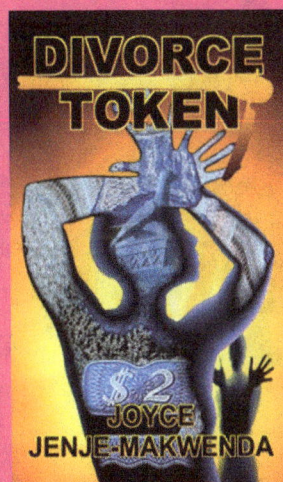

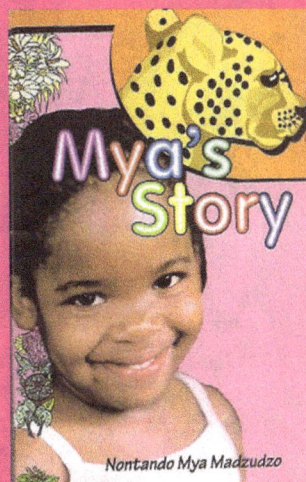

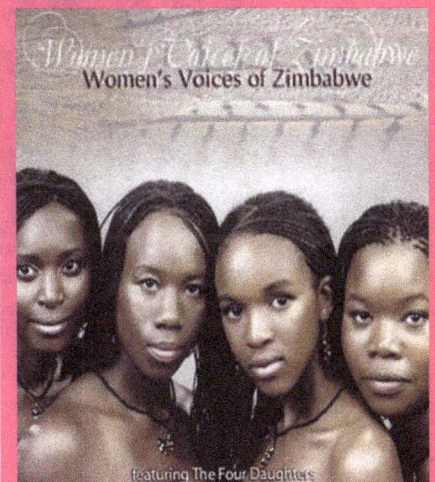

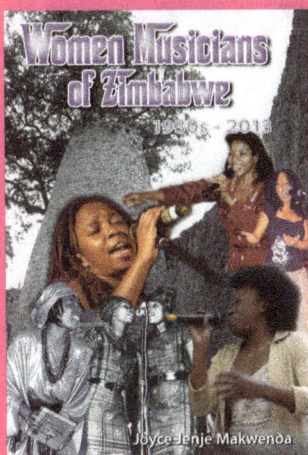

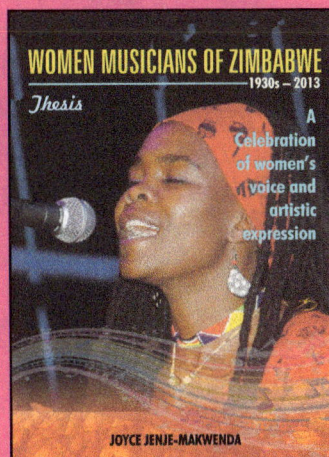

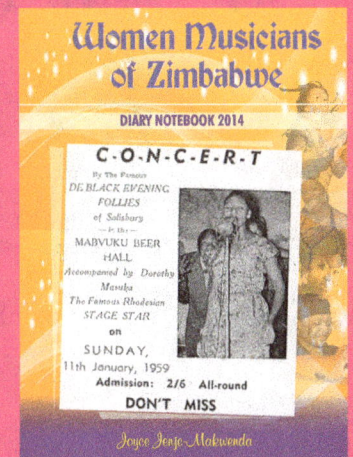

Chiwoniso Maraire
(5 March 1976 – 24 July 2013)

Introducing your title track *Rebel Woman* – this is what you said:
... but it is also a tribute to strong women who suffer because they do not follow the restrictions society tries to place on them. "The truth is that when you are a strong woman you might lose your husband, your home, because the way the systems are structured you're not allowed to be strong as a woman, unless you follow the rules. This song is about changing those rules." Chiwoniso Maraire 2008
Part of the song goes:
But as you weep rebel woman

www.ingramcontent.com/pod-product-compliance
Lightning Source LLC
Chambersburg PA
CBHW080844270326

41929CB00017B/2920